HIP-HOP ARCHITECTURE.

HIP-HOP ARCHITECTURE.

Sekou Cooke

BLOOMSBURY VISUAL ARTS
LONDON · NEW YORK · OXFORD · NEW DELHI · SYDNEY

BLOOMSBURY VISUAL ARTS
Bloomsbury Publishing Plc

50 Bedford Square, London, WC1B 3DP, UK
1385 Broadway, New York, NY 10018, USA
29 Earlsfort Terrace, Dublin 2, Ireland

BLOOMSBURY, BLOOMSBURY VISUAL ARTS and the Diana
logo are trademarks of Bloomsbury Publishing Plc

First published in Great Britain 2021

Copyright © Sekou Cooke, 2021

Sekou Cooke has asserted his right under the Copyright, Designs and
Patents Act, 1988, to be identified as Author of this work.

For legal purposes the Acknowledgments on pp. xviii–xxi
constitute an extension of this copyright page.

Cover design by Namkwan Cho
Cover image: Graffiti text at the AIANY Center for Architecture by
David "CHINO" Villorente, © David "CHINO" Villorente

All rights reserved. No part of this publication may be reproduced or transmitted in any
form or by any means, electronic or mechanical, including photocopying, recording, or any
information storage or retrieval system, without prior permission in writing from the publishers.

Bloomsbury Publishing Plc does not have any control over, or responsibility for,
any third-party websites referred to or in this book. All internet addresses given
in this book were correct at the time of going to press. The author and publisher
regret any inconvenience caused if addresses have changed or sites have
ceased to exist, but can accept no responsibility for any such changes.

A catalogue record for this book is available from the British Library.

A catalog record for this book is available from the Library of Congress.

ISBN: HB: 978-1-3501-1615-3
PB: 978-1-3501-1614-6
ePDF: 978-1-3501-1617-7
eBook: 978-1-3501-1616-0

Typeset by Lachina Creative, Inc.
Printed and bound in the U.S.A by Sheridan, Chelsea, Michigan

To find out more about our authors and books visit
www.bloomsbury.com and sign up for our newsletters.

For Mummy, Daddy, and Nina.

viii	**ILLUSTRATIONS.**	
xiii	**FOREWORD.**	
xviii	**ACKNOWLEDGMENTS:**	
	SHOUT OUTS, BIG UPS, AND THANK YOUS.	

I

001 *Ready or Not*: **An Introduction to Hip-Hop Architecture**

01 DISCLAIMER.	003
02 MANIFESTO.	005
03 PROLOGUE.	007

II

011 *Step into a World*: **Perspectives and Narratives from the History and Theory of Hip-Hop Architecture**

01 LEGITIMACY.	013
02 AUTHENTICITY.	017
03 GODPARENTS.	023
04 RACE.	031
05 GENDER.	039
06 NOSTALGIA.	045
07 COMMODITY.	059
08 GRIDS + GRIOTS.	065
09 TECHNOLOGY.	073
10 CONTRADICTION.	079

083 ***As I Manifest*: Contemporary Speculations on Hip-Hop Architectural Education and Practice**

01 FORM.	085
02 IMAGE.	097
03 PROCESS.	111
04 IDENTITY.	137
05 URBANISM.	159
06 SPACE.	177

183 ***Flipping to the B-Sides*: Tangents to and Projections from Hip-Hop Architecture**

01 KANYE.	185
02 DECONSTRUCTIVISM.	191
03 AFROFUTURISM.	197
04 INFORMAL SETTLEMENTS.	201
05 ACTIVIST ARCHITECTURE.	207
06 NEO-POSTMODERNISM.	215
07 OUTRO.	223

231	**APPENDIX.**
233	**NOTES.**
251	**BIBLIOGRAPHY.**
254	**INDEX.**

ILLUSTRATIONS.

II.001 The Sugar Hill Gang (Getty Images / Anthony Barboza) (p. 016)
II.002 KRS One with a copy of The Gospel of Hip-Hop (© Nicci Cheeks) (p. 019)
II.003 Screenshot of MinnPost article "What's Hip-Hop Architecture? 'Hip-Hop Culture in Built Form.'" (© 2015 MinnPost.com) (p. 021)
II.004 Robert Moses looks over model of Battery Bridge (p. 025)
II.005 Model of Le Corbusier's Plan Voisin (Image courtesy Siefkin DR via Wikimedia Creative Commons CC BY-SA 4.0 https://commons.wikimedia.org/wiki/File:Plan_Voisin_model.jpg) (p. 025)
II.006 Screenshot from "Mo Money Mo Problems" music video ("The Notorious B.I.G - Mo Money Mo Problems" directed by Hype Williams © WMG (on behalf of Bad Boy); LatinAutor - SonyATV, EMI Music Publishing, Sony ATV Publishing, BMI - Broadcast Music Inc., SOLAR Music Rights Management, PEDL, UNIAO BRASILEIRA DE EDITORAS DE MUSICA - UBEM, CMRRA, LatinAutor - Warner Chappell, ASCAP, Warner Chappell, LatinAutor, and 14 music rights societies 1997. All rights reserved) (p. 035)
II.007 Bass Odyssey sound system (Image courtesy Yaniq Walford via Wikimedia Creative Commons CC BY 3.0 https://en.wikipedia.org/wiki/File:Bass_Odyssey_Sound_System_speaker_column,_Tropical_Hut,_St._Mary,_May_2012.jpg) (p. 049)
II.008 Screenshot from "Rapping, deconstructed: the best rhymers of all time" (Video © Vox Media 2016) (p. 050)
II.009 Still from "Beat Street" ("Beat Street" directed by Stan Lathan 1984 © Orion Pictures) (p. 052)
II.010 Diagram of object-discipline relationships (Craig L. Wilkins. Reproduced with permission) (p. 057)
II.011 Dapper Dan in his studio (© Wyatt Counts) (p. 061)
II.012 Installation view of the exhibition, "The New City: Architecture and Urban Renewal." The Museum of Modern Art, New York, January 1967 through March 13, 1967, Photographic Archive. The Museum of Modern Art Archives. Photographer: George Cserna (Digital Image © The Museum of Modern Art/Licensed by SCALA / Art Resource, NY) (pp. 066–067)
II.013 J Dilla's MPC3000 (Video © Vox Media 2017) (p. 073)
II.014 Ice Cube in the Eames House (Ice Cube Celebrates the Eames House © The New York Times Company 2011) (p. 078)

II.015 5Pointz Image courtesy of Ezmosis via Wikimedia Creative Commons. CC BY-SA 3.0. (https://commons.wikimedia.org/wiki/File:View_of_5_Pointz,_January_20,_2013.jpg) (p. 080)

II.016 MERES mural at Museum of Street Art (© Sekou Cooke) (p. 080)

III.017 Exterior view of *Close to the Edge: The Birth of Hip Hop Architecture* (© Erik Bardin) (pp. 086–087)

III.018 Interior view of *Close to the Edge: The Birth of Hip Hop Architecture* (© Erik Bardin) (p. 088)

III.019 Detail view of *Close to the Edge: The Birth of Hip-Hop Architecture* (© Erik Bardin) (p. 089)

III.020 "I Know You Seen Me on Your Videos" (© Erik Bardin) (p. 090)

III.021 "Black Noise" (© Erik Bardin) (p. 091)

III.022 "B-Sides" (© Erik Bardin) (p. 092)

III.023 "On Form" (© Anthony Turner) (p. 093)

III.024 *Harlem: the Ghetto Fabulous* (PHAT is: Nathaniel Q Belcher, Stephen M Slaughter, David Mesfin, Adam Wheeler) (pp. 098–099)

III.025 Poster for *Het Wilde Wonen* (Maurer United Architects) (p. 100)

III.026 Poster for *P2001* (Maurer United Architects) (p. 101)

III.027 Poster for *Zedzbeton 3.0* (Maurer United Architects) (p. 102)

III.028 "The Hive" (Zvi Beling) (p. 103)

III.029 "The End to End Building" (Zvi Beling) (p. 104)

III.030 Detail view of "City Thread" (Photo by Justin Harris) (p. 105)

III.031 "City Thread" (Photo by Benjamin Chase) (p. 105)

III.032 Matrix 1 - Row F (John Szot) (pp. 106–107)

III.033 Still from "Architecture and the Unspeakable – Part 1" (John Szot) (p. 108)

III.034 Still from "Architecture and the Unspeakable – Part 1" (John Szot) (p. 108)

III.035 *Color(ed) Theory* Palette (Amanda Williams. Courtesy of the artist) (p. 112)

III.036 Color(ed) Theory: Pink Oil Moisturizer (fall) (Amanda Williams. Courtesy of the artist) (p. 112)

III.037 Dorchester Projects (Courtesy of Rebuild Foundation) (p. 113)

III.038 Sanctum (© Max McClure) (p. 114)

III.039 "The Urban Porch," collage and drawing (Nina Cooke John) (p. 115)

III.040 Model of "The Urban Porch" (Nina Cooke John) (p. 115)

III.041 Model of "Remixing Architecture – Main Hub (Andrea Bulloni, Marco Papagni) (p. 116)

III.042 Appropriated Tekniques_Zamora (Copyright © 2019 Mauricio D. Zamora. All rights reserved) (p. 117)

III.043 Appropriated Tekniques_Zamora (Copyright © 2019 Mauricio D. Zamora. All rights reserved) (p. 118)

III.044 "Found Object Models" (Chris Cornelius, Associate Professor, University of Wisconsin-Milwaukee) (p. 119)
III.045 S.N.A.F.U drawing (Chris Cornelius, Associate Professor, University of Wisconsin-Milwaukee) (p. 120)
III.046 Museum design, final section drawing (Chris Cornelius, Associate Professor, University of Wisconsin-Milwaukee) (p. 121)
III.047 *Elementz* installation (Stephen Slaughter. Reproduced with permission) (p. 122)
III.048 Stephen Slaughter with *Elementz* design team (Stephen Slaughter. Reproduced with permission) (p. 122)
III.049 B-boy diagram (Stephanie White and Sabrina Reyes) (p. 123)
III.050 Student installation in Slocum Hall (© Sekou Cooke) (p. 124)
III.051 3D printer tests (Joshua Siev) (p. 125)
III.052 Catalog of laser cutter effects (Reide McClain) (p. 125)
III.053 Graffiti in the city diagram (Nathaniel Banks) (p. 126)
III.054 Drawing study of graffiti installation (Noah Anderson and Shao Li) (p. 127)
III.055 Diagram of "My Block" (Elizabeth Mandato) (p. 128)
III.056 Diagram of "Planet Rock" (Scott Krabath) (p. 129)
III.057 Axonometric view of "Third Space" (Scott Krabath and Renata Ramela) (p. 130)
III.058 Diagrams of "Adams Morgan Re-coded" (Evelyn Brooks) (p. 131)
III.059 Site plan of "Adams Morgan Re-coded" (Evelyn Brooks and Richard Kim) (p. 132)
III.060 Streetscape perspective views of "Adams Morgan Re-coded" (Evelyn Brooks) (p. 132)
III.061 Final presentation, "Adams Morgan Re-coded" (Evelyn Brooks © Sekou Cooke) (p. 133)
III.062 Graffiti hierarchy diagram (Kyle Simmons) (p. 134)
III.063 Building section, "Ivy City Redux" (Kyle Simmons) (p. 135)
III.064 Final presentation, "Ivy City Redux" (Kyle Simmons © Sekou Cooke) (p. 136)
III.065 "The Growth Game" (© 2014 Tajai Massey) (p. 139)
III.066 'S' Chair Iteration (Anthony "YNOT" Denaro and Van Escobar) (p. 140)
III.067 "Freestyle Archityper" (Carlos "Mare139" Rodriguez) (p. 142)
III.068 Exothermic (Boris Tellegen) (p. 143)
III.069 "Ego" installation, part of "A Friendly Takeover" (Boris Tellegen) (p. 144)
III.070 Berlaagen (Boris Tellegen) (p. 144)
III.071 Homecore (© Laurent Clement) (p. 145)
III.072 Bow House (© Laurent Clement) (p. 146)
III.073 A-Kampa47 (Malka Architecture) (p. 147)

III.074 "Sittin' on 24s" (James Garrett Jr.) (p. 149)
III.075 Perspective view of "Juxtaposition Arts Center" (4RM+ULA, LLC) (p. 149)
III.076 *SCHMO 15: surface, stratum, time* (© Rik Sferra Photography) (p. 150)
III.077 *Lauren Halsey: we still here, there* (Installation view of *Lauren Halsey: we still here, there*, March 4–September 3, 2018 at MOCA Grand Avenue. Courtesy of The Museum of Contemporary Art, Los Angeles. Photo by Zak Kelley) (p. 151)
III.078 Crenshaw District Hieroglyph Project (Prototype Architecture) (Photography: Brian Forrest; Courtesy of David Kordansky Gallery, Los Angeles and Hammer Museum, Los Angeles; © Lauren Halsey) (p. 152)
III.079 *Surface Armatures* (Olalekan Jeyifous. Reproduced with permission) (p. 153)
III.080 *Shanty Mega-Structures* (Olalekan Jeyifous. Reproduced with permission) (p. 154)
III.081 "Political Impermanence of Place (P.I.M.P.)" (Olalekan Jeyifous. Reproduced with permission) (p. 155)
III.082 *Hip-Hop Ar(t)chitecture Signifyin'* (Nathan Williams. Reproduced with permission) (p. 157)
III.083 Genesee Street perspective view (Sara Zewde. Reproduced with permission) (p. 160)
III.084 Watercolor rendering of elevation view, "Hip-Hop Park" (Craig L. Wilkins. Reproduced with permission) (p. 161)
III.085 The Bottega (Ujijji Davis. Reproduced with permission) (p. 162)
III.086 Cottage Grove Strip (Rui Li) (p. 163)
III.087 Strip Diagram (Angela Murano) (p. 164)
III.088 Neighborhood Diagram and Precedents (Ashley Dunkwu) (p. 165)
III.089 Graffiti and B-Boy Diagram (Xinyao Wang) (p. 165)
III.090 Graffiti and B-Boy Diagram (Bohan Li) (p. 166)
III.091 Hip-Hop Call and Response Diagram (Elise Zilius) (p. 166)
III.092 Strip Diagram (Rui Li) (p. 167)
III.093 Remixable Housing Modules for Southside Chicago (Alexander Sheremet) (p. 168)
III.094 Remixable Housing Modules for Southside Chicago (Alexander Sheremet) (p. 169)
III.095 Cottage Grove streetscape perspective view (Timothy Mulhall) (p. 170)
III.096 Exploded axonometric view of "Intrusion" (Xiangyao Wang) (p. 171)
III.097 Rooftop Legends (© Sekou Cooke) (p. 179)
III.098 Rooftop Legends (© Sekou Cooke) (p. 179)
III.099 During and after, *Close to the Edge: The Birth of Hip-Hop Architecture*, Saint Paul (left: © Sekou Cooke, right: © Chad Holder) (p. 181)
IV.100 Kanye West at GSD (© Noam Dvir) (p. 187)

IV.101 Yeezus Tour Stage (Image courtesy of ZiaLater via Wikimedia Creative Commons. CC BY-SA 3.0. https://commons.wikimedia.org/wiki/File:Yeezus_Tour_Stage.jpg) (p. 189)

IV.102 Still from "Sweetheart" music video ("JD & Mariah Carey – Sweetheart" directed by Hype Williams © SME (on behalf of Columbia); LatinAutor - UMPG, Spirit Music Publishing, UMPG Publishing, LatinAutor - Warner Chappell, Warner Chappell, ASCAP, PEDL, LatinAutor, UMPI, UNIAO BRASILEIRA DE EDITORAS DE MUSICA - UBEM, and 14 music rights societies 1998. All rights reserved) (p. 191)

IV.103 Capital City Towers (Image courtesy of IndexxRus via Wikimedia Creative Commons. CC BY-SA 3.0. https://commons.wikimedia.org/wiki/File:Capital-citytowers-moscow-indexxrus.JPG) (p. 193)

IV.104 Screenshot from "Black Panther" ("Black Panther" directed by Ryan Coogler © Marvel Studios; Walt Disney Pictures 2018. All rights reserved) (p. 199)

IV.105 City model from "Art and Society: Bodys Isek Kingelez: City Dreams" (Digital Image © The Museum of Modern Art/Licensed by SCALA / Art Resource, NY) (p. 199)

IV.106 Model of "Porto Seguro Social Housing, Brazil" (Courtesy Christian Kerez GmbH) (p. 201)

IV.107 Torre de Davide (Image courtesy of EneasMx via Wikimedia Creative Commons. CC BY-SA 4.0. https://commons.wikimedia.org/wiki/File:Torre_de_David_-_Centro_Financiero_Confinanzas.jpg) (p. 203)

IV.108 Quinta Monroy before and after (© Cristóbal Palma) (p. 205)

IV.109 Still from *Do the Right Thing* ("Do the Right Thing" directed by Spike Lee © 40 Acres & A Mule Filmworks 1989. All rights reserved) (p. 208)

IV.110 Cross-Border Community Station – Tijuana (Estudio Teddy Cruz + Fonna Forman. Reproduced with permission) (p. 209)

IV.111 Hotel Fouquet Barrière (© Laurian Ghinitoiu) (p. 216)

IV.112 Caixa Forum (Image courtesy of Luis García via Wikimedia Creative Commons. CC BY-SA 3.0. https://commons.wikimedia.org/wiki/File:CaixaForum_Madrid_(Espa%C3%B1a)_01.jpg) (p. 216)

IV.113 Model of "House No. 64" (Kyle Miller) (p. 218)

IV.114 Model of "House No. 77" (Kyle Miller) (p. 218)

IV.115 Best Sandwiches study model (Jennifer Bonner/MALL) (p. 219)

IV.116 Haus Gables (Jennifer Bonner/MALL, photo by Tim Hursley) (p. 220)

IV.117 Roy and Diana Vagelos Education Center (© Sekou Cooke) (p. 221)

IV.118 Community "takeover" event at *Close to the Edge* exhibition (Aaron Price for NetWirth Ent.) (p. 225)

IV.119 Community "takeover" event at *Close to the Edge* exhibition (© Carl Atiya Swanson) (p. 225)

IV.120 Community "takeover" event at *Close to the Edge* exhibition (© Carl Atiya Swanson) (p. 226)

FOREWORD.

Building Blocks
By Michael Eric Dyson

Let's build. I often say that to my younger colleagues in circles that don't qualify for AARP membership. I try to keep abreast of the linguistic currents of rap music since I still teach it and swore to myself decades ago that I wouldn't become one of those grizzled heads who gets stuck in earlier artistic eras sounding like a hiphoposaur. But I must confess that until reading this book, I hadn't given much thought to the architectural features of "build" as a term that signals a communion of sorts among likeminded folk—to sit down and build and talk and develop deeper kinship. Now I hear the resonances of construction and design and shaping a future by building it a certain way. And in an instant, new meanings flood my mind and reveal dimensions of hip-hop that were always there but awaiting the right approach to bring them to life. It's apparent that hip-hop builds, and is built, by architects of sound and speech, of signifying and testifying, who call upon a vast array of verbal tools and rhetorical craft to construct their art. It is an art where metaphor reigns, and to shift metaphors from architecture to biology, hip-hop is a sublimely generative culture.

Hip-hop scholarship, like the culture that birthed it, has been determinedly fertile and relentlessly creative. The culture produces and reproduces. It mixes and remixes. Hip-hop scholarship embraces an ethic of creation and a morality of invention that flow through its veins and, to mix metaphors, resounds throughout its sonic built environment. In fact, the mixed metaphors of production and construction offer a scholarly scaffolding of sorts to approach the birthing and building of an art form. Hip-hop scholarship only exists because the culture it studies exists. But that scholarship must bring to the culture sharp insight and healthy skepticism.

There is already vigorous dispute about the place of hip-hop in the larger cultural firmament and especially in the broader academic universe. Another way of saying this is that there is bitter argument about what place hip-hop holds in the edifices of American university life or, to dramatically shift metaphors again, whether hip-hop is an illegitimate offspring of academic forces forging illicit connections. Questions of birth and invention, of pedigree and stature, dog the production and construction of hip-hop in the halls of ivy to this day. Often seen as even more destructive than a bull in a china shop, hip-hop scholarship has been accused of throwing out the baby of academic disciplines and the knowledge they generate with the bathwater of oldfangled ways of thinking about the world. Alas, that metaphor doesn't walk on all fours. Instead, hip-hop scholarship has birthed new epistemologies of race and place—and space—that have led to the construction of new towers of reflection and new arenas of academic investigation.

Hip-hop scholarship has also done its share of deconstruction, especially by questioning formal bodies of knowledge and rigid disciplinary boundaries. Hip-hop scholarship, partly by design and partly by virtue of its sheer existence—and the social logics it unleashes, the epistemic approaches it endorses, the existential crises it reveals, the moral dilemmas it addresses—shakes the foundations of American scholarship. It also wreaks havoc on the byzantine and esoteric constructions of academic discourse. It significantly shifts and challenges what we think we know and why we know it and for whom that knowledge is important and to whom it is responsible.

Into this building—both the thing that is being constructed and the thing already finished, or at least seemingly so—steps Sekou Cooke, a man with a fresh voice, a fresh vision, sketching fresh vistas. As a theorist and practitioner of architecture writing about hip-hop architecture, he expands our awareness and deepens our consciousness. Despite rap legend Nas chiding rap legend Jay-Z for duplicating the efforts of rap legend KRS-One on his classic album subtitled *The Blueprint*, Jay-Z made his own album named *The Blueprint* and thus created another classic. In that moment he showed us that there are many blueprints for many constructions and reconstructions of sonic architectures. Cooke's *Hip-Hop Architecture* offers one such blueprint for the construction of the culture. It introduces a voice that vibrates in swagger, a narrative voice as cocky as Kanye's, as hypnotizing as Biggie's, as complex as Rakim's, as authentic as K-Dot's, inflected with the ingenuity of Rapsody and the impressionistic fire of Young Thug. To borrow further from Nasir "Nas" Jones, Cooke "ethers" this project. That means that he sets fire to any preconceived notions about the limits of hip-hop culture. He also rips off the facades of the often oddly cloistered world of architecture and its romanticized brigand of outlaw theorists. For all of its colorful challenges to how we think of the built environment or design practice, mainstream architectural theory has curiously neglected Black culture. Cooke and his cohort of willing architectural accomplices are here to change all of that. They are here to plot a new course or, keeping with our metaphor, to erect a new intellectual edifice on the grounds of Black urban logic, of Black sonic utterance, and of Black spatial resistance. This book is both the blueprint and the structure, or, at least, one take on the structure, of hip-hop architecture.

Hip-Hop Architecture is dope—by design. That may sound corny, but blame my word choice and not Cooke's vision. Cooke seeks to establish a design-build for hip-hop scholarship that reflects the culture that inspires it. Thus, instead of mere chapters, there are *volumes* of insight and information to absorb. There are also intriguing excerpts, samples of lyrics, hip-hop scholarship, and other edifying or instructive quotations. All of these are seamlessly woven into the design of a book whose intent is to reflect the styles, themes, methods, approaches, and characteristics of hip-hop culture. And all of this further establishes the burgeoning field of hip-hop architecture.

I'm hardly an architect, though I've engaged from time to time with theories of the built environment and taken in the work of Modernists like Mies Van Der Rohe and Frank Lloyd Wright, Postmodernists like Denise Scott Brown and Robert Venturi, and the communal aesthetic of one of the foremost Black architects, my late friend Phillip Freelon, who helped to design the National Museum of African American History and Culture. I know that after a design is architected, stakeholders must secure permissions for the build. Cooke deftly illumines this process throughout the book even as he interrupts and deliberately distorts the White racial gaze that has sought to contain the bodies and buildings of Black folk. Even more gallantly, Cooke seeks no permissions and asks no one for forgiveness. Instead, he clears space to speak his truth and to channel the voices of thinkers and designers too often relegated to the margins of our culture and to the corners of architectural theory and practice. Cooke says that architecture has been captive to privileged White male scholars and that "only about 2 percent of all registered architects in this country identify as Black." Cooke clarifies the grounds on which hip-hop architecture is established and points to the stretches of space that his work touches like the tallest skyscrapers in the known world.

There are two noteworthy and foundational pillars to his work that stand tall and strong throughout the book. First, there is Cooke's encyclopedic grasp of the historical interface between the fields of hip-hop culture and architecture. Cooke has seen and sampled it all, from the hallowed halls of Cornell University's groundbreaking architectural program to the more obscure academic conferences on the subject to the corrugated streets from which sprang hip-hop culture. His immersion in his field is impressive, and his work in hip-hop architecture is rigorous. To paraphrase Jay-Z, you can't talk like Cooke talks because you have not been where he has been. And the insights he has gleaned in his fieldwork have given him a comprehensive overview of the profession that is striking. He writes with the bravado of a battle rapper but delivers his insights with the compassion of a wizened veteran in the newly curated collaborations on social media known as Verzuz. Second, Cooke is highly skilled at the "clapback," or speaking back and Black, to the powers that be in his field and beyond. Equally satisfying is his astute chronicling of the necessary "clapbacks" in the world of architectural studies. From his redress of comments made at a panel discussion related to the *Close to the Edge* exhibition to his recounting of the critical interventions made by the Women in Design group about the Pritzker Architecture Prize, Cooke outlines and provides critical context for why *Hip-Hop Architecture* matters.

As Cooke narrates overlooked stories, unearths hidden histories, deconstructs destructive myths, and counteracts racist cant, he also manages to cite other work that bolsters his case while using it to extend his theoretical and epistemological reach. He acknowledges, for instance, Murray Forman's *The Hood Comes First: Race, Space and Place in Rap and Hip-Hop* and then skillfully builds on that work to establish a scholarly doorway into architectural studies. He skillfully shows how work that has already been done has opened up avenues into the work that excites him: Cooke argues that Forman's discussion of rap flow as bricolage logically leads to a discussion of architectural forms. Cooke says that "[u]nderstanding flow as bricolage that seamlessly blends disparate inputs gives us a clearer image of [rap's] architectonic potentials." Cooke is invested in form and space, both of which provide grist for his epistemic mill as a scholar of architecture and as a hip-hop intellectual.

Impressive, too, are Cooke's scope of work and his design finishes, suggesting that an intellectual builder and designer and architect of the first order is at work. As Cooke revisits the concept of the grid in architectural design, he highlights the ubiquity of the concept—and the oppressive power of conventional academic discourse that erases Black and Brown experiences. Not only does Cooke critically engage and, when needed, refute narrow academic convention, but he also smashes intellectual delusions with the aid of a hearty roster of rap artists and other scholars, generously acknowledging their crucial contributions. It is a majestic way to evoke the hip-hop cipher in curating a colloquy of voices as he takes on some of the most pressing issues in hip-hop scholarship and architectural theory.

Building in hip-hop culture is about coming together to think together. The call to build, like my opening line to this brief essay, is a call to come together and think as a community. When we build in hip-hop, we make change happen in the world through our collective efforts at rethinking our experiences and reshaping our understanding of what those experiences mean. But for every effort to build, there is a corollary effort to tear down monuments to a destructive past and to a hateful heritage. Cooke is obviously interested in the vital intersections between hip-hop culture and architectural theory and practice. He also reminds us how our built environments are not merely constructed on noble ideals and uplifting aspirations but reflect a culture's and nation's racial and political priorities as well. The grave controversy over Confederate monuments in our time of racial reckoning is an important reminder that statues are, in miniature, an extension of the beliefs and values on which our society is erected.

Even more important is the built environment that, without explicit political meaning, takes on huge consequence in light of our racial history and the uses to which this physical environment is put. A street corner and pavement become the killing ground for George Floyd. The apartment of a young Black woman becomes the architectural coffin of Breonna Taylor. A fast food restaurant in Atlanta becomes the *mise en scene* for the cop killing of Rayshard Brooks. And the viewing of a not-yet-completed home in Georgia by Ahmaud Arberry in part motivates his hunting and killing by father-and-son vigilantes.

Cooke's book is a timely reminder that how we build what we see is a reflection of invisible ideals come to life in the architecture of our various and, at times, competing built environments. Hip-hop is a culture that is deeply attuned to the rhythms of existence in bodies that boast and bleed, in voices that sing and cry, in mouths that curse and bless. Architecture is the literal projection, in raised structures, of our beliefs about what settings we should live in and look at; what abodes we should make permanent, at least for a while, paradoxically enough; and what structures we should view as the realization of civilization's imagination about itself and its values. *Hip-Hop Architecture* reflects the values and visions of hip-hop culture, a social force that for too long was easily dismissed but that, now, has seized the reins of the culture and has made it look and listen. Cooke's book uses the historically reviled culture of hip-hop—a culture that, despite its recent acceptance, is still misunderstood and sometimes grossly underestimated—to look at the deeply admired discipline of architecture. It is the measure of this delightful text that it makes us think of both in new and energizing fashion.

ACKNOWLEDGMENTS: SHOUT OUTS, BIG UPS, AND THANK YOUS.

As with any major project in hip-hop or architecture, there are several contributors and collaborators who participate in creating a book. An undertaking of this magnitude (bigger than anything I've done previously) requires a long list of acknowledgements.

The first big shout out has to go to my immediate family: my mother, Cynthia Cooke, who is my biggest advocate and has set a bar of activity, achievement, and excellence that is difficult to top; my sister, Nina Cooke John, who paved the many roads to architecture that lay ahead of me beginning when she was 16 and I was 11; and my father, Leroy Cooke, who has read more books than anyone I know, published his first book in 2018, has been one of my few readers during the writing process, and who volunteered to compile this book's index—a meticulous job that I wouldn't trust to anyone else.

Big up and thanks to the HHA crew—my Hip-Hop Architecture brain trust—Amanda "Big Ro" Williams for constantly keeping me in check throughout my journey with this topic, for encouraging me to dive headfirst into this adventure, for dropping several knowledge bombs along the way, and for saying "yes" to me when, at times, she should have said "no"; Craig Wilkins, a true elder statesman of Hip-Hop Architecture, for being involved in all my events since the first, for tapping me into a world of scholarship awaiting my discovery, and for being incredibly generous and supportive as one of this book's primary readers; James "SCHMO" Garrett, Jr. for leading the cause of Hip-Hop Architecture in his practice and in the world of the AIA, for keeping me on point with his vociferous support of my writing, lecturing, and exhibitions, and for defending the topic against posers and charlatans; and to the brainiest of the brain trust, Andrés "Signifying Monk" Hernandez, who gave me some of my first in-depth education on hip-hop while I was at Cornell, and for providing some of the most important academic perspectives for contextualizing the work of this book.

More shout outs to the participants of the various events I've planned over the years: Olalekan "Lek" Jeyifous, an original member of the "Ripense 4" and the man producing the most compelling Hip-Hop Architectural imagery; Lawrence Chua, a gracious colleague and generous supporter of this work; Jack Travis, who is a pioneer for the causes of Black architects across the country, who is responsible for getting my toe in the door at the Center for Architecture, and with whom I share a healthy disagreement about many things worth debating; Michael Ford, who has done more to motivate my work in this area than perhaps anyone else; Shawn Rickenbacker; Héctor Tarrido-Picart; Travis Gosa; Harry Allen; Felecia Davis (also my undergraduate thesis advisor); Rayvon Fouché; Lauren Halsey, one of the key future voices of the topic; Open Mike Eagle; Tajai Massey; Nathan Williams, who laid the foundation for Cornell's role as the nexus of Hip-Hop Architecture; Mitesh Dixit, a dear colleague who had my back at a time when most didn't; Stephen Slaughter; Jennifer Newsom; and Ujijji Davis, another young voice of the topic, and a staunch advocate of this work.

Shout outs to the rest of the Ripense 4/Freeform Deformers: Efrain "EONER" Perez, who dragged me out of a safe job and challenged me to produce "real" architecture; Emanuel "GRUFF" Pratt the McArthur genius; and Anaelechi "AN.A.LAY" Owunwanne. Shout outs also to the other Cornell blackitects: the matriarchs, Nsenga Bansfield and Hansy Better Barraza, Peter Robinson, Nate Johnson, Lance "El Capitan" Collins, Nate Johnson, Omar Isaac (RIP), Scott Ruff, Oneka Horne Tolentino, Lisa Cholmondeley, Antoine "Kool Papa" Bryant, and Ife Ebo to name only a few. And a special shout out to Dr. Raymond Dalton who is singularly responsible for our deep numbers at such an exclusive program.

Special thanks to Ilgaz Kayalp and Sarah Aziz who helped me formulate my thoughts and focus my arguments as I began to write. Sarah spent more time and effort reading and providing feedback for my pre-editorial writing than anyone else. My interns and staff have also been instrumental in the compilation of this material over the past few years. Cesi Kohen, Emma Stoll, Sabrina Reyes, Garrett Wineinger, Karina Roberts, Stephanie White, Julia Ocejo, Vasundhra Aggarawal, Erin Doherty, Noah Anderson, Katrina Abad, Isaac Howland, and Toni Jones have each been key to the success of this project. Kyle Simmons has been a progressive thinker on the subject as a student and an intern. Adam Lee Secor and Shauneil Williams, I can't thank you two enough for being as organized as you have been in compiling the images, rights, and releases for this publication.

A shout out to each student who has participated in the various Hip-Hop Architecture seminars and studios I've taught over the last five years and who have attended the various events at the School of Architecture. Your ideas, thoughts, questions, and insights have been critical in shaping my own thoughts on the topic. More shout outs to my other (current and former) faculty colleagues at Syracuse who have participated on reviews and provided support to the work in other ways: Joseph Godlewski, Liz Kamell, Amber Bartosh, Greg Corso, Molly Hunker, Kyle Miller, and Britt Eversole among others. Also, to Julia Czerniak, Julie Larsen, Ted Brown,

Anne Munly, Larry Bowne (who convinced me to go to Harvard), Mark Robbins, Jonathan Massey, Marc Norman, and Randall Korman (who all helped me get into Harvard), thanks for helping me stay the course. I must also mention the excellent Syracuse Architecture staff, particularly Katryn Hansen, who is always patient with my unorthodox ways, and Karen Baris, who has often made the impossible possible.

Big ups to my west coast foundation crew. To Lisa Findley, who gave me my first studio teaching gig at CCA, Mark Donohue, who first taught me how to teach, and Jason Anderson, who was an early supporter of my work and a dear friend when I was in need. Shout out to Kory Beig, Maxi Spina, Antje Steinmüller, Mabel Wilson, and Sandra Vivanco my California colleagues.

Thanks to all the institutions and organizations that have also supported the work over the past few years including the DC Office of Planning (Eric Shaw and Thor Nelson), GTM Architects (Colline Hernandez-Ayala), Greenling USA (Lamell McMorris and Sean Harden), Autodesk, Inc. (Erica Nwankwo), The Knight Foundation (Priya Sircar), The Graham Foundation (Sarah Herda), The Museum of Contemporary Art (Amanda Hunt), The Museum of Modern Art (Sean Anderson, Arièle Dionne-Krosnick, and Aaron Smithson), AIANY Center for Architecture (I'm incredibly indebted to Ben Prosky, Berit Hoff Lavender, and Katie Mullen for their work putting together the *Close to the Edge* Exhibition), Springboard for the Arts (Laura Zabel and Carl Swanson), AIA Minnesota, AIA Saint Paul, Minnesota Architectural Foundation (all three run by the incredible Mary-Margaret Zindren—you're a rock star!), and, of course, Syracuse Architecture, whose Dean, Michael Speaks, has been more supportive of my academic career than any other colleague or administrator. This publication in particular was made possible through a grant from the New York State Council on the Arts (NYSCA).

Big ups to my chosen family in the Global Information Network (GIN) and The Alchymist Society. You are each more important to my life than I can express in words and too many to name individually. Camille Duplessis, Christie Trinh, Jason Gant, Alexandra Bijland, Chow Li Ng, Mike Uruski, Ngub Nding, James Eisenberg, Tarjei Flove, Aline Dalbiez, Jean-Luc Scheefer, Jonathan August, Marion Llopis, Martin Fredette, Dean Maser (who provided a crash pad and chauffeur services in Saint Paul), Dr. Tom Morter, Dr. Ted Morter, Blaine Athorn, Ed Forman, Earlene Vining, and Kevin Trudeau are just a few from those incredible organizations who have supported my growth in tangible and intangible ways. Cindy Reed has also been incredibly generous in volunteering to be another academic reader of this material. Special big up to my Syracuse GIN family, Rochette Withers, Neal Powless, and my dearest friend Michelle Schenandoah.

Thanks to the professors I've had over the years who have encouraged me and shaped me as an architect and educator, especially those who believed in me where others didn't. Val Warke and Andrea Simitch hold a special place in my heart. Milton Curry supported me even when I didn't produce work worthy of his support. Henry Richardson, Vince Mulcahy, and George Hascup most heavily influenced my undergraduate career. Eric Höweler, as my undergrad TA and my grad school thesis advisor, continues to be a model for my development as a professor. I also deeply idolize his practice and would be happy to model his success in my own studio. Jacques Herzog and Pierre de Meuron showed me that it was possible to "teach" architecture. Ben Van Berkel proved to me that it was possible to be simultaneously a famous architect, a great teacher, and a decent human being. I consider myself extremely fortunate to have met Sanford Kwinter and taken his "How to Do Things with Words" course at Harvard. It was the wackiest, least organized, and most enjoyable class I'd ever taken and the first venue to give me confidence that I was, indeed, a writer.

Finally, I'd like to thank each of the participants and interviewees whose words and images are included herein. Without your work and insights none of my work is possible. And to those deeply interested and invested in Hip-Hop Architecture, who have followed the topic, my work, and its trajectory over the last few years (some I've met and some I haven't as yet), thank you!

Ready or Not: An Introduction to Hip-Hop Architecture

VOLUME I

Track List   **Page**

01 DISCLAIMER.   003

02 MANIFESTO.   005

03 PROLOGUE.   007

01

DISCLAIMER.

This book is not for you. It is not for architectural academic elites. It is not for those who have gentrified our neighborhoods, overly intellectualized the profession, and ignored all contemporary Black theory within the discipline. You have made architecture a symbol of exclusion, oppression, and domination rather than expression, aspiration, and inspiration. This book is not for conformists—Black, White, or other. It is not for those who practice blind adherence to guidelines, rules, codes, and ordinances. It does not relegate itself to standard procedures for winning government contracts or gaining commissions to deliver services to clients in the one percent.

This book is for those who wanted to enter your academy and you told them they were "too ethnic." For those who have continually shaped their own environments and you dismissed it as "primitive" or "outsider." For those who never got a grade higher than a B- because they didn't conform to Corbusier's five rules. For the inner-city kid who spent her whole life as a product of public housing and social programming, never understanding why public space didn't feel public. This book goes beyond the confines of ivory tower classrooms, academic conferences, and limited-circulation journals to engage those who bear the brunt of architecture's most egregious crimes.

This book does not depend on the standard canons of architecture and philosophy to ground its arguments. You will not find extensive references here to Eisenmann, Corbusier, Semper, Lefebvre, Foucault, Hegel, Heidegger, or Locke. Instead you will find references to the pioneers of a new canon—Wilkins, Walker, Rose, Chang, Williams, Wilson, hooks, Dyson, Gooden, Fouché, Hernandez, Garrett, and Jeyifous. I also reference here several other voices outside of academia that deserve to be elevated to the level of critical scholarship. There are more than enough ideas that exist in these realms of otherness—beyond the White, male, Western *literati*—within which to position this book.

This book is not written in the journal standard third person. I am second or third to no person. Like Charlie Kaufman in *Adaptation,* I have written myself into the script. It is written in my voice—an avatar for the voice of the people. It is not a book about my work. Indeed, it is a collection of the works and accomplishments of several participants. However, it is a book that includes samples of my work, not as an exemplar, but as a proponent of the movement. I am not a Hip-Hop Architect. I am not even a Black Architect. I am an architect. And this is a book for, by, and about architects, though they may define their architecture differently than you have.

■ ■ ■

— Nas[1]

02 MANIFESTO.

Hip-Hop Architecture goes far beyond the mere novelty of combining two seemingly dissimilar terms. It seeks to redefine the way we think about both hip-hop and architecture—expanding the limits of both disciplines. Its primary objective is to elevate the ideas, cultures, and practices of marginalized peoples to the level of prominence and dominance previously reserved for Western ways of thinking. It rejects notions of equality and universality—the idea that "we are all the same" dilutes the cultural richness of humanity—but holds true to the promise of an equitable society. It takes every opportunity to challenge the "White spatial imaginary"[2] and all other assumed baselines, defaults, or normative positions. It imagines a world designed by the many instead of the few.

In an age of heightened White fragility, this is not the time to shy away from progressive worldviews. This is the time for Black people to more actively participate in the architecting of their environments. In the search for a "Black Architecture" we do not, however, need to limit our vision to Africa's ancient empires or primordial dwellings, nor do we have to emulate the practices of those who have played the coded game of their White educators and contemporaries. There is already an architecture that has been brewing in the bellies of Black designers for almost 30 years, that has been expressing itself in the underground, that is poised to define a generation of American architects—hip-hop is its muse.

Hip-hop is the dominant cultural product of our era. All contemporary advances in music, dance, art, literature, fashion, and theatrical performance can trace a direct line of influence from hip-hop—the blueprint of the twenty-first century.[3] Like every dominant cultural force before it, hip-hop will also shape the way architecture is produced. In the words of Andrés Hernandez, "This is not a style; it is a way of working. We are not constructing a way to design; we are designing a way to build."[4] The pages that follow point the way forward while, like the Sankofa bird, looking to our past, with Hip-Hop Architecture as its detailed blueprint.

■ ■ ■

– *Drake*[5]

PROLOGUE.

In case you were tripping on the title of this book, Hip-Hop Architecture is neither a new term nor a novel idea. The term can be traced back to the early 1990s and the idea that hip-hop and architecture are related (or relatable) fields should be implicit in the nature of hip-hop's roots within uniquely constructed urban contexts. This book spends most of its energy illustrating the myriad points of overlap and channels of expression that open up wherever hip-hop and architecture collide. This opening volume prepares readers for the dynamism of worlds colliding by first providing a few disclaimers that position the book within its intended space of acceptance. Next, it includes a manifesto to describe the fundamental attitudes of Hip-Hop Architecture, and this prologue as a basic outline of the book's organizational structure. Each of the volumes is presented as a collection of essays (sometimes referred to as "sections" or "tracks") covering various aspects of the overall topic. Whereas Volume I provides an introduction, Volume II establishes the historical and theoretical confines of the topic, Volume III describes some of the work produced on the topic, and Volume IV includes perspectives on other movements that may be adjacent to or tangential from Hip-Hop Architecture.

Volume II opens with a series of shorter texts that clarify basic positions within the book on identity, authenticity, race, and gender—each an area that impacts the writing in subsequent sections. A few important definitions are established within these first sections, such as those for the words, "Black," "hip-hop," and "architecture," critical to the development of more complex ideas and arguments proposed later on. The section entitled "GODPARENTS." is also included among these opening sections as a way of marking an important starting point for the topic and distinguishing its central arguments from those made by other proponents of Hip-Hop Architecture. The next group of sections on the nostalgia latent in any hip-hop-based study, on the commodification of hip-hop (and potential commodification of its architectural products), on the relationship between the grid and the Black body in space, and on Hip-Hop Architectural Technology expand on the basic concepts from the early sections and seeks to move beyond talking about what Hip-Hop Architecture *is* to talking about what Hip-Hop Architecture can *do*. The section on technology is particularly explicit about a single area in which hip-hop attitudes and approaches can completely transform the nature of architectural practice if properly understood and applied. The final section in Volume II addresses the fundamental contradiction within the term Hip-Hop Architecture and re-questions its legitimacy and authenticity from this new vantage point.

Volume III organizes as many examples of Hip-Hop Architectural Practice as have been identified thus far (and can fit within these pages) into the categories of form, image, process, and identity. It includes work first collected for the *Close to the Edge*[6] exhibition, additional work from later iterations of the show, and other work that for various reasons wasn't exhibited but fit within the given classification. The next section introduces the idea of Hip-Hop Urbanism, an approach to urban design, closely associated with Hip-Hop Architecture, with the potential to produce its own stand-alone movement. The volume ends with assertions of the importance of qualifying space within any architectural movement and speculations on the nature of hip-hop space. The provocations in this section may prove to be the most important for establishing the direction of Hip-Hop Architectural Practice and measuring its eventual effectiveness.

Volume IV reframes Hip-Hop Architecture through the lens of related architectural movements and ideologies: Deconstructivism, Afrofuturism, the architecture of informal settlements, activist ideals within architecture, and Neo-Postmodernism. Each section provides a brief introduction to the basic precepts of these topics before connecting them to readings (and misreadings) of the book's primary topic. The volume opens with a positioning of the work of hip-hop artists venturing into architectural arenas (also tangential to Hip-Hop Architecture). This section uses Kanye West as the archetypal hip-hop figure with design aspirations and draws on previous assessments of his work in design fields to derive new conclusions about how a Hip-Hop Architect is defined. The closing section of this volume is the closing statement of the book and presents some final reflections on the book's content and the topic's importance, impact, and ultimate audience.

Each section contains citations from books, articles, essays, interviews, lectures, symposia, movies, television shows, social media posts, and hip-hop lyrics[7] mixed in with the main body of the text. Between sections you will also find a series of interludes—quotations from several of the sources listed above—carefully selected to match the theme of each section and to include various relevant voices. These sources are intentionally eclectic as a reflection of the vast musical and sonic vocabularies of any hip-hop construction. Like a DJ, I have sampled, juxtaposed, and layered the voluminous amounts of reference material collected and repackaged it into an easily digestible form. My hope is that you will enjoy the journey through this topic, as I have over the past several years of study, regardless of whether you include yourself within its intended audience.

■ ■ ■

■ "This is your last chance. After this, there is no turning back. You take the blue pill—the story ends, you wake up in your bed and believe whatever you want to believe. You take the red pill—you stay in Wonderland, and I show you how deep the rabbit hole goes. Remember: all I'm offering is the truth. Nothing more."

    – *Morpheus,* The Matrix[8]

■ "____"

    – *Common*[9]

Step into a World: Perspectives and Narratives from the History and Theory of Hip-Hop Architecture

VOLUME II

Track List	Page
01 LEGITIMACY.	013
02 AUTHENTICITY.	017
03 GODPARENTS.	023
04 RACE.	031
05 GENDER.	039
06 NOSTALGIA.	045
07 COMMODITY.	059
08 GRIDS + GRIOTS.	065
09 TECHNOLOGY.	073
10 CONTRADICTION.	079

01

LEGITIMACY.

"So why hip-hop?" was his first question to me. "It's so filled with misogyny, and homophobia, and violence." My initial reaction was shock, especially since I had just spent the previous hour explaining in detail the many theories I had developed connecting the worlds of hip-hop and architecture. I had just taken an audience of faculty and students through a four-year journey to bring the nascent field of Hip-Hop Architecture to an academic audience; grounded it in work that had been published on the topic in various journals, lectures and books; expanded on it through examples of work done by students, academics, and practitioners for over two decades; and described my own design tests funded by granting organizations and private clients alike. Yet, there I sat, in front of a committee of five tasked by the faculty to evaluate my trajectory along the track to tenure, still buzzing off the high from a well-received public presentation, now forced to be an apologist for the sins of an entire culture.

I'm sure I'm not the first one ever to be put in that position. Georgetown University Professor, author, and "the 'hip-hop intellectual'"[1] Michael Eric Dyson has built much of his career on understanding and explaining the intricacies of hip-hop culture to the masses. He too has had to face continual inquiry about the legitimacy of hip-hop as a site of academic study. His prelude to *Know What I Mean? Reflections on Hip Hop* deftly fends off jabs by jazz musician Wynton Marsalis and his ilk "who dismiss hip-hop as adolescent 'ghetto minstrelsy,'"[2] and others such as social critic Stanley Crouch who "claim that the deficits of hip-hop blare beyond the borders of ugly art to inspire youth to even uglier behavior."[3] A.D. Carson, who famously presented his 2017 PhD dissertation as a rap album[4] contends with continual challenges to his academic credentials based solely on the delivery method of his work rather than its content. Others who have dared bring hip-hop into academic institutions (Tricia Rose, Murray Foreman, Bettina Love) or other intellectual spaces (Jeff Chang, Dan Hancox, Roy Christopher) have met similar resistances—forced to first argue for the legitimacy of their chosen topic of investigation before any merit-based evaluation of the scholarship they have produced.

So, what was I to do in that moment? Cuss him out? (Naw kid, I didn't have the balls. That's when I realized I'm bumpin' too much Biggie Smalls.) My response to the offending question was a meandering explanation of the inherent dualities and contradictions in hip-hop and, by extension, Black culture. It was something about how we've always had to deal with the dual realities of sexism and feminism, of violence and anti-violence, Malcolm and Martin, exclusivity and universality—how we have to accept the good with the bad. In that moment, I felt the judgement of the myriad "scholars, researchers, and journalists," discussed by Christopher who "have always had a tumultuous relationship with hip-hop. [Who] quickly point out its negative traits: its violence, vulgar language, misogyny, and heteronormativity."[5] I sought solace in the fact that "while it's true, it's not exactly news or insightful critique."[6] I felt compelled, like Rose, to "ignor[e] some of the most highly publicized issues in rap music, as media attention on rap music has been based on extremist tendencies within rap, rather than the day-to-day cultural forces that enter into hip-hop's vast dialogue."[7] I considered critically distancing myself from the topic in alignment with David A. M. Goldberg's attempts to separate rappers and their lyrics from hip-hop DJs and their techniques in forwarding his analysis of the technological innovations spawned by the hip-hop generation. "Despite the difficulties inherent in representing its multiple layers of cultural practice as a monolithic form," he writes of rap music, "it has become a site for critical engagements with the mechanisms of white supremacy, issues of class mobility in the postindustrial urban landscape, and the mass distribution of violent, misogynist, and homophobic narratives."[8] Though he recognizes it as a "delicate operation," his "extrication of the rapper's ego and role as media avatar from the sonic backdrops that support them"[9] echoes my own deflection when faced with the harsh realities of hip-hop's most famous shortcomings.

A much more empowering posture (and more poignant response to my colleague's question) didn't come to me until directly after the interview while teaching my weekly seminar course. I was unable to hide my unnerved state from my students while attempting to direct the day's conversations about the pervasiveness of graffiti within the built environment. After about five minutes, I interjected to relay the source of my consternation: the question that stayed with me throughout the rest of the interview and that bled into my class time. Without hesitation, one of my more vocal students gave the perfect answer: "Why architecture? Architecture is just as violent, just as misogynistic, just as homophobic." Right then and there I had my "jerk store"[10] moment. I was under as little obligation to apologize for hip-hop as I was to apologize for architecture since I am not the sole representative of either cohort. Also, while the hip-hop community has had to continually confront its negative aspects and answer for its mere existence, the architectural discipline has been so self-involved that it has yet to recognize its own bigotry. Internally, it elevates itself to the level of visionary, savior, hero, the conscience of the age, and the liberator of the masses. Meanwhile, it lacks the self-awareness to recognize its increasing irrelevance, its impotent effect on the collective consciousness, and its economic unsustainability. Instead of being implicitly suspicious of each new idea added to the architectural landscape, architecture needs to more thoroughly investigate the dominant ways of thinking, doing, and being in the world today and rethink its place within this current reality.

"It's an age-old argument," Dan Hancox writes, "but the case that music with morally unpalatable messages merely reflects reality, rather than glamorizes, or incites amorality, seemed more important than ever." Hancox continues, "If, as Martin Luther King wrote, 'a riot is the language of the unheard,' a result of 'living with the daily ugliness of the slum life, educational castration and economic exploitation,' then [hip-hop is] Dr. King's language rendered as art, and set to music."[11] My intention, therefore, is not to define hip-hop's legitimacy or its worthiness for architectural study, but to argue for architecture's inclusion within a growing list of hip-hop-based forms of cultural expression. Can Dr. King's language also be rendered in built form? "If we take hip-hop as a community of practice," Christopher posits, "then its cultural practices inform the new century in new ways."[12] Let's hope hip-hop can show the kind of flexibility that architecture hasn't and allow architecture to be included on its list of cultural practices.

■ ■ ■

"On the way over here from Ithaca, NY, I was listening to the new Kendrick Lamar CD. Has everyone downloaded this? Everyone's talking about it. This album begins with a sample of 'Every Nigger is a Star.' I think about how he uses that, echoing back with collective memory of Sly and the Family Stone. I think about how The Roots remade 'Everybody is a Star.' These two tensions between having the crown, wearing the crown, being the best vs. being someone who is always challenging the best through imagination and cultural inversion. To flip something means to attack form and tradition in a way that people say, 'Oh! I can't believe this shit! This is ill! How did he do this? I gotta emulate this!' This is why I think, when I have audacity to listen to rap music after 1996, that Iggy Azalea is not hip-hop. Because in every interview she says, 'Oh, I'm not the best rapper. I'm ok.' No, that is not hip-hop. You have to understand that tension between 'Everybody is a Star' and always going for that crown. Being the freshest kid in the skate park. Being the illest is something we have to deal with as academics. Because I know we all come from fields in which there seems to be that one voice—that one monologue. How do you flip it academically? How do you get ill, go def, get stupid, act a fool, and still get tenure? This is what a lot of us are still trying to figure out as hip-hop academics."

– *Travis Gosa*[13]

II.001 | The Sugar Hill Gang
Getty Images / Anthony Barboza

02 AUTHENTICITY.

Depending on who you ask, the Sugar Hill Gang were either pioneers of a cultural revolution that gave voice to a new generation, or complete sell-outs who plagiarized their way to stardom [II.001]. Objectively, Sugar Hill brought a level of commercial success to rap music unimagined during its early years. However, within the hip-hop community, they were universally regarded as phonies. Tricia Rose recounts their "sudden, albeit short-lived success"[14] from the perspective of hip-hop insiders:

> According to number of rappers and DJs from this period, the three members of Sugar Hill Gang were not local performers. One of the members, Hank was a doorman/bouncer at a rap club in New York and had access to bootleg tapes that he played back in northern New Jersey, an area that at this point had no local rap scene. Sylvia Robinson heard one of Hank's tapes and approached him about recording a rap single.[15]

Grandmaster Caz tells the rest of the story in Steven Hager's *Hip Hop*:

> "Later, I asked [Hank], 'Whatsup?' and he said, 'Sylvia already has two rappers and she wants one more. And she asked me to do it.' So I said, 'Well, okay, I understand that.' If it was me, I would have done the same thing. And he said, 'Well, I want to use some of your rhymes.' I threw my rhyme book on the table and said, 'Take what you want.'"
>
> Before long Robinson created the Sugar Hill Gang, a group composed of Hank, Wonder Mike, and Master Gee. Their first record, "Rapper's Delight," unexpectedly sold two million copies . . .[16]

Sugar Hill's story raises several key points about the importance of authenticity that are critical to hip-hop's definition and evolution. What and (at times, more crucially) who is hip-hop is a subject that provides perpetual fodder for debate in fora from barbershops to lecture halls. Is there a price of entry into the hip-hop firmament? Can a creative product legitimately remain part of a subversive counterculture while retaining its commercial viability? Is it possible or necessary to delimit the borders of hip-hop production while still "keeping it real?"

Architecture, too, has grappled with similar questions of authenticity within its practice, profession, and discipline. In my first essay on the subject, *The Fifth Pillar: A Case for Hip-Hop Architecture*, I insist: "To properly define Hip-Hop Architecture we must first define each of its component terms."[17] The subsequent two paragraphs compare the relative consistency of definition ascribed to hip-hop and the surprisingly inconsistent definitions of architecture gleaned from a variety of sources:

> Definitions of the word "architecture" tend to be vague and cumbersome, even when they exclude misnomers like "web architect", "information architect", "lash architect", or "architect of the Iraq war." For example, The Oxford Dictionary of Architecture and Landscape Architecture provides a 200-word explanation of the term beginning with a reference to an 1849 work by Ruskin and ending with a cynical quote from Philip Johnson defining architecture as "the art of how to waste space." A singular AIA sanctioned definition is difficult to find . . .[18]

Though architectural education has strayed from the notion that architecture is fundamentally about people, I will define here that architecture, in each of its movements, epochs, and manifestations, is the physical embodiment of dominant culture—the will of the people made visible. What defines that dominant culture and who shapes that will is the subject of later sections of this volume.

> Hip-hop's definition is far less vague. It is unanimously recognized by reference standards, from Webster's Collegiate Dictionary to urbandictionary.com, that hip-hop, though exemplified by rap music, includes all four stylistic elements or "pillars" [deejaying, emceeing, b-boying, and graffiti]. Hip-hop is a subculture—a movement that comprises an entire generation of performers, artists, thinkers and designers, and began with young urban Blacks and Latinos.[19]

Both hip-hop and architecture, however, have strict implicit and explicit codes of inclusion and exclusion. Though it may be more accurate to call the constituents of hip-hop "powerless" than those within architecture, Christopher's statement that "in a rhetorical environment of domination, powerless groups voice their resistance in coded forms"[20] may apply equally to both cohorts. The legal death grip with which architectural licensing boards across the United States have held the words "architect," "architecture," and "architectural," along with the very existence of KRS One's *The Gospel of Hip Hop: First Instrument* [II.002], is testament to how important self-definition is to either group. For architecture, protection of its legal definition is the last line of defense against impending irrelevance. Many practitioners would find themselves perpetually unemployed if municipalities no longer required their signature and stamp for issuance of permits. Hip-hop has a few contradictory challenges tied to its version of self-definition. On the one hand, clearly defined limits of who's in and who's out allows for an internal

II.002 | KRS One with a copy of *The Gospel of Hip-Hop*
© Nicci Cheeks

sense of quality control, authenticity, and autonomy. Being able to define itself on its own terms enables a level of power and agency necessary to remain relevant. On the other hand, much of this determinism is driven by the market and corporate interests. It's easier to sell a product when the outcomes are consistent, much like tomatoes, avocados, or bananas genetically engineered to be more easily packaged, shipped, and marketed if their size, color, and flavor are unvaried.

At each critical juncture of the topic's public life, architectural academics, critics, and journalists have repeatedly requested a singular definition for Hip-Hop Architecture—a request that I have repeatedly sidestepped. Confronting the question would first require a singular definition of hip-hop. Hip-hop, however, in its most authentic form (KRS One notwithstanding) has continually defied definition and confounded attempts at unilateral categorization throughout its five decades of existence. What constitutes hip-hop has expanded over the years to include everything from styles of music and dance to fashion and even yoga. "Experts" have variably labeled anyone from Tupac and Biggie, to Banksy and Iggy Azalea as hip-hop. Concurrently, each of the original four hip-hop elements has evolved into increasingly unrecognizable forms. Those that preserve a nostalgic allegiance to the pioneering 1970s or attempt to recreate the magic of the 1990s (hip-hop's so-called "golden era") reinforce the misguided notion that hip-hop can be limited to just one thing. "[W]hite people were the first to construct this reality that was concrete, had reason and form and hierarchies and categories," postulates MC Ish Butler of Shabazz Palaces, formerly of Digable Planets, "That just wasn't something that African motherfuckers were concerned with."[21] This lack of categorization is a theme that proliferated throughout each aspect of Black music and into the hip-hop era. Even at its birth, hip-hop's DJs befuddled partygoers with their eccentric musical tastes. The eclecticism of Afrika Bambaataa's record selections, drawing samples from exotic and obscure artists, balanced Kool Herc's love of 1960s funk and Grandmaster Flash's fusion of contemporary rock, classic soul, and TV show themes. "Since they were only playing a few, often unrecognizable, seconds from each song," Joseph Schloss highlights, "they were no longer bound by the more general constraints of genre or style."[22] Hip-hop is, in essence, genre-less and is anything but singular.

A more appropriately multiplistic definition of hip-hop comes from Yasiin Bey (then known as Mos Def) on the introductory track of his 1999 album, *Black on Both Sides*:

Listen, people be askin' me all the time,

'Yo Mos, what's gettin' ready to happen with hip-hop?'

'Where do you think hip-hop is goin'?'

I tell em, 'you know what's gonna happen with hip-hop?

Whatever's happening with us.'[23]

Bey's definition distills all the varied and often contradictory expressions of hip-hop ("If we smoked out, hip-hop is gonna be smoked out. If we doin' alright, hip-hop is gonna be doin' alright")[24] into one cognitive thread: that of common lived experience. That these experiences are particular to Blacks and Latinos in America, and that they are urban and youthful, is implicit in the rest of Bey's work and connects them to the legacy of the South Bronx.

As hip-hop evolves from counterculture to subculture to the dominant cultural force of our time, it must continue to resist capitalist tendencies for singular definition. Similarly, Hip-Hop Architecture must continue to avoid limiting definitions in determining the authenticity of its products. Otherwise, it risks having a similar fate to that of the engineered produce, filtered from all heirloom varieties, and stripped of its variegation and multiplicity. It must instead adopt hip-hop's core attitude, spirit, and legacy within each of its manifestations. And, like other forms of architecture, it must also transmute these into immediately discernible spatial experiences.

Despite all my resistance, side-stepping, and turns of phrase in avoidance of defining Hip-Hop Architecture it does get exhausting having to give a dissertation each time the question is asked. After five years of reading, speaking, and writing on the topic I finally gave a bite-sized description that remained loose enough to be reconciled with my unwavering positions against singularity stated previously. During an interview for MinnPost about the Saint Paul edition of the *Close to the Edge: The Birth of Hip-Hop Architecture* exhibition, I was once again pressed for definition. The answer was clear enough and short enough as a soundbite to be used in the article's title: "What's Hip-Hop Architecture? 'Hip-Hop Culture in Built Form.'"[25] [II.003]

■ ■ ■

▮ **David Letterman:** Hip-hop is all biographical. Am I right about that?

Jay-Z: Ah, no. It pretends to be. A lot o' guys are just telling stories. Very few people are telling their real true story.

DL: Really? Even in the beginning when kids are starting out?

JZ: Yeah. Lyin' . . . nine times out of ten.[26]

▮ "_____"

– *Lupe Fiasco*[27]

II.003 | Screenshot of MinnPost article "What's Hip-Hop Architecture? 'Hip-Hop Culture in Built Form'"

02 AUTHENTICITY.   021

03

GODPARENTS.

When asked what he wanted to be when he grew up, young Nathan Williams would either say, "an artist," or "a DJ." Both were natural choices for him having shown early signs of natural artistic talent and having come of age during the early days of hip-hop's success. Like most Black families, the Williamses couldn't imagine art as a legitimate career path for their child. Thoughts of young Nate pursuing art fulltime would only conjure up stereotypical images of the "starving artist" and were, thus, completely forbidden. Equally unthinkable (if not more so) was any idea of a career in hip-hop as a DJ. Unlike most Black families, however, who can only image few successful careers for talented children (doctor, lawyer, or engineer; either you slinging crack rock or you got a wicked jump shot), their attempts to ground 12-year-old Nate on a more secure foundation led them to get him a job in an architect's office running the blueprint machine. By his first year at Cornell Architecture in 1987, Williams was finding ways of bringing his love for all things hip-hop into his design studio class. The "Sound Project" assigned in ARCH 101 provided the perfect opportunity to transform his deejaying aspirations into visualizations of the sonic space of hip-hop—"both disruption and redirection of datum and theme in the DJ's scratch."[28] By his second year, he reinterpreted the bridge project assigned by Prof. Wolfgang Tschapeller into another Hip-Hop Architectural exploration. To do so, he tracked the work of local graffiti crew, "Dog Soldiers," who had tagged the bridge from the assignment, to multiple sites around Ithaca. His design, a lodge space for the Dog Soldiers, fittingly sited on the underbelly of the bridge, was a physical interpretation of their graffiti style mixed with historical references to "ancient Egyptian rites, initiations, and African cultural practices."[29] The design also came with its own soundtrack, a remix of The 45 Kings' "The 900 Number" with layers of West African percussive rhythmic communication, created as part of the design process.

By his final year at Cornell, Williams was able to fully express his ideas for an architecture based in hip-hop culture outside a prescribed studio pedagogy. At 7:00 a.m. on a December morning in 1993, in Sibley Hall room 157, Cornell Architecture's marquee review space at the time, a DJ began playing selected hip-hop beats that exemplified the wide range of Afrodiasporic sound before ending with an original composition by Soul Urge Productions (a Cornell DJ crew including Williams, Andrés Hernandez, current architecture professor Scott Ruff, and Victor LaValle, now an acclaimed author). "The specific act of appropriation of sound and space was as much a protest as it was a celebration, a call to arms and call to action."[30] Williams would then begin presenting the visual component of his undergraduate thesis, *Hip-Hop Architecture*, at the scheduled time of 9:00 a.m., two hours after the sonic incursion commenced. The audience of fellow architecture students, thesis critics Val Warke, Andrea Simitch, and Vince Mulcahy, invited guest critics, and additional professors, students, and guests were entirely unprepared for the revolutionary party/protest atmosphere they were entering, or for the historical significance of that moment.

For Hip-Hop Architects, Nate Williams' thesis presentation deserves as much reverence and heraldry as DJ Kool Herc's legendary birthday party for his sister at 1520 Sedgwick Avenue on August 11, 1973, the mythical birthdate of hip-hop.[31] Though many other factors, events, and developments converged at different moments along hip-hop's timeline, the title "originator," "pioneer," or "forefather of hip-hop" is best placed on the crown of the Black teenagers who scripted that singular event. My early writing on the topic misguidedly asserted that "the true father of hip-hop is [former New York City public works official Robert] Moses"[32] [II.004] paralleling similar assertions by Michael Ford placing Swiss architect Le Corbusier as a figure central to hip-hop's inception.[33] I have rethought this assertion for two reasons. First, similar to Schloss, who states, "I am not so much interested in the conditions themselves as I am interested in the way hip-hoppers, given these conditions, were able to create an activity that was socially, economically, and artistically rewarding,"[34] I am more interested in the potential architectural products of hip-hop than the nature of the architecture that spawned it. Second, though both men (Moses and Corbusier) were deeply influential in shaping the environments against which hip-hop culture emerged as a counterpoint—Corbusier via his initial conception of *Ville Radieuse*, or "towers-in-the-park" urbanism [II.005] and Moses via his realization of a radically interpreted form of Corbusier's vision across the five boroughs of New York City—the invocation of their names is mere empty provocation aimed at architects who have trouble imagining new forms of architecture coming from sources other than White male elites. In truth, there have been multiple points during hip-hop's evolution where young pioneers like Nate Williams have attempted to exploit intersections between the two worlds.

Craig L. Wilkins, an architect and academic, who has written most extensively on the subject of Hip-Hop Architecture, first attempted a speculative redesign for a park in Chicago using hip-hop principles in 1993. That same year, Stéphane Malka, who started as a graffiti artist in 1986, applied to art school in Paris. Malka had already used the vast expanse of vacant lots across Paris over that seven-year timespan as a training ground for honing his craft, and now felt ready to test those skills in a more academic setting. After viewing his portfolio of graffiti tags and pieces, the interviewers

II.004 | Robert Moses looks over model of Battery Bridge

II.005 | Model of Le Corbusier's Plan Voisin
Image courtesy Siefkin DR via Wikimedia Creative Commons CC BY-SA 4.0 https://commons.wikimedia.org/wiki/File:Plan_Voisin_model.jpg

at his art school immediately rejected Malka, offering that he was "lucky they didn't call the police" to report his multiple acts of vandalism. Malka then crossed the street and entered the architecture school instead.[35] Many others, before the time of Malka, Wilkins, and Williams, were introduced to the worlds of hip-hop and architecture simultaneously while attending The High School of Art and Design in Manhattan. The school was a virtual breeding ground for talented visual and performing artists during the early days of hip-hop's formation. Students there between the 1970s and early 1980s participated in exchanging graffiti books in the lunchroom or rap and b-boy battles in the schoolyard. The architecture class, however, as recounted by Carlos "MARE 139" Rodriguez, was a "discriminatory space." "Architecture classes were too meticulous and dry and lacking excitement," he recalls, "It was a challenge for anyone in those classes to practice anything related to hip-hop."[36]

Many others since that time have felt the compulsion to express their hip-hop cultural identities within their work only to be discouraged and ridiculed for not grounding their ideas in established academic knowledge or holding on to the notion that any connection between hip-hop and architecture even existed. A few contemporaries of Nate Williams at Cornell like Amanda Williams and André Gould were emboldened by the revolutionary thesis they had witnessed as freshmen and inspired to explore other aspects of hip-hop culture in their own thesis projects. Those outside of the Cornell bubble of the 1990s were either confined to using references from entirely outside of architecture or forced to position themselves as lone wolves who had invented the concepts all on their own. Not until the year 2000, when Wilkins published his seminal essay *(W)rapped Space: The Architecture of Hip Hop* was there any traditionally academic foothold for expanding the topic. By 2005 two other treatises seeking to discover the architectural space and language of hip-hop—one by Jabari Garland, the other by James Garrett, Jr.—found their way into academic journals. The current landscape of written, auditory, and visual content accessible to an increasing number of students interested in studying Hip-Hop Architecture includes essays by Wilkins and Kara Walker in Walker's 2014 *Ruffneck Constructivists*; Wilkins' books *The Aesthetics of Equity* and *Diversity among Architects*; Lawrence Chua's chapter in *Archi.pop*; lectures, presentations, and an entry in the 2017 issue of *Platform* by Michael Ford; documentation from courses taught by Chris Cornelius at the University of Wisconsin-Milwaukee and by Stephen Slaughter at the University of Cincinnati; excerpts of the 2015 *Towards a Hip-Hop Architecture* symposium; documentation of the *Close to the Edge* exhibition; and many other interviews, podcasts, panels, lecture, and TED talks seeking deeper understandings of the topic.

Over the last three decades the hip-hop generation has become increasingly effective at developing and disseminating work about Hip-Hop Architecture, each step bringing us closer to its establishment as canon and combating the disciplinary resistance that has discouraged so many passionate students from expressing their own hip-hop–based ideas of architecture and dissuaded so many others from architecture all together. We have many forbearers to thank for this improved position including the official "Godfather of Hip-Hop Architecture"[37] Nate Williams. Ironically, for Williams, the biggest hurdles weren't particular to hip-hop culture. "The conflicts that I faced were more about the legitimacy of there being any kind of African American culture in design, as opposed to legitimizing hip-hop. The hip-hop part didn't even matter. People were struggling with the idea that there was any type of feasible or cohesive and continuative concept of design and culture [particular to] being African in the Americas. Once they got past that everything else was easy."[38]

■ ■ ■

Jack Travis: When I first heard [Michael Ford] say ["Le Corbusier is the Forefather of Hip-Hop"[39]] in Philadelphia in October, I'm sitting there listening to this and I'm going: "what the fuck is going on here?" And then I thought about when John Lennon said, "The Beatles are more famous than Jesus Christ." It's exactly what you [Michael] just said. You are looking at a deeper meaning than who the forefather is. It's a bigger broader sense for you. But I was thinking that there needs to be another word in that sentence before the word forefather. There is something that has to go in that for me. Then you said f-o-u-r fathers, "the four fathers." And if there is a word before that one, I think I could come up with something like "original." "The four original fathers of hip-hop." But there has to be another word there, and I don't know what that word is for Le Corbusier. I think that's really the search for you.

Shawn Rickenbacker: I don't think I know [what that word is] but I have two images that are associated with this statement. One, clearly, I might agree with you that he is the unintended forefather of hip-hop by circumstance. Then the other thing is that less than a half-mile away from Sedgwick Ave. there were other crews living in low tenement buildings and inherited domiciles. For every tenement building there were probably five or six 40-foot by 100-foot empty lots before you got to the next one. This was the South Bronx and the eighties. This is what was. Still, coming out of that, I was thinking: "Ok, we can draft Robert Moses into this.

We can draft urban policies and those sorts of things." But clearly the identifiable marker, which I would agree with you, would be the high-rise. And to that extent, interestingly enough, trying to understand the evolution of a culture that was literally trying to express their frustration with their environment. And through that came the birth of hip-hop. Had there been more tools or more economic structure, I guarantee you we might have been looking at some versions of Eames structures in the South Bronx. This is exactly why I became an architect. I saw a bunch of empty land. I thought to myself: "Oh my God! Something can be done." I'm running around the streets getting stuck up—the conversation that we had on the bus. This was my life. Now, to a certain extent, I knew it could be and should be better. Really, where it started was with my immediate environment. This is a true story. I'm not making this up. About three or four of us, when I was growing up, in one of these empty lots, were cobbling together broken bricks to see if we could get the damn wall to stand up, thinking we could do something. No mortar. No epoxy. Just balance. "Step back! No! No!" I'm getting off track, but this image sat with me. I actually read it before I heard you say it. I thought, "well of course." But those same guys I grew up with, the same guys I still know now, they don't know who Le Corbusier is.

Andrés Hernandez: I feel some kind of way, as they say, about this. I've heard the conversation and I think it's really interesting as a provocation. I appreciate what you're saying about it opens the door for these other things. One of my concerns about some of our conversation though is: where is the agency of people to actually do their thing? We are really putting architecture on a level where basically we're just reproducing whatever the architecture did for them. And that's a dangerous slope to go down. There are ways of being in space, there are ways of understanding space, that have nothing to do with modernism. So when it's applied we understand that it has these implications. But when it isn't a modernist principle organizing the world it has a different implication. I want to make sure that we bring to the surface that there are other ways of being and thinking about space that have nothing to do with Corbusier or Moses or whatever. I do understand that it's the perfect storm of policy, building, law, and everything else that comes together to create these environments. But, at the same time, I want to make sure there is room for us to talk about our own power and our historical power to design and occupy space in ways that make sense for us, separate from what everyone else thought of. If that's on the table, I'm down with it.

Craig Wilkins: I just wanted to get to the point about other ways of being. I think this is the interesting thing about Mike's take on this. The nexus of that oppressive structure, whatever that is—whether it's Corbu's towers-in-the-park, or whether it's the vacant lots [in the South Bronx], or in Detroit the dilapidated buildings—is the spatial practices that are laid upon that and the way you respond to these particular things. So, I don't think it's ever off the table. I think it is part of the conversation. Say you did predict that people would rage against living in this way, but because it was a particular kind of people who have a particular kind of spatial practice. That was how they raged. You have another group of people who have another way of raging because they have another kind of making space. So, I don't think it's ever off the table.

James Garrett, Jr.: I'm one of the people who disagree with the statement. I feel like architecture does not necessarily create the social relationships and the social network that is necessary in order for a cultural movement to begin. Perhaps in some kind of a happenstance way some people might have lived in buildings or co-op towers that were reminiscent of some of the social housing projects Le Corbusier was imagining in 1920s France. That's fine. I would also agree with you that modernism needs to be destroyed. There are some real serious implications to taking the people whose culture is generally about the street and interacting in the street and the block parties. It's a culture that really lives and breathes, derives its energy, from the street, from its relationships, from the people. It doesn't derive its energy in any way from the housing blocks. The other thing I would say is that when these housing blocks were new, they were heralded as modernity. There are all these old archival photos of happy brown-faced people in these buildings that were really proud of these. In Chicago. In New York. In Minneapolis. So that rage wasn't immediate. It wasn't like they were being incarcerated and warehoused. This was seen as the new technology. This was the new thing. People were happy to have something that wasn't a tenement at the time. And over generations of poor maintenance some of those energies started to build up and some of the responses maybe fueled hip-hop.[40]

04

RACE.

Iggy Azalea was the name most often mentioned throughout the two-day symposium *Towards a Hip-Hop Architecture*, hosted by Syracuse University's School of Architecture in the spring of 2015. This happened not because she somehow embodies any critical aspects of Hip-Hop Architecture's history, theory, or its evolution into practice, but because she serves as a reminder of the significance of race within hip-hop culture and increased misunderstanding of that significance over time. Much like the Sugar Hill Gang, she has been the source of continued debate around who can legitimately occupy the space of hip-hop celebrity. Beyond the dubious nature of her rise to stardom (produced by established rap artist T.I., a seemingly more legitimate option than the White industry outsider Sylvia Robinson who produced Sugar Hill) and the apparent inauthenticity of her rapping accent, the fact that she is a blonde-haired, white-skinned Australian calls her entire hip-hop credibility into question. The most significant part of this debate (which I have dubbed the "Iggy Azalea Conundrum") is the question: "Is hip-hop is an exclusively Black/Brown/minority enterprise?" It may be convenient to place all White rappers under the same heading as Dan Hancox does in describing the "wigga" (White nigga). "US rap has numerous discussions of the phenomenon of the 'wigga,'" he states, "and the disproportionate media prominence and industry support given, Elvis Presley-style, to white rappers from Vanilla Ice to Eminem, by an at best cynical and at worst racist music industry."[41] This attitude misses the critical subtleties determining hip-hop's rejection of the former artist and acceptance of the latter. A quick analysis of the perceptual difference between Vanilla Ice and Eminem will reveal a clearer understanding of racial politics within the hip-hop establishment. Vanilla Ice will continue to be the ultimate caricature of White rappers given the inauthentic persona he created to be more saleable to mass audiences (claiming that he "grew up in the ghetto" when he was actually "a middle-class kid from Dallas, Texas").[42] Meanwhile, the authenticity of Eminem's path to success, having come up through the Detroit underground battle-rap scene, the undeniable superiority of his technical skill, and the uniqueness of lyrical narratives have earned him unchallenged entry into hip-hop's inner sanctums.

For Rose, hip-hop is unapologetically Black. "Rap music is a black cultural expression," she writes in *Black Noise*, "that prioritizes black voices from the margins of urban America."[43] Though she consistently refers to its pioneers as both African-American and Afro-Caribbean, she also routinely positions hip-hop within general understandings of "Blackness" and "otherness" in describing the Afrodiasporic influences on its forms. Joseph

Schloss concurs with Rose through his statement, "hip-hop is African American music" and similarly connects the form to Black Americans, Puerto Ricans, and West Indians.[44] "As a result," he continues, "African-derived aesthetics, social norms, standards, and sensibilities are deeply embedded in the form, even when it is being performed by individuals who are not themselves of African descent."[45] Similarly, for Hancox, "Grime is black music (even if it's not always made by black people)."[46] In framing his own definition of a hip-hop generation, Jeff Chang highlights the challenges to Baraki Kitwana's definition of "African Americans born between 1965 and 1984"[47] by those excluded without proper acknowledgment. "How could one accept a definition of a Hip-Hop Generation which excluded the culture's pioneers, like Kool Herc and Afrika Bambaataa, for being born too early? Or one that excluded those who had come to claim and transform hip-hop culture, but were not Black or born in America?"[48] Though many practitioners of hip-hop culture are not of African descent, hip-hop heads who don't personally identify as Black must retain an awareness of hip-hop's African lineage.

Being Black, for our purposes, does not exclude the contributions of the Latino community, many of whom were pioneering DJs, graff writers, and b-boys, each integral to the creation and evolution of hip-hop culture. Nor does it ignore other pioneers like TAKI 183, a Greek immigrant who brought early notoriety to urban graffiti writing. Blackness here can be understood as a state of being that is common to the marginalized, underprivileged, and institutionally underserved and that is rooted in the trauma of those stolen from their West African homelands and brought to the continents and islands of the European colonies in America. For my purposes, and the purposes of this book, I see the word Black through this lens. This liberates Black from being a skin-color tested against brown paper bags, or a box on a form requesting self-identification in opposition to Hispanic, Asian, or Pacific Islander, or a DNA–tested heredity rooted only in those parts of Africa considered to comprise the "dark continent." It connects Black people to a common struggle for self-determination within a system of oppression and control. (You know when some White dude says some really ignorant shit like asking "where are you from?" when he really means "what racial or ethnic box can I put you in?" or a White woman has no clue that her Whiteness comes with privilege ("Oh they didn't let you in?"), you can just look across the way, catch an eye, and give a nod. That's the kind of Black I'm talking about.)

The "double-consciousness"[49] required for being Black and an architect at the same time intensifies the calculus of success in America—an existence based on promises of prosperity rather than oppression, exclusion, and otherness. This desire to succeed echoes Du Bois' description of the African American: "He simply wishes to make it possible for a man to be both a Negro and an American without being cursed and spit upon by his fellows, without having the doors of opportunity closed roughly in his face."[50] My expanded definition aside, only about 2 percent of all registered architects in this country identify as Black.[51] This is a statistic that has only slightly increased from the 1 percent figure at the time of Whitney Young's famously exhorting keynote address to the American Institute of Architects (AIA) in 1968. "One need only take a casual look at this audience," he observed, "to see that we have a long way to go in this field of integration of the architects."[52] Though precise numbers are difficult to source in a single location, the percentages of self-identified Black architecture students is only slightly higher, making architecture one of the most underrepresented professions of our time. This is unsurprising given the historical nature of architecture institutions catering primarily to White males, and the profession being established as a vocation for elites. Further, the discipline of architecture has promoted "shared vocabulary, history, references, techniques, practices, and codes of conduct"[53] from a position of Western idealism. Many have managed to exist simultaneously as successful architects and Black. Few have managed to express their Blackness through their architecture. Within hip-hop culture lies the blueprint for an architecture that is authentically Black with the power to upend the racist structures within the architectural establishment and ignite a new paradigm of creative production.

One of the more forward-thinking exhibitions in recent times to include hip-hop attitudes and present the work of Black architects and designers was The Studio Museum in Harlem's *harlemworld: Metropolis as Metaphor* in 2004. Museum director, Lowery Stokes Sims, introduces the work of the eighteen participants by describing "The history of African Americans in architecture and urban design," as a history of "struggle, both a struggle for recognition with these arenas; and a struggle to achieve a synthesis between an Afrocentric sensibility of mutability and eco-compatibility and a European statement of permanence and dominance (or the illusion thereof)."[54] This struggle for synthesis is common to anyone attempting to bring an identity heavily influenced by Black culture to the field of architecture, dominated by Eurocentric points of view. The work included in the exhibition and the essays published in the final catalog describe a complex tapestry of Black history and culture mapped onto a twenty-first-century urban landscape—an architecture of the city understood only through Black identity and hip-hop sensibility. Thelma Golden, the show's curator, explains that the show's title comes from a Ma$e lyric on The Notorious B.I.G.'s "Mo'

Money Mo' Problems" [II.006] referencing "Harlem World."[55] Greg Tate's essay describes Harlem as "a world within a world within even the Black world . . . that can, when it chooses, negate anything from the outside world that is not coming from hip-hop, Hollywood, or live Africans."[56] Tate later connects Harlem's historical capacity for musical production to the physical nature of the streetscape:

> The freedom its folk feel to be as loud and Black as they want to be in this space of their own making . . . creates those eddies and energies of utter Negrocity that jazz, blues, gospel, hip-hop, salsa, and house have taught us can rhythmically structure the flow and curvature of information, space, and identity in galaxies far beyond the real estate known as Harlem.[57]

Other work in the show by young practitioners imagined contemporary hip-hop readings of Harlem such as *Silver Shoe Mantra* by Amanda Williams, re-envisioning 125th Street with samples from Los Vegas, Bilbao, and the mythical land of Oz; *(Counter) insurgents: "Dispossess the Natives"* by Olalekan Jeyifous' mixing various three-dimensional narratives of insurgents and their tools used to re-inhabit the city varying from highly engineered structures to graffiti; and *Harlem: The Ghetto Fabulous* by PHAT (a collaboration between Nathaniel Belcher and Stephen Slaughter) envisioning glamorous penthouses depicting hip-hop "bling" lifestyles overlaid atop the city grid. Works by more established academics, Milton S.F. Curry and Darell W. Fields, grappled with more fundamental questions of defining Blackness within architecture. Curry presented theories of Black Futurism and Afromodernity: "blackness is about space—its occupation, inscription, description, thickness and depth; it is no longer about a failed nostalgic conception of visual representation in the form of skin."[58] Fields' rhetorical poster for the exhibition asks, "If architecture were black, how would you recognize it?"[59]

Black people in the United States have been engaged in a century-long struggle for acknowledgement and relevance within architectural practice. Our ranks include several competent and highly accomplished individuals who have found remarkable levels of success within an overwhelmingly White profession.[60] Those who have succeeded, like Hilyard Robinson and Paul Revere Williams, though "Ignored by the architectural elites for [most] of their careers,"[61] have based their designs and processes on an assimilated Western norm. Others fully accepted within the *starchitect* category don't fully identify as African American, like Ricardo Scofidio of Diller Scofidio + Renfro who "is African American in heritage but does not identify as African American,"[62] and David Adjaye who identifies as British-Ghanaian.

II.006 | Screenshot from "Mo Money Mo Problems" music video
"The Notorious B.I.G - Mo Money Mo Problems" directed by Hype Williams © WMG (on behalf of Bad Boy); LatinAutor - SonyATV, EMI Music Publishing, Sony ATV Publishing, BMI - Broadcast Music Inc., SOLAR Music Rights Management, PEDL, UNIAO BRASILEIRA DE EDITORAS DE MUSICA - UBEM, CMRRA, LatinAutor - Warner Chappell, ASCAP, Warner Chappell, LatinAutor, and 14 music rights societies 1997. All rights reserved

Few have attempted to base an entire career on being Black, doing so mainly by looking to their African ancestry for a sense of legitimate aesthetic expression. Jack Travis, architect, educator, and author of *African Americans in Current Practice*, has spent much of his career "trying to flush out [his] own interpretation of what might be considered the basic beginnings of a Black aesthetic approach to the visual expression of environmental design disciplines."[63] David Hughes, author of *Afrocentric Architecture: A Design Primer*, like Travis, continues to espouse the idea of grounding African American architectural expression in Western, Eastern, Central, and Southern African imagery.

These essentializations of Black aesthetics leaves clear openings for design parody. As Mabel Wilson puts it, "Whether discovered in the ghetto, the colony, or remote regions, blackness and black building forms, in their vital simplicity, provided white architects with conceptual and formal inspiration to advance their cause of social progress and technological advancement in the metropole."[64] Mario Gooden adds: "architecture can neither be essentialized to race nor racial representations" and "the politics of 'Black Style'" cannot be relegated to aesthetics.[65] "Rather," he posits, "it is a politics that refers to spatial praxes and resistance. This is the manner in which blacks occupy and move through space, negotiate spatial relationships, and create alternative spaces for creative expression and daily affirmation of life in American society."[66] The promise of Hip-Hop Architecture is in its ability to establish a way of working that is recognizably Black beyond mere aesthetics—an architectural practice, profession, and discipline deeply connected to the legacy of displaced African peoples in the Americas and legible in its production process and spatial resonance.

If Hip-Hop Architecture does become solidified and recognizable in purely aesthetic terms, there remains the constantly looming fear of cultural appropriation. During the two-part symposium event after the Saint Paul opening of *Close to the Edge,* I was asked the same question phrased in almost the exact same way by two separate White male architects, once during the presentation session at the exhibition space and again during the continued conversation at the University of Minnesota. Each was seeking to know how they as representatives of the dominant majority could practice Hip-Hop Architecture. I felt a bit of internal pride feeling that the topic had somehow "arrived" after several years of being mocked and discouraged. That feeling was quickly overtaken by a simmering rage at the thought of being once again trumped by The Man. "Why would you even want to?" was my ultimate response. "Y'all are doing just fine."

■ ■ ■

Tya Winn: I also think that we are a field that has been a stranger to talking about race in a qualitative and serious way. Our field has been against talking about socio-economic issues. And I wonder, one, how can we—if architecture can address the root of the issue that sparked the movement—really start to create an architecture around it? But two, I think right now as an idea, Hip-Hop Architecture is protected. I mean, look around this room. This is the most Brown people in a room I've seen in a lecture on architecture in my life. It's pretty much stayed within the culture—minority culture. It has been protected by the people that lived it and experienced it. Are we ready to mainstream? I mean, right now Hip-Hop Architecture is underground hip-hop. And hip-hop has gone through a lot of growing pains. Craig touched on a lot of them earlier. For every J. Cole there is an Iggy Azalea. Then it gets even worse—you get the appropriation of Miley Cyrus. And it's not bad music, but it's different. Are we ready yet? Have we defined it yet within this house to put it out to the public and open it up for critique and open it up for remixing from other cultures? And then once that happens, where are we going to go from there?

Craig Wilkins: I don't know if the argument here is necessarily about mainstreaming anything. There is always a danger when you talk about anything that somebody might overhear and find it is interesting and useful and take it on themselves. One could argue, literally, that's what happened to hip-hop. Let's just say that the evolution has been that somebody found it useful, interesting, and figured out a way they could make money on it and corporatized it. I think there is always that danger. But I don't think that's what we are talking about here. I think these kinds of conversations absolutely have to happen. Maybe they don't need to happen in the university or the institution. But if they want to provide the resources for it, God bless 'em. Thank you. But we still need to have these conversations. And part of what you may have heard, or hopefully you have heard, from each of the presenters is how important it is to hold on to it, to define it, to make sure that the folks who produce it, the folks who live it, the folks who suffer the consequences of it, remain front and center, and clearly own that idea and whatever comes out of that idea. To a certain degree it's almost anti-architectural. It really is. But I don't think the conversation here was about, or hopefully it didn't come off as, we need to do this and show the world that it can be done. No, we need to do this so we can see that it is done.

Andrés Hernandez: I do think that the people are begging for something like this. That is what is coming out of this; that this is about empowerment. So, they may not necessarily know they are begging for it in terms of saying, "I want that." Like that building that we saw yesterday with the graffiti façade. But I think that people know that they are desiring something because they are making those spaces on their own now. They are looking to the profession saying, "What are you going to do for us? We are doing a little bit of this, but how can y'all make it better?"

CW: Well there is just one more point on this. Are the cameras on? Cut the cameras. I don't wanna be on camera when I say this. They didn't cut it? Alright, you can edit it out later. You promise? Liar! Anyway, whatever.

We're not allowed to have diddlysquat. We are not. Historically, whatever you can have. How many people in here have seen *Raiders of the Lost Ark*? You remember that point where Dr. Belloq takes the skull, after [Indiana Jones] gets past the rolling stone and he comes out? Belloq takes the skull and says, "Dr. Jones, I have proven that there is nothing that you have that I cannot take away." That's what I feel about what happens to many of the things that come out our experience.

If you talk to people about the history of rock music, rock historians will downplay the influence of African Americans in that field. They will just downplay it. You really can't do it with jazz because that's just denying an entire thing. But here we have Macklemore winning, Iggy Azalea being nominated. You can play and sing whatever you want. It's the discourse around them that troubles me. It's like, "if we can erase that troublesome part then now it's great." I don't want to see that happen with this possibility of a Hip-Hop architecture.

I'm not for necessarily saying nobody outside of what you might consider the hip-hop community. You may even argue that I'm not part of that, and that's fine. But what I am for is always the acknowledgement and the respect of where this comes from. I think that's the problem with Azalea, is that she just thinks that "well, this is just music and I can just do whatever I want with it," and people are trying to tell her "no, it comes from some place that you need to at least acknowledge." I don't want to have that in my discipline. This is a moment where we get to make some choices, we get to make some decisions, we get to decide how certain things should happen and how they shouldn't happen. I want us to take advantage of that.[67]

05 GENDER.

In 2013, Women in Design, a group comprising students at Harvard University's Graduate School of Design, gained international attention with the circulation of their petition to the Pritzker Architecture Prize committee to retroactively acknowledge Denise Scott Brown's contribution to the work of the firm Venturi Scott Brown and Associates. "Women in architecture deserve the same recognition as their male counterparts," the petition demanded. "Denise Scott Brown's contributions were seminal to her partner Robert Venturi winning the prize in 1991."[68] Scott Brown herself criticized the Pritzker jury, after Zaha Hadid became the prize's first female recipient, as having "a certain definition of architecture, an almost 19th century notion of great men and of design that is generated through the genius of one mind. It's taken a long time to find a woman to fit these notions."[69] More than 20,000 individuals signed the petition including Hadid, notable female architects like Farshid Moussavi, and even Venturi. However, the petition was not universally embraced by the architecture community. The reaction by one particular Pritzker laureate, for example (here quoted anonymously) was, "they don't give prizes to the wives."

Widely recognized as the highest international honor in recognition of architects, the Pritzker has a 40-year lineage of White and Asian male honorees (Hadid won in 2004, and until 2020's award to Yvonne Farrell and Shelley McNamara, there have been only two other women recognized, both as partners in collaborative practices).[70] There isn't enough space in this book (or expertise by this author) to thoroughly scrutinize the state of gender relationships within architecture.[71] However, there are a few key statistics worth reiterating as often as is necessary for them to improve. Though highest among engineering-related occupations as categorized by the Bureau of Labor Statistics, the percentage of "full-time wage and salary workers" in architecture who identified as women was only 24.2 in 2016[72] despite the fact that 40 percent of those who had completed the pre-licensure qualifications in that same year were women.[73] All this, coupled with the statistics cited earlier for Blacks in architecture, makes Black women virtual snow leopards of the field. As of this writing, only 470 are licensed to practice in the United States.[74]

A definitive scrutiny of hip-hop's dubious track record with female inclusion would be similarly challenging to include within these pages. The references I include in this section are just the beginner texts on a topic that has both been thoroughly interrogated by bona fide experts and easily appreciated by casual observers of hip-hop culture. However, sidestepping the subject of gender in a work seeking to connect two disciplines with equally offensive shortcomings would be unnecessarily evasive and unprofessional.

In her introduction to *Black Noise*, Rose offers her interrogation of hip-hop through the complex lens of her own identity as an "African-American woman of biracial parentage."[75] Race, gender, and the contradictory forces within race and gender, carve her path through hip-hop's tangled landscape. While repeatedly highlighting the contributions of women in all aspects of hip-hop culture throughout its history (from pioneering female DJs, MCs, b-girls, and graff writers to contemporary producers, radio personalities, and academics), Rose also reminds readers of the often undervalued and overshadowed positions hip-hop's women have held and the need for more direct confrontation of sexism within the music industry.

Bettina Love discusses the recondite relationship Black women have with hip-hop. In doing so, she also highlights the role of capitalism in forming hip-hop's most distasteful imagery. "The race-specific sophisticated marketing of rap music by corporate America transmits more than just 'hood stories of violence, gangs, crime, and womanizing," she contends. "It draws from a legacy of patriarchy, corporate greed, and the White exoticization of the Black female body."[76] Neither rap music nor hip-hop culture created sexism and misogyny as one might glean from dominant public perception. Instead, they are "a reflection of the prevailing values in our society" as bell hooks claims; "values created and sustained by white supremacist capitalist patriarchy."[77] Love defines for her readers the growing field of Hip-Hop Feminism using foundational texts from Gwendolyn Pough and Whitney Peoples to ground her arguments. "Simply defined," she states, "Hip Hop feminism seeks to examine rap music and culture through a Black feminist lens and questions the misogyny and sexism within the art form but recognizes the sexual agency of women who utilize the culture to express themselves and their sexual desires."[78] In this way hip-hop can be called to task for its negative attributes while simultaneously used to empower Black women. Pough ("my development as a Black woman and a Black feminist is deeply tied to my love of hip hop"[79]) and Peoples ("hip-hop feminists contend that hip-hop is also a site where young black women begin or further develop their gender critique and feminist identity"[80]) both corroborate this point of view.

Dyson dedicates an entire chapter of *Holler If You Hear Me: Searching for Tupac Shakur* to the question of Tupac's controversial and contradictory attitudes towards women. He paints a complex picture of the rap artist: raised by a former Black Panther Party member, ex-convict, drug-addicted single mother who taught him to respect and cherish women; raised in the streets of Harlem, the Bronx, Baltimore, and Marin City, California, which taught him to defend his masculinity through the objectification and subjugation of women. In recounting his teenage pursuits of the opposite sex Dyson quotes Shakur:

"I was liking this girl . . . and I'm extra nice. Extra gentleman. I'm extra just, like, 'Oh, you're beautiful, and you deserve the best.' And she told me I was too nice. I couldn't believe it. It wouldn't work because I was too nice. . . .

"I went through a week of just going, 'Forget it. I'm just going to be like [the bad boys] because they seem to get the girls, and the call girls the b word, and they smack and beat [them], and they're getting girls. And I'm going, 'Peace,' and 'I think you're beautiful,' and they're going, 'Well, I like him because he's masculine.'"[81]

The "masculine" image to which Shakur refers is an artificial construct. Shabazz' *Constructing Blackness* provides a clear historical contextualization of this contemporary Black male identity—one rooted in a legacy of incarceration and slavery, each system intent on stripping the masculinity of its subjugates. For Shabazz, gender disparity and homophobia within hip-hop culture exists less as an intentional disparaging or exclusion of the female or gay than an over-amplification of a reactionary, unambiguously heterosexual, male figure.[82]

I imagine that Rose, Dyson, Love, Pough, Peoples, and Shabazz have had to continually play the role of apologists for each of their controversial male subjects to a much greater degree than I have had to in defense of Kanye West.[83] Even in clarifying his position that "Hip-hop has been distinguished by an assault on women that is remarkable for its virulence as for its crushing lack of creativity,"[84] Dyson will be forever associated with the most distasteful attributes of Shakur's character in the minds of those too invested in their own victimhood to appreciate the circumspection of his arguments.

Unlike these other authors, Dream Hampton has been willing to reject hip-hop all together if it can't separate from its most troubling aspects. In 2012, Hampton announced publicly that she was "done with hip hop and men who collude to silence women."[85] Though that statement proved to be less definitive than it seemed at the time,[86] Hampton has remained uncompromising in calling out misogyny and other good-old-boy shenanigans deeply embedded within the culture, most famously bringing R. Kelly's decades-long criminal activity back into public consciousness in "Surviving R. Kelly."[87]

Like Hampton, Hip-Hop Architecture must resist the pressure to shy away from hip-hop's darker side. Only by facing racism, sexism, homophobia, and other forms of physical and psychological violence in both hip-hop and architecture will their effects be understood and neutralized.

■ ■ ■

■ "I like this idea of somebody's mama making something out of nothing. Who really made it possible for these wonders to be created and recreated on our corners? It may be the forefathers—intentional or unintentional. But what about the girls who were on the corner with the songs of double-dutch; with the hand games that provided the rhythms that would become part of everything up until Nelly ruined every childhood song I've ever heard. I blame Nelly. Who has been left out of this narrative? I would say we have to start asking, 'who were the foremothers of architecture and hip-hop?' One of the things I've had the honor of doing over the past few years at Cornell University is to be able to meet people like Sha-rock and Queen Lisa Lee. It goes on and on and on, the people who get left out of this story. I think we have to do the work of not just reimaging hip-hop history as something other than people raging against the machine. These are street hustlers right who knew that you could kill somebody with a mike or kill somebody with a gun. Which one is going to be more profitable? I think we have to reimagine and re-gender this story.

"The last thing I'll say is that I think the places that get left out of hip-hop history are the gay clubs that actually nurtured this new form of music. That [is something] no one wants to talk about. We imagine it went from the block parties straight to MTV. Black radio wasn't having it. Heterosexual clubs didn't want to hear this noise. I'm a big critic of Russell Simons on everything—everything he's done since "Def Comedy Jam." He is a culture vulture. But what I do like is that he has used his newfound wealth to recreate that history to say that between '77, '78, and '79 it was those queer clubs that really provided the space for people to quickly emerge on the scene. So I think we have to begin reimagining, re-gendering, and re-queering what has otherwise become the standard history 101 of where we're at."

– Travis Gosa[88]

■ "As the lone girl in the crew, I would say that feminism isn't necessarily something that I have with a capital F sitting in my studio. But it's definitely something that comes into play when I think about the problems that hip-hop started to have for me when I started to evolve and grow. I didn't feel this music was the soundtrack of my entire life. What were some of the things that didn't sync? One of them is the Biggie song ["One More Chance"] "Navajos creep me in they tepee," but Navajos actually live in hogans. Then there's the shape of the tepee and the idea of what he is suggesting sexually. This is me pretending to beat Biggie up. . . . The other piece I did with Krista Franklin called "Frozen Assets" or "Lemme Ice You Like Kobe Wife," in which we recreated the 1996 Lil' Kim cover as a piece of ice for the intro to our show. It was a huge hit with my daughter who was two at the time."

– *Amanda Williams*[89]

06

NOSTALGIA.

At the 1998 annual conference for the National Organization of Minority Architects (NOMA) in Washington, DC, a panel of three recent Cornell and Syracuse University graduates challenged the audience with a more progressive vision of Black architecture than they had ever considered. Amanda Williams, Andrés L. Hernandez, and Brian C. West each delivered presentations grounded in a defiant, unapologetic, and irreverent attitude with new hip-hop-based architectural theories.[90] Having been incubated for several years in the halls of Sibley and Rand in Ithaca, and expanded to Slocum in Syracuse and Wurster in Berkeley, Hip-Hop Architecture was now ready for its first public moment. That conference session is solidified in my memory as an epic battle between the "young guns" and the "old heads." A highlight for me was Earl Bell's comments during the Q&A: "if I chat like this, that's hip-hop. If I walk like this (skanking across the floor), that's hip-hop. So anything I do, art, architecture, music, whatever—that's hip-hop." He killed it! The professional NOMA members, being more content to find ways of survival within a White-dominated profession, were not very welcoming to the radical ideas posited by Williams, Hernandez, and West. The organization itself, formed almost thirty years earlier "to fight discriminatory policies that limit or bar minority architects from participating in design and constructions programs,"[91] tended to hold more conservative perspectives. Some members, like David Hughes and Jack Travis, were seeking to ground all Black practice in Afrocentrism or to create a singular Afrocentric aesthetic. Students and younger professionals in attendance were more compelled by Hernandez' "10 Points of Hiphopitecture" (what some called the idea at the time) than any professional ethics workshop, government contracting seminar, or back-to-Africa idealist theory on offer.

1. Hiphopitecture must be grounded in the realities of urban experiences—it must "keep it real" but never create fiction, "represent" these experiences in their totality, and should allow and account for the diversity of these experiences.
2. Hiphopitecture must allow and account for the evolution and revolution of the communities within which it occurs—it must concern itself with elevation, not stagnation and "nostalgic paralysis" of itself as a culture and within the community.
3. Hiphopitecture must build on existing foundations—it must recognize that there are no *tabula rasas* and take into account the myriad histories and perspectives that drive communities and serve as an educational precedent.

4. Hiphopitecture must never allow itself to be controlled by elements and forces outside of the cultures within which it occurs—it must ultimately and most importantly be defined and determined by the people in order for it to remain authentic and relevant to the community.
5. Hiphopitecture must wed theory and practice with social responsibility—it must set out to solve society's myriad problems, but particularly those of underrepresented and marginalized communities.
6. Hiphopitecture must occur as cooperative, not competitive, processes—it must lend itself to building and sustaining communities, to be affirmative, not detrimental or destructive.
7. Hiphopitecture must be equally educational and functional—it must serve a purpose, namely the elevation of underrepresented and marginalized communities, and should not only be judged according to its aesthetic value or worth.
8. Hiphopitecture must be accessible to the communities in which it occurs, and clear in its actions and intentions—it must allow and account for the participation of communities and as such, must be fully comprehended by these communities.
9. Hiphopitecture must result in processes and products that reflect the communities within which it occurs—it must concern itself with the aesthetics, values, and philosophies of these communities.
10. Hiphopitecture must occur by any means necessary—it must be.[92]

Hernandez' 10-point platform would be the first in a series of treatises aimed at codifying the main tenets of an architectural movement yet to be realized at the time. The next surfaced two years later in Wilkins' *(W)rapped Space*, where he outlined "four primary principles necessary for the manifestation of Hip Hop space"[93] listed under the following section titles:

Hip Hop Architecture: Palimpsestic

Hip Hop Architecture: Anthropomorphic

Hip Hop Architecture: Performative

Hip Hop Architecture: Adaptive[94]

Each has proven to be a productive design tool for architects and students invested in creating hip-hop space since its publication. Additionally, the four principles represent the starting point for subsequent treatises by Garland and Garrett, Jr. Garland's *Flow-Tektonics* explains and expands three of Wilkins' principles while connecting it to another set of principles forwarded by Sharon Pat West, then an architecture student in Halifax, Nova Scotia.

Anthropomorphism is analogous to West's principle of Community.

- Physically wrapping, touching, or penetrating neighboring buildings.
- Allowing views deep into a building to demystify its functions and thus help prevent community alienation.

Performative is analogous to West's principle of Public Expression.

- Be physically open or at least able to be visually penetrated to help develop a relationship between the user and passer-by, much like the tradition of call and response, which invites participation in the event.
- Contain elements for public announcement such as videos monitors, message screens or other places to broadcast information.

Adaptive is analogous to West's principle of Adaptation.

- Reusing existing buildings wherever possible.
- Using pre-fabricated material not normally used for construction.[95]

Garrett, Jr. begins his 2003 treatise on Hip-Hop Architecture, titled *Resonant Spaces/Dynamic Flows*, with the four elements of hip-hop, which he re-labels "turntablism, rapping, muralism, and break-dancing."[96] He takes a step away from pure nostalgic reference to early hip-hop culture by grounding his definition of Hip-Hop Architecture in attitudes rather than techniques:

> I see Hip-Hop architecture, ultimately, as a communic8ion of movement and flow from the perspective of the artist/designer. I see the Hip-Hop architect as a medi8or, transl8or and incub8or of this energy flow—a go-between, oscillating back and forth between the art 4rm and the building process. [sic][97]

Most ideas and experiments in hip-hop-based architectural production have maintained similarly nostalgic connections either to hip-hop's original composition or to its "golden age" between the late 1980s and the mid-1990s. Beginning with the four elements is a natural entry point since they each represent a physical manifestation of an intangible cultural force present at hip-hop's birth and transmitted across the globe. In "The Fifth Pillar," I make direct connections between each of the four elements and architectural expressions as a way of beginning to image works that would qualify for inclusion: "Remix is renovation . . . Rap is construction . . . Breakdance is form . . . Graffiti is surface."[98] As we will see, further investigation of each connection reveals a series of methodologies ripe for exploitation within architectural design.

Remix Is Renovation

The DJ, or disk jockey, existed long before hip-hop. DJs have been selecting records and segueing between them with witty introductions on the radio and at parties since vinyl recordings became commercially available. Like many aspects of hip-hop culture, hip-hop deejaying finds its roots in the Jamaican dancehall [II.007]. "Hip-hop came out of Trenchtown,"[99] Kool Herc admits. Dancehall sound systems comprising oversized speakers, re-engineered amps, turntables, and crates of records (mostly 45-rpm "dub plates") travelled across the island playing at primarily outdoor venues and featured elaborate toasts and braggadocious chants by celebrated DJs (aka "selectas"). Hip-hop DJs, beginning with Kool Herc, followed this formula, expanded their musical vocabulary, and eventually evolved (and revolutionized) the entire pursuit through a succession of innovative manipulations. Chang gives us one of the earliest examples. "In a technique he called 'the Merry-Go-Round' Herc began to work two copies of the same record, back-cueing a record to the beginning of the break as the other reached the end, extending a five-second breakdown into a five-minute loop of fury."[100] Contemporary hip-hop DJs and producers use the entire history of recorded sound as the material library for their compositions and manipulate each sample using breaks, cross-fades, slip-cues, needle drops, backspins, and the iconic scratch.[101] Architecture has long been adept at transforming verbs into design operations, making each DJ technique an easy analog for design processes. Beyond these technique-based corollaries to architecture, the construction of hip-hop music is heavily precedent based. DJs and producers continually decode, recode, elevate, and amplify lost or forgotten pieces of musical history. The parallel attitudes for architects engaged in renovation, restoration, or adaptive reuse projects are implicit. As improvisational artists, hip-hop DJs are also invested in the real-time responses of their audiences. This may not be as easily achieved within traditional relationships between architects and users, but it does provide an exciting model to which designers can aspire. Finally, hip-hop DJs are pioneering hackers of phonographic technology, "continuing a tradition of previous misuses of technology by the Black diaspora such as broken bottlenecks on Blues guitar necks, oil drums as steel drums, and so on."[102] This attitude toward technology brings deejaying in line with architecture's long-standing interest in creating new modes of practice through the assimilation of available material and fabrication technology. The vast potentials of this technology-based connection between hip-hop and architecture are more thoroughly discussed in later sections.[103]

II.007 | Bass Odyssey sound system
Image courtesy Yaniq Walford via Wikimedia Creative Commons CC BY 3.0
https://en.wikipedia.org/wiki/File:Bass_Odyssey_Sound_System_speaker_column,_Tropical_Hut,_St._Mary,_May_2012.jpg

Rap Is Construction

Emceeing is unquestionably the most recognizable and consumed element of hip-hop culture; so much so that rap and hip-hop have become almost synonymous. Rap stems from a legacy that interconnects Jamaican dub poetry, toasting, signifyin', and playing the dozens, all forms rooted in West African oral traditions. These "ancient traditions of the motherland," notes Christopher, "had to be remembered because the artifacts . . . couldn't be carried [to the New World]."[104] The structural relationship between the rhymes within a verse and the beats within its accompanying music presents a likely entry point into the architecturalization of rap. The Vox video, "Rapping, deconstructed," spends twelve minutes dissecting and analyzing the relationships between the rhymes of "the best rhymers of all time" and the structure of the musical bars. It includes structural comparisons of tracks from The Notorious B.I.G., Rakim, Eminem, André 3000, and the immensely talented underground rapper, MF Doom. ("I'll bet a million dollars on Doom against Lil' Wayne," proclaims Yasiin Bey in one of the video's

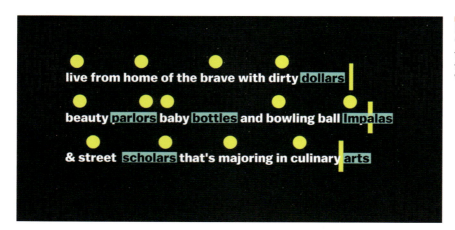

II.008 | Screenshot from "Rapping, deconstructed: the best rhymers of all time"
Video © Vox Media 2016

clips.) The diagrams accompanying the video content could each easily be modified into an architectural partí [II.008].

Schloss reminds us that "the culture's participants have invested a great deal of intellectual energy in the development of elaborate theoretical frameworks to guide its interpretation."[105] This includes the language-based, poetically coded nature of emceeing, which allows the artform to dovetail with other narratives and theories of grammar, syntax, and semiotics in architecture. As such, a decoding of rap's linguistic structure can be easily reinterpreted as diagrammatic content used in the generation of architecture. Other design techniques and processes can be extracted from rap's multiple embedded references to architecture and the built environment. From Melle Mel's gritty descriptions of life in the projects on Grandmaster Flash and the Furious Five's hit, "The Message," to contemporary references by Kanye West to Swiss starchitects Herzog & de Meuron, rap lyrics have a conscious connection with many aspects of architectural production. The unique perspective that MCs bring to architectural matters, therefore, invites interpretation through a close read of their narrative content. A final avenue of exploration latent in rap music is the nature of flow and its potential to be made tangible. Flow, however, is one of the more challenging aspects of rap and (by extension) hip-hop to quantify. Here, Garland offers a useful definition:

> Flow is defined as the combination of style, skill and emotion expressed in a clearly delineated fashion. Flow can be as smooth as a light eddy or as rough as a torrential downpour. However, a discernable pattern lies at the core of flow. A rapper's flow, or lack of, can make and/or break a style.[106]

If this particular facet of hip-hop culture were transmuted into architectural form and/or space any architecture based in hip-hop would be much more easily recognized. A key in doing so may lie in Murray Forman's interpretation of flow. He posits that "rap music's 'flow' is relevant to the discussion of discursive space, for rap artists are actively and intentionally involved in what might be termed discursive bricolage, enacted through the accumulation of fragments and shards from an array of social discourses and stylistic elements of popular culture."[107] Understanding flow as bricolage that seamlessly blends disparate inputs gives us a clearer image of its architectonic potentials.

Breakdance Is Form

Many dance forms typically associated with hip-hop are deeply rooted in battle dances common among gang members in the 1960s and '70s South Bronx and can be traced back to traditional African and Afro-Caribbean forms. Once these dances (most recognizably, the "Uprock") made their way into early hip-hop parties, a sacred relationship between DJs and b-boys was ignited. The DJ's ability to extend "the breaks" (the instrumental portions of mainly funk records) and allow b-boys (a contraction of "breaker boys") to corporally express themselves on the dancefloor is the primordial battery of early hip-hop culture. B-boys' inventive modes of occupying and appropriating public space should be of primary interest to architects and urban designers. Powerful attitudes common to all forms of hip-hop expression—unbounded bravado, boastfulness, and self-confidence—allow b-boys to reconceive the intended use of inherited spaces. This phenomenon was dramatically visualized in 1984's *Beat Street*. One of the most iconic scenes in the film depicts a spontaneous parting of the crowd on the main dancefloor of The Roxy in Manhattan, making way for two b-boy crews to begin their epic dance battle [II.009]. Steven Hager describes the real-life events at the legendary Negril nightclub in 1981 upon which this fictional scene may have been based. "Negril's greatest moment probably came the night the Rock Steady Crew battled the Floormasters, a crew from the Bronx later known as the New York City Breakers. For the first time the audience got a taste of the competitive nature of breaking."[108]

Beyond the physical nature of the spaces that hosted early b-boy battles and the ways that hip-hop bodies appropriate space, other technical aspects of b-boy performances can provide formal inspiration for architects. The four-stage evolution of each performance, their derivation from other indigenous forms of dance, along with the structural and formal complexities suggested by b-boys' contorted bodies each indicate an additional area of potential design investigation. "Starting upright in the top-rock, hands up stabbing like a gang-member in motion, feet moving side to side like Ali in a

II.009 | Still from "Beat Street"

'"Beat Street" directed by Stan Lathan 1984 © Orion Pictures

rope-a-dope, dropping down like James Brown, turning hurricanes of Spy's Boricua footwork, exploding into a Zulu freeze, tossing in a spin and punctuating it all with a Bruce Lee grin or a mocking Maori tongue—the entire history of the hip-hop body in a virtuoso display of style."[109] Imagine the kinds of built environments that would warrant such a dynamic description!

Graffiti Is Surface

Like every other element of hip-hop culture, the story of graffiti extends well beyond 1520 Sedgewick Avenue. TAKI 183 made his New York City debut sometime around 1969, CORNBREAD began writing his name in Philadelphia's public spaces a few years before that, and Kilroy began way back in the 1950s. Others, like Rammellzee and KRS-One, connect graffiti's legacy back even further to the Gothics[110] and the Egyptians.[111] Though it was late in being assimilated as part of hip-hop culture (many graff writers didn't see the connection at all), it may be the element most easily associated with architecture, based on both their connections to the visual arts and graffiti's use of the built environment as its primary canvas. Jeff Chang gives a vivid description of graffiti artists' motivations and its relationship to the urban fabric:

> Roaming through gang turfs, slipping through the long arms and the high fences of authority, violating notions of property and propriety, graffiti writers found their own kind of freedom. Writing your name was like locating the edge of civil society and planting a flag there. In Greg Tate's words, it was "reverse colonization."[112]

The architectural study of graffiti parallels the study of breakdancing in many ways, since both are anthropomorphic in nature, both bend public space to their will, and both embody a similar formal aesthetic. Additionally, many b-boys were also graff writers. The implicit formalism and codification of graffiti letters, the temporality of its layering and transformation of surfaces, and the recoding of cities based on accessibility, non-surveillance, and visibility of graffiti works are each potent areas of design investigation.

Blind adherence to interpretations of hip-hop elements is not, by itself, enough to reflect the totality of hip-hop's transformative powers. Hip-hop culture exists outside of traditional understandings of linear or singular time. "With its infinitely recombinant and revisable history," Christopher notes, "the music represents futures without pasts."[113] He later states that "Of all the things anticipated and invented in the South Bronx so long ago, a crippling nostalgia was not one of them." Two treatises discussed here that are fully liberated from nostalgic allegiance to any of the four elements or any particular era of hip-hop culture both appear in the same publication. The exhibition catalog for Walker's *Ruffneck Constructivists*, an exhibition of photography, video, and installation art at the Institute of Contemporary Art at the University of Pennsylvania, opens with two powerful essays by Walker and Wilkins. Though not an explicit exploration of Hip-Hop Architecture, the show included work by artists interested in hip-hop culture or reflective of hip-hop ideals, opened with music from DJ Questlove and members of Okayplayer, and included within the exhibition text clear connections to architecture. Walker admits therein that the title itself is a mash-up of the Russian Constructivist architectural movement and the hip-hop/dancehall idea of the ruffneck. Her selection of Craig L. Wilkins to pen the only other catalog essay is also telling. Wilkin's essay, *Cuirass Architecture* begins: "I am an architect. I should say that up front"[114] and continues with one of his most compelling arguments for Hip-Hop Architecture. Unlike his four principles of *(W)rapped Space*, which describe essential characteristics of or methods for creating Hip-Hop Architecture, the quartet outlined in *Cuirass Architecture* describes the essential attitudes of hip-hop *space*. With this four-step progression he outlines a transition from "(the ideal) space," the assumed normative condition, through "(we'll just deal) space," a space of segregated experience, to "(it just got real) space," where truth is spoken to power, and finally to "(we'll just steal) space,"[115] the space of the ruffneck, where marginalized people exercise unlimited agency over their environments.

Walker is most explicit in her opening essay, Ruffneck Constructivism, when she introduces the exhibition's manifesto, which, as she states, is "in search of a movement," and "proposing a theory of architecture based around a ruffneck, antisocial, hip-hop, rudeboy ethos."[116] Though no hip-hop architects were included in the show, her manifesto and its introduction are critical inclusions in any written documentations of Hip-Hop Architectural theory. As such, it is included here in its original form and suggested as a guiding philosophy and fundamental attitude in the production of hip-hop space.

RUFFNECK CONSTRUCTIVISTS

ARE DEFIANT SHAPERS OF ENVIRONMENTS. RUFFNECKS POSITION THEMSELVES AT ODDS WITH DOMINANT CULTURE. THEY RELY HEAVILY ON OFFENSIVE GESTURES. IF THE WORLD SAYS PANTS UP, THEY PULL THEIR DRAWERS DOWN.

WHATEVER THEIR GENDER AFFILIATION, RUFFNECKS GO HARD WHEN ALL AROUND THEM THEY SEE SOFTNESS, WEAKNESS, COMPROMISE, SERMONIZING, POVERTY, AND LACK. THE RUFFNECK RULE: GET RICH OR DIE TRYING. RUFFNECKS DON'T CHANGE THE WORLD THROUGH CONSCIOUS ACTIONS, THEY BUILD THEMSELVES INTO IT ONE ASSAULT AT A TIME. THEY ARE TOP DOGS.

THERE IS NO ROOM FOR FAILURE. EVEN GETTING CAUGHT IS AN OPPORTUNITY.

PRISON IS THE TRAINING GROUND FOR CONSTRUCTIVISTS, WHETHER THAT PRISON IS THE PENITENTIARY, THE PROJECT, THE FAVELA, THE TOWNSHIP, THE "SYSTEM," OR THE SOUL. RUFFNECKS ARE IN PERPETUAL LOCKDOWN, PERFECTING THEIR MEANS OF ESCAPE WITH LIMITED RESOURCES.

WE HAVE NO POLITICAL AFFILIATION, ONLY DEEP LOYALTIES TO SPECIFIC ENTITIES—FAMILY, MOTHER, GOD, UNIT, CELL BLOCK, RACE, TEAM, NEIGHBORHOOD, GANG, OURS IS A LIMITED TERRITORY. WE ROAM IT WITH IMPUNITY. WE GIVE LITTLE VOICE TO THE FRAGILE, AND YET THEY HOUNT US AND HOUND US.

"BY ANY MEANS NECESSARY" IS A MOTTO WE HOLD CLOSE TO HEART. WE WEAR IT ON OUR ARMS AND FLEX FUCK-YOUS IN THE DIRECTION OF ADVERSARIES. WE ARE PREPARED TO FIGHT AND PEPPER OUR SPEECH WITH EPITHETS AND SLURS. LIKE CALIBAN, WE CURSE.

THE SHAPE OF THE SYSTEMS THAT BIND US IS HINTED AT, DARKLY, LIKE SHADOWS VIEWED FROM THE FAR END OF A DARK ALLEY. WE ARE NOT WITHOUT CONTEXT, BUT THE PLACES WE BUILD, THE FORTRESSES OF SELF, ARE ERECTED TO SHUT OUT THE TYRANNY OF A LOSS OF SELF-CONTROL.[117]

■ ■ ■

"So, every discipline, every profession has an object, right? There's something that you focus on and that's why we do what we do. And around that object this collection of knowledge. You become the expert about that particular object. For us its architecture or the architectural object, however you define it, but that's what we do. And there is in a sense, and we can make generalizations and we can parse things together as much as we want, but in order to have this conversation there's three avenues in which you focus your expertise in hip-hop. One is the application, which would be the design ideal. The second one is the theory. Why do we do what we do? Why did we make this choice? Why did we do this? And then the other is the pedagogy. How do we teach ourselves and teach other folks who want to be a part of this discussion to do what we do? And these things are flowing. They all sort of flow into each other. They flow backwards, they flow forwards, sometimes they can flow across but it's all circulating around the object itself.

"But we know that these objects don't exist in abstraction, they exist in a world. They exist in a society. And within that society there are some stories that are told and some stories that aren't told. There are some things that we do not focus on. And so, if we look at the sort of circular area around the object, the things on the edge of that circle are things that we necessarily do not tackle in this profession. We don't talk about them. we don't talk about the wealth making, we don't talk about environmental protections, we don't talk about food security, we don't talk about social sponsorships, we don't talk about mass incarceration, we don't talk about the old population, we don't talk about the consecration of thought. Those are things that exist on the edges of what we feel we need to know to practice our craft. This is where Hip-Hop Architecture comes in because Hip-Hop Architecture situates itself in that zone.

"I'm glad you mentioned this idea of Hip-Hop Architecture being 'culture in built form' because it ties into something I was telling the opposite team. So, a lot of people when you talk about Hip-Hop Architecture, or make that statement or something similar, they say 'I don't really get that, I don't really understand it.' And they still conflate the culture with the music and that's a problem because it's a part of it. It's almost like saying Classical architecture is about Classical music. That's not true. We know that's not true, right? It's about a whole lot of things about which the music comes out. So, first thing is to switch our mindset and not talk about hip-hop and Hip-Hop Architecture as rap. Rap is part of it. In this field we have seen this kind of movement, for lack of a better term. So, Constructivism, its whole purpose, if you had to boil it down to a phrase or statement, is the desire to make a just, egalitarian society with an emphasis on the people. So, it's about trying to create a classless society. Modernism is the attempt to create a new and just order with an emphasis on the common man, but a universal society. These are the tenants and the things that come out of that are all focused on trying to make that statement a reality. Architecture is one part of that. So, then we have Deconstructivism. It's a critique of art and there is no '-ism.' We are a decentered society and their work reflects that way of thinking.

"So now we have hip-hop. I hate to use the word 'hip-hop-ism,' because I don't want to throw the word '-ism' into the mix. But it's part of that thing—that ideological, cultural language. And this is what's going to include full participation of marginalized, disenfranchised communities with emphasis on the community without creating a just society and an equal society. So, if we go back to this image of where wealth and health and equities and environmental issues sit on the outside of the focus of architecture, both the study and the practice of architecture, that's where Hip-Hop Architecture situates itself, right? It sits right there in that space and its pulling architecture so that it's going to encompass these things. And what we end up having is that. Does that make sense? We end up having that, and the focus on our object gets bigger as well. Does that make sense? [II.010]

"So, this is why my statement I made the other day, I would bring that back. This is my point. Architecture should do this, period. It just should. That is what it's supposed to do. You shouldn't need

Hip-Hop Architecture for you to do that. That's why my point is that Hip-Hop Architecture should just be architecture.

"So, if you take nothing away from this, one of the things I think about Hip-Hop Architecture is that it combines the visual aesthetic with the visible ethics."

– Craig Wilkins[118]

II.010 | Diagram of object-discipline relationships
Craig L. Wilkins.
Reproduced with permission

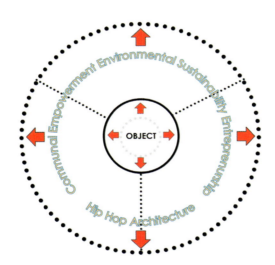

07

COMMODITY.

Like chivalry, disco, and God, hip-hop has been pronounced dead on multiple occasions. Most famously, the legendary Brooklyn rapper, Nas, dedicated his entire 2006 album to the notion by titling it "Hip Hop Is Dead." Though he very quickly qualified his declaration in the outro to Dyson's *Know What I Mean?* the sentiment lingers in the collective imaginations of countless hip-hop heads.

> Some folks got angry when I told them that hip hop is dead. Other folks got confused when I told them that hip hop is dead. Still others knew that I was right. People disagreed and spilled ink on magazine pages freely like cheap wine or young blood to argue with each other and with me. Although the voices may have clashed, the one constant in the clamor was that all of these people out there felt that hip hop was worth fighting over and fighting for.[119]

The exact time and date of hip-hop's death is more at question than whether it is indeed a dead form. "Making rap records tore everything apart," Bambaataa laments. "It tore all of us apart. That's what killed hip hop."[120] If we imagine hip-hop to be a culture exemplified by creative acts that are performative, improvisational, temporal, and reactive to unpredictably changing conditions—hip-hop happens in real time—then the act of solidifying it in any reproducible format would exist outside of that image. Referring to "Rapper's Delight" as an object of consumption rather than a "practice in action," Russell Potter suggests, "Hip-hop was something goin' down at 23 Park, 63 Park, or the Back Door on 169th Street,"[121] not something that could be packed and consumed. The unquenchable capitalist desire to commoditize all creativity proved to be hip-hop's death knell long before Nas "called it."

There is no greater paradox in hip-hop culture than that of being a "sellout." Hip-hop gives pounds to its most "conscious" artists with one hand, while signing massive record deals and endorsement contracts with the other. Being true to your roots and being unapologetically capitalist occupy equal space at the core of hip-hop's creative expression. "Hip-hop is a bridge across the breadth between art and commerce," Christopher writes, "in a bohemia always assimilated by and always assimilating both culture and business."[122] In Mark Fisher's essay *It's Easier to Imagine the End of the World Than the End of Capitalism*, the author critiques hip-hop's multiple understandings of "the real." Authenticity within "the first version of the real," Fisher states, "enabled [hip-hop's] easy absorption into the second, the reality of late capitalist economic instability, where such authenticity has proven highly marketable."[123] Hip-hop's success, therefore, makes it the least natural voice for anti-capitalist criticism. We conveniently blame Sylvia Robinson for creating the Sugar Hill Gang, or Patti Astor for bringing graffiti art to Soho galleries, or other White speculators for exploiting Black and Latino kids growing up in poverty, without criticizing the capitalist system that compels these kids to sell their most valuable assets to the highest bidder, or celebrating their ingenuity in working that system. Fred Braithwaite, aka Fab Five Freddy, was one of the first to develop a legitimate hustle for graffiti artists. As Hager recounts in *Hip Hop*:

> Fred Braithwaite kept returning to see [noted gaff writer, Lee] Quinones. "He said he knew a way to make money with graffiti. I started thinking about what he was proposing and said, 'Well, let's give it a try.'"
>
> A few weeks later, Braithwaite appeared with a clipping from the *Village Voice*. In the February 12, 1979, "Scenes" column was a photo of Braithwaite standing in front of one of Lee's murals. A brief article by Howard Smith followed.
>
> "We call ourselves the Fabulous Five and we're the best at what we do—graffiti. Just recently we decided to start selling our services for $5 per square foot, and already we've got several commissions."[124]

Black producers were also behind some of hip-hop's most remarkably profitable yet inauthentic fabrications like ABC (Another Bad Creation), Kris Kross (included here because of their gimmicky personas, but those kids were proper rappers), Vanilla Ice, and (I hesitate to mention her again) Iggy Azalea.

Hip-hop's pioneers have been engaged in heavy salesmanship from the moment they became public figures. Each created a new identity projecting an image of competence, style, and cool with new names to match. Rose cites an extensive list of early rapper, DJ, graff artist, and breaker pseudonyms, each seeking to reframe their identities to promote a "fuse [of] technology with mastery and style," "suggest street smarts, coolness, power, and supremacy," "critique society," or to "highlight their status as experts." "Taking on new names and identities," Rose explains, "offers 'prestige from below' in the face of limited access to legitimate forms of status attainment."[125] The persona is thus amplified to create a larger-than-life image that overshadows one's current situation. Commodification is probably at its most apparent in hip-hop fashion where being larger than life is par for the course. Dapper Dan became legendary in the early 1980s by exploiting the label-consciousness of Harlem residents [II.011]. His jackets, pants, and jumpsuits covered with repetitive pirated Gucci, Louis Vuitton,

II.011 | Dapper Dan in his studio (Facing page)
© Wyatt Counts

and Fendi logos became a must-have for anyone wanting to prove they were *a la mode* or ballin'. Oversized logos, repetitive logos, bright colors, bold patterns, heavy gold chains, excessively gemmed jewelry, and overly visible certificates of authenticity become mainstays of hip-hop fashion—originated in the streets of Harlem, Brooklyn, and the Bronx only to be imitated later by the same labels originally being knocked off.

Commodification in hip-hop depends on limited definitions, replicable products, and pre-packaged methods, formats, and technologies. The easiest way to draw architectural connections to hip-hop culture is by translating such definitions, products, and methodologies to architectural corollaries. Such translation typifies many misguided attempts at creating a Hip-Hop Architectural product. I have often been implored by older Black architects to profit as much as I can from Hip-Hop Architecture, to "own" the topic, and protect it from others seeking to do the same. Locking in its limits, its aesthetics, and its rules is the inevitable path suggested for doing so. This, for me, would be tantamount to creating what Hernandez calls "architecture in blackface."[126] It is far more challenging to first uncover the implicit set of qualitative attributes that exist at hip-hop's core and reflect those in new attitudes for design and construction. Confronting this challenge, however, will protect hip-hop–based architectural production forms from blind appropriation and capitalist consumption. Additionally, since those most adept at cultural appropriation already control architecture's institutions and dominate its practice, Hip-Hop Architecture will have to be especially vigilant in determining its constitution. It must continue to resist forces from within and without seeking to assign it a singular face.

Hip-Hop Architecture must also resist the tendency to wait for a patron. Though hip-hop culture has created Medicis, Rockerfellers, and Vitras of its own, hip-hop architects may need to adopt a Nipsey Hussle attitude towards advancing their agenda. "For the community to claim what was theirs, Hussle realized, they would have to forge their own path forward. Remaining fiercely independent, never compromising his voice, retaining full ownership over his artistry, brand, and output, uplifting those around him, and being the blueprint for others to follow was his contribution to that larger mission."[127] If this can be successfully emulated within architectural practice, there will be no limits to the commercial value of Hip-Hop Architecture while it remains in the hands of its original innovators.

■ ■ ■

🟥 "Where is the Maybach music? That was all a seductive description of urbanism that goes from the slave ships to the tenement houses. But two-thirds of what I have to change the station for is about Maybachs and jetting off to wherever. I think you have to add that in as well. . . . I take Condoleezza Rice with my Lena Horne. I take them both. You know what I mean? It's all me."

– *Amanda Williams*[128]

🟥 "_____"

– *T.I.*[129]

08 GRIDS + GRIOTS.

Like many thought leaders of the Hip-Hop Architecture movement, Amanda Williams studied architecture at Cornell in the mid-90s, a time when the architectural thought pervasive among the faculty was directly descendant of Colin Rowe's Postmodernist ideals. Ironically, Williams believes that the experimental nature of the faculty at the time allowed space for more transcendent ideas. "That time was coincident with Deconstructivism," she reminded me, "You have to remember how architecture was being taught."[130] In her presentation at *Towards a Hip-Hop Architecture,* she reflected briefly on her education by forming a new reading of "The Whites" and "The Grays." Architectural heavyweights "The New York Five" (Peter Eisenman, Michael Graves, Charles Gwathmey, John Hejduk, and Richard Meier) captured the attention of architectural theorists for many years after the CASE group (Conference of Architects for the Study of the Environment) first discussed their work at the Museum of Modern Art (MoMA) in 1969. Their redirection of the functionalism introduced by early Modernists a half-century before, toward more formalist methods of producing architecture, dominated discourse within the discipline for the rest of the 1900s. Extensive use of purist geometries and surface materials earned them and others exuding similar operational tendencies (including Rowe and Kenneth Frampton) the nickname "The Whites," setting off a pseudo-rivalry with other less puritanical practitioners, such as Robert Venturi, Robert Stern, and Vincent Scully, contrastingly dubbed "The Grays." Debates about their ideologies and methodologies were so compelling that another half-century later, theorists continue to cite their writings and philosophies. Emanuela Giudice's admission, for example, that "the debate that elapsed between the 'Whites' and 'Grays' showed the need to re-establish . . . a discipline devoid of identity"[131] reads as a damning indictment of architectural responses to the Postmodern movement. Their guiding attitude assumed that removing identity would result in a more evolved architectural expression and that design, in practice and theory, can and should be ethically neutral. As Williams put it, "I was always so offended when they talked about [Whites and Grays] as if it had nothing to do with race."[132] For her, now a practicing painter, installation artist, and color theorist, any conversation about the "Whites" and "Grays" was incomplete without discussing "The Blacks."

One of the most ubiquitous of all supposedly neutral tools that Modernists and Postmodernists used in their pursuit of "a discipline devoid of identity" is the grid. It was the predominant tool used in the 1967 MoMA exhibition, *The New City: Architecture and Urban Renewal*, which included works by many soon-to-be-called Whites and Grays representing teams from Cornell, Columbia, MIT, and Princeton, just two years before CASE. With Harlem, East Harlem, Washington Heights, and the South Bronx as their primary targets, "The architects reconfigured neighborhoods by inserting large white grids and primary-colored geometries outlining block-busting mega-projects"[133] [II.012]. The perceptual relationship between

II.012 | Installation view of the exhibition, "The New City: Architecture and Urban Renewal."
The Museum of Modern Art, New York, January 1967 through March 13, 1967, Photographic Archive. The Museum of Modern Art Archives.
Photographer: George Cserna
Digital Image © The Museum of Modern Art/ Licensed by SCALA / Art Resource, NY

white grids and black and brown bodies was rendered as oppressive, and each project affirmed Wilson's assertions that "In the public arena 'urban renewal' was code for 'Negro removal.'"[134]

The grid's ubiquity and oppressiveness, however, is not limited to twentieth-century architecture. The history of the grid as a design and planning tool extends from ancient global civilizations to iconic contemporary streetscapes such as Barcelona and Manhattan. Its proliferation across the American continent can be traced back to Thomas Jefferson and the Land Ordinance of 1785, the effects of which are clearly visible today. One simply has to browse Google Maps for aerial photographs of the American Midwest, flip through the pages of James Corner's *Taking Measures Across the American Landscape*, or peek out the window during a transcontinental flight to appreciate the grid's visual dominance.

When viewed holistically, the shared history of Black people in America and the grid is a markedly contentious one. Yasiin Bey, in rapping about the gridded pattern of a newfound fabric, artfully summarizes this relationship in *A Soldier's Dream*:

> If you look closer, you'll notice that this pattern resembles
>
> Tenement row houses, project high-rises, cell block tiers
>
> Discontinued stretches of elevated train tracks
>
> Slave ship gullies, acres of tombstones[135]

Each item on Bey's list is a reminder of a four-hundred-year hardship. From the moment Blacks were packed onto slave ships they were met with this prevalent system of neutrality, order, and efficiency. From tightly confined slave quarters and shotgun houses designed for maximum efficiency, to public housing, public schools, and private prisons, each with spatial logics and security features (bars on windows, chain-link fences, etc.) exemplifying hyper-rationality and utility, it's easy to image blanket rejection of "dropping gridded megastructures . . . from above."[136] Though the grid itself cannot bear responsibility for each oppressive act, its legibility within the previously listed forms belies the assumed neutrality of its existence. One could even argue this as a motivation in the Michael Brown shooting.[137] In refusing to conform to the prescribed paths of the gridded sidewalk and instead creating his own path along the street he was confronted, shot, and killed.

Architectural historian Lawrence Chua, who also analyzes *A Soldier's Dream* in his chapter on hip-hop's utopian aspirations, helps to connect this latest rebellion to the cultural production of the South Bronx in the early 1970s. "The ordinary image of the neo-liberal utopia," he argues, "the seamless, ahistorical façades of its urban plan, and the 'towers in the park' reveal a more critical history of modernism upon closer inspection by [Bey]"[138] As argued in *The Fifth Pillar*, hip-hop culture can be seen as a direct response of Black and Latino youth to the oppressive nature of these gridded Modernist environments. Hip-hop's pioneers developed their own defiant forms of artistic expression against a backdrop of the ubiquitous grid. DJs, MCs, b-boys, and graff writers envisioned a world completely oppositional to the grid—a space of breaks, scratches, and flows. Grid-laden concrete surfaces became canvasses for tags, throw-ups, and pieces, or stages for breaking, popping, and locking. Pure whites and grays were shunned for neon pinks, yellows, and lime greens, or for Cross Colors in black, red, green, and gold. Hip-hop culture provides a welcome antithesis to the grid's legacy and holds the power to coopt architecture from its affluent, White, male figureheads who continue to profess neutrality and universality.

This rejection of tools and systems primarily associated with Modernism has earned hip-hop a Postmodernist reputation of its own. The promotional video for the 2011 exhibition at the Victoria and Albert (V&A) Museum in London entitled *Postmodernism: Style and Subversion 1970–1990* could well be a promo for the beginnings of hip-hop. Its opening scene, a series of controlled implosions of brick, concrete, and steel towers, also included an iconic clip of Pruitt-Igoe Houses suffering a similar fate—the moment Charles Jencks famously dubbed "the death of modern architecture." Jencks, when interviewed in the V&A video, admits that Postmodernism became an "umbrella term for rethinking."[139] Others, including Andre Craddock-Willis, cited by Rose in *Black Noise*, locate hip-hop under the postmodern umbrella. "In describing rap music as 'an expression of the complexity of post-modern African-American life,' Willis argues that rap's contradictory stance toward capitalism, its raging sexism, and other 'non progressive' elements are unresolved postmodern contradictions"[140] Rose quickly challenges Craddock-Willis' assertions by noting that these "contradictory stances . . . have *always* been part and parcel of jazz, the blues, and R&B, as well as any number of other nonblack cultural forms" that contradictions that are central to hip-hop are "not unique to postmodernity," and that "his identification of rap as a postmodern form is not consistent with his previous formulations of jazz, blues, and R&B as forms that are rooted in economic relations, power relationships, and social struggle."[141] Distinguishing rap from other postmodern forms (removing it from a singularly postmodern classification) frees it from a dependence on Western formulations of Postmodernism, postmodern rhetoric, and postmodern theory. We can now more appropriately "consider it a direct extension of African-American oral, poetic, and protest traditions."[142] Therefore, like rap music and other associated forms of hip-hop cultural production, Hip-Hop

Architecture can anchor itself on Black cultural traditions instead of White ones, which it appropriates, samples, and transforms.

One such tradition, evident in all aspects of hip-hop culture, is that of the *griot*. The griot is a critical character in pre-colonial West African communities. They were storytellers, poets, musicians, travelers, and teachers who drew wisdom from centuries of oral tradition for which they were the trusted keepers. The legacy of the griot has evolved in the Americas to include caricatures of tricksters, confidence men, and mystics. Their stories are told in African-American and Afro-Caribbean folktales through protagonists like Br'er Rabbit, Anansi, Shine, Stagger Lee, and the Signifyin Monkey. As discussed earlier, the content, contexts, and methods of telling these stories are the predecessors of rap. Paul D. Miller, aka DJ Spooky That Subliminal Kid, draws additional connections between griots and hip-hop DJs, calling them "The New Griots." "The best DJs," he claims, "are griots"[143] linked to the traditional practices of public narrative, storytelling, and educating through samples from contemporary and archival sources. The stories told by the DJ, however, "might be called 'music before the impact of language,' or pre-linguistic stories."[144] Adam J. Banks builds on Miller's colocation of the griot and the DJ in his 2011 book, *Digital Griots: African American Rhetoric in a Multimedia Age*.

> The griot has survived the middle passage, slavery, and centuries of American apartheid and has diffused into many different spaces and figures: storytellers, preachers, poets, standup comics, DJs, and even everyday people all carry elements of the griot's role in African American culture. As historians and archivists, they interpret current events, raise societal critique, entertain, and pass down communal values. . . . The "digital griot," an amalgamation of all of these figures, offers a useful model for conceptualizing black rhetorical excellence bridging print, oral, and digital communication.[145]

Various modes of adapting DJ techniques into architectural design processes have already been discussed earlier in this section. Reinterpreting the role of the DJ within hip-hop into that of a "digital griot" opens up additional techniques and (more importantly) attitudes for approaching architecture. Banks lists a few of these, presenting them as "metaphors for writing practice."[146] When considering this list (with my emphases), we can easily extend the metaphor to include architectural practice.

- *the shoutout* as the use of references, calling the roll, and identifying and declaring one's relationships, allegiances, and influences as tools for building community and locating oneself in it

- *crate digging* as continual research—not merely for songs, hooks, breakbeats, riffs, texts, arguments, and quotes for a particular set or paper but as a crucial part of one's long-term work, of learning, knowing, and interpreting a tradition
- *mixing* as the art of transition and as revision in the Adrienne Rich sense of writing as re-vision
- *remix* as critical interpretation of a text, repurposing it for a different rhetorical situation as 2010 Conference on College Composition and Communication chair Gwen Pough challenged the field to "remix: revisit, rethink, revise, renew" in the conference call
- *mixtape* as anthology, as everyday act of canon formation, interpretation, and reinterpretation
- *sample* as those quotes, those texts, those ideas used enough, important enough to our conceptions of what we are doing in a text (or even in our lifelong work) to be looped and continually repeated rather than merely quoted or referenced[147]

Each technique—the shoutout, crate digging, mixing, remix, mixtape, sample—is mute without their underlying attitudes. Griot attitudes towards gridded spatial paradigms invented hip-hop. Within these attitudes we can find the answers for combatting the oppressive tendencies of Modernist architectural practice. The myth of rational neutrality will be busted, not by the wild defiance of Postmodernism, but through an adoption of griot-derived hip-hop traditions like defamiliarizing the familiar, taking the given and reshaping it in your own image, "making do," or, as they say in Jamaica "tun yu han' mek fashion."

■ ■ ■

James Garrett, Jr.: For me, looking at this particular quote [Bey, from *A Soldier's Dream*], I am just thinking three-dimensionally in terms of what vision I get from tenement row houses, project high-rises, cellblock tiers. I'm thinking now in terms of fractal geometry and looking at varying scales and cell replication. This is a very graphic quote that has a lot of fodder and possibility for exploration in terms of an organization of spaces—an expression of perhaps even an aesthetic of a multiplication of these individually contained entities.

Lawrence Chua: It is also worth pointing out that this is very much a historical perspective on things that are built. And I think it's that historical consciousness that allows an artist like Mos Def [Bey] to look beyond the façade, perhaps in a way that a practitioner isn't able to.

Shawn Rickenbacker: That's a very good point. What I was struggling with is that all of those [items listed], from a historical perspective, are, and have been, inherited spaces. Those aren't spaces that we have created for ourselves. So to what extent do I want to accept that kind of representation as being bestowed upon me? I understand where Mos Def is coming from. These spaces are very familiar. I grew up in the Bronx. Then there is also, as you [Amanda] mentioned or alluded to the goal of aspiring out of those situations. So to speak about their aesthetic value undermines the desire to then grow beyond that. I'm posing that more as a question than as a definitive statement.

Andrés Hernandez: I'm really interested in what the last quote said. It's funny, I felt like Mos Def was breaking down the grid for us. Like, what is the dominion of the grid and what does that mean in an urban space? We are in a school of architecture. We can we talk about the 7.5-degree shift and all that. I want to connect us back to the point that the grid is what really has impacted urban culture to the point that we are looking at the school system and the grave yard and the prison industrial complex as all the same. What does it mean to build spaces like that and how does that have dominion over people's lives? I think when we look at Dr. Wilkins' quote—this idea of hip-hop being this way of understanding our world and particularly in our urban world, or even the outside or exurban world—I think about what that mean in terms of its impact and what people are experiencing in the world, and what that means for us designing around that. I think that comes from a lot of different areas. And hip-hop is right for that. It doesn't mean that hip-hop is the only way to think about how we actually design our world, but it is really interesting to think about how people think about space, occupy space, and visualize space, especially in vIdeo. I mean, it's really interesting to see how that can be applied to the work we do as designers and architects. But I think this grid piece is really interesting. He had some really critical theory right there in the form of lyrics.[148]

09

TECHNOLOGY.

J Dilla, one of the most prolific and admired hip-hop producers of the 1990s and 2000s,[149] is best known within the industry for his humanistic approach to digital technology. His dexterity with the MPC3000 drum machine was so distinctive and revolutionary that his machine is now enshrined in the Smithsonian National Museum of African American History and Culture in Washington, DC. As Brian "Raydar" Ellis explains in the Vox video, *How J Dilla Humanized His MPC3000* [II.013], "He figured out how to humanize the drum machine by avoiding certain things that he could have done to make it more robotic, make it more stiff."[150] For example, Dilla decided to ignore the manufacturer setting called *quantization*, designed to minimize or eliminate human error from manual drumbeats played slightly off tempo—a bit like snapping the drum samples to a grid of beats and bars. "Dilla was like, 'yeah, I'm just gonna turn this off,'"[151] recounts Ellis. "The result," the narrator states, "is a discography with incredibly off-kilter drums."[152] This effect can be best appreciated in the track *Baby* on Dilla's 2006 album, *The Shining*. Though the sample here is a vocal instead of a drum, the inconsistently interspersed "baby" (a distortion of the word "maybe" sampled from The Stylistics' *Maybe It's Love This Time*) is a clearly recognizable trace of Dilla's analog fingerprint.

Off-kilter, distorted, and inconsistent with manufacturer recommendations, Dilla's music makes audible his defiant approach to technology. This approach closely aligns with those taken by generations of Black inventors

II.013 | J Dilla's MPC3000
Video © Vox Media 2017

and innovators transplanted to the Western world as highlighted by Rayvon Fouché in his essay on "Black Vernacular Technological Creativity." From design to production to consumption, from cotton farming to hip-hop music, Blacks in America have maintained a distinctive otherness relative to mainstream technological products. In his reading of Amiri Baraka's 1970 essay *Technology & Ethos*, Fouché notes "Baraka felt that the West had long ago gone down the wrong path in attempting to technologize humanity rather than humanizing technology."[153] We can trace this technologization of humanity from military indoctrination and slave labor to public school curricula, standardized tests, and industrialized workforces. Humanizing technology, for Baraka, was a product of reflecting on and projecting through creative forms of Black cultural expression. "The actual *beginnings* of our expression," he claims, "are post Western (just as they certainly are pre-western)."[154] To crystalize this point, Fouché excerpts a section from Baraka's text that uses the typewriter as an example:

> A typewriter?—why shd it only make use of the tips of the fingers as contact points of flowing multi directional creativity. If I invented a word placing machine, an "expression-scriber," *if you will,* then I would have a kind of instrument into which I could step & sit or sprawl or hang & use not only my fingers to make words express feelings but elbows, feet, head, behind, and all the sounds I wanted, screams, grunts, taps, itches, I'd have magnetically recorded, at the same time, & translated into word—or perhaps even the final xpressed thought/feeling wd not be merely word or sheet, but itself, the xpression, three dimensional—able to be touched, or tasted or felt, or entered, or heard or carried like a speaking singing constantly communicating charm. *A typewriter is corny!!*

> The so called fine artist realizes, those of us who have *freed* ourselves, that our creations need not emulate the white man's, but it is time the engineers, architects, chemists, electronics craftsmen, ie film too, radio, sound, &c., that learning western technology must not be the end of our understanding of the particular discipline we're involved in. Most of that west shaped information is like mud and sand when you're panning for gold! [sic][155]

Noted hip-hop journalist and "media assassin"[156] Harry Allen places hip-hop culture at the epicenter of contemporary humanizations of technology. "Hip-hop humanizes technology and makes it tactile," he proclaims. "In hip-hop, you make the technology do stuff that it isn't supposed to do."[157] Instead of reinventing the typewriter, hip-hop's pioneers adapted conventional phonographic equipment (turntables, mixers, drum machines, etc.) into post-Western typewriters of their own. This ingenuity is clearly evident in Kool Herc's description of his first sound system. "What I did was I took the speaker wire, put a jack onto it and jacked it into one of the four channels, and I had extra power and reserve power. Now I could control it from the preamp. I got two Bogart amps, two Girard turntables, and then I just used the channel knobs as my mixer. No headphones. The system could take eight mics. I had an echo chamber in one, and a regular mic to another. So I could talk plain and, at the same time, I could wait halfway for the echo to come out."[158]

Tricia Rose cites this attitude of Black and Caribbean peoples toward technology as one of the main catalysts in the creation of rap music—a form connecting deejaying and emceeing, two of hip-hop's original four elements. "Rap's black sonic forces," she states, "are very much an outgrowth of black cultural traditions, the postindustrial transformation of urban life, and the contemporary technological terrain."[159] She later explains that "hybrids between black music, black oral forms, and technology that are at the core of rap's sonic and oral power are an architectural blueprint for the redirection of seemingly intractable social ideas, technologies, and ways of organizing sounds along a course that affirms the histories and communal narratives of Afro-diasporic people."[160]

The arguments outlined by Vox, Fouché, and Rose each call for a relationship between (wo)man and machine that is reflective of cultural values long embedded within human DNA. Each also offers hip-hop as an exemplary mediator of this relationship. Hip-hop, the most authentically anthropomorphic[161] of contemporary cultural lenses, is uniquely qualified to bring humanity to technology. As such, hip-hop attitudes toward digital technology provide possible answers to Baraka's questions: "But what is our spirit, what will it project? What machines will it produce? What will they achieve? What will be their morality?"[162]

In proposing his own answers, Fouché introduces scratching, a technique pioneered by hip-hop DJs, as an especially generative interface between the manual and the mechanical. "When DJs began scratching," Fouché posits, "they subverted the fundamental meaning constructed for record players as well as for that of the LP records."[163] A passive means of listening to prerecorded music is thus transformed into an instrument of musical performance. Several additional arguments made in Fouché's essay reinforce hip-hop's position as protagonist in the struggle for technological agency. First, he discusses the significance of hip-hop in not only reimagining uses for existing technology but also in promoting technological change.[164] He recalls DJ Grandmaster Flash, one of hip-hop's patriarchs and pioneer of some of the most legendary technological advances in deejaying over several decades, who later partnered with DJ equipment manufacturers to help their technology keep up with industry trends. Next, by recounting in detail Flash's collaboration with the Rane Corporation in the development of their Empath mixer, Fouché underscores the sensitivity with which the human-machine relationship was navigated. He then concludes: "the vernacular technological creative innovations of hip-hop musicians have deeply imprinted black cultural aesthetics, priorities, values, beliefs, and sensibilities on the dominant culture."[165] In other words, the general posture of hip-hop practitioners toward technology is to have it reflect their individuality.

This posture establishes a new imperative for hip-hop's influence on other creative fields, especially those, like architecture, typically held beyond hip-hop's reach. Architecture has long been interested in creating new modes of practice through careful adaptation of available technology. From the introduction of computer-aided drafting, through the proliferation of parametric modeling, to digital fabrication and the nascent incorporation of AR and VR into architectural practice, the discipline has continued to question the relationship between the use of digital tools and their impact on architectural production, what the chairs of the ACADIA (Association for Computer Aided Design in Architecture) 2018 call "the technological 'arms' race."[166] Our collective disposition toward these tools, however, has been that of the passive consumer—fascinated by the possibilities they bring to architectural thought and practice but limited by their predetermined functionality. This gives the tool designer (software developer, manufacturer) greater agency over the architectural product than architects should allow.

This tool-designer/tool-user dialectic is even further limited by its internal biases against minority consumers. As Ron Eglash explains in the introduction to his co-edited volume *Appropriating Technology: Vernacular Sciences and Social Power*, "First world consumers, especially those from the White middle class, rarely realize the extent to which their technological access is ensured simply by their status as 'the user' foremost in so many [tool] designers' minds."[167] When White product developers exclusively design our tools for consumption by White architects this leaves little room for meaningful innovation. If viewed using the criteria previously discussed—humanizing technology, embracing a post-Western mindset, and reflecting cultural values within creative products—architecture's current relationship with technology remains myopic.

Hip-hop, with all of its requisite humanistic (social, cultural, and political) imperatives, presents an ideal lens through which to view and guide true technological innovation within architecture. Though we may easily dismiss Rose's reference to "an architectural blueprint," Baraka's inclusion of "architects" in his call to action, or Vox's description of snapping to a grid as tangentially relevant to architecture itself, it is also easy to acknowledge the applicability of the various hip-hop–based techniques and attitudes cited by all three to architectural practice. Application of these techniques provides a new avenue for Black vernacular technological creativity within the practice, profession, and discipline of architecture. Fouché's assertion that "resistance has been a motivating factor for musicians in the reconception of technological artifacts, practices, and knowledge"[168] hints at a way forward. Hip-Hop Architects, like musicians, must continue to use resistance to shape their attitudes towards technology.

■ ■ ■

■ "My mother and father were architects. The guy next door to my parents when I was growing up, he was a carpenter, he was an architect, because we were building and making our own communities, because nobody else would come in and make our community. And the reason my parents were architects and couldn't even pronounce the word—when I told them I was going to go to school to become an architect, they said "archy-tek"—it's because as a carpenter that gentleman would not do the entire building. He would leave a little bit of the interior for us to try and figure out and navigate. Or we would move into a building that was so dilapidated that we had to figure out a way to make it livable. And, in that respect, we become interior decorators; we become interior designers, interior architects, and ultimately architects and urban planners, even when the social spaces aren't working in our communities. This what we have been doing, and we continue to do these things."

– *Jack Travis*[169]

■ "I've had long conversations with Jack about this and this is part of what has come out of these conversations. Why is this [the Eames "Case Study" house, II.014] not a model for practice, period? Why aren't we learning or mining from this the idea, which is a very strong theme in the hip-hop community, about self-sufficiency and doing for yourself? You make a mix-tape, you go out there and you hustle it and you sell it, because you own it—it is yours. Why isn't this a model for hip-hop practice? I can go out and build my house, but I can also go out and build a neighborhood. Why do I have to wait for a client? Why do I have to wait for somebody to co-sign me doing what I want to do? They [the Eames] didn't wait. It wasn't like they went out and got special materials from some place. They would have gotten it from Home Depot if Home Depot were around. We have Home Depot. We have all these CNC routers. We have all this technology that allows you to go ahead and do your thing. Why isn't this, this? What I take from this is that this is what someone did for themselves. Fine. Great architects have been doing that forever. But when you have the opportunity now with mass-production of materials and mass-customization we can do this every weekend if you wanted to. You can own it; it's yours. You can change your whole community in two years. You can do that. And it is something that you can have a practice in. You own it and you get paid for it. And then you just flip the script."

– Craig Wilkins[170]

II.014 | Ice Cube in the Eames House

Ice Cube Celebrates the Eames House © The New York Times Company 2011

10 CONTRADICTION.

Long Island City, Queens may not seem the most likely location to erect a monument to hip-hop culture, yet 45 Davis Street could eventually prove to be as important a hip-hop landmark as 1520 Sedgewick Avenue. The former home of 5Pointz (aka "The Institute of High Burnin'") stood as a "world-class museum . . . that's open 24/7 and that shows the top artists in their field" where "the art is constantly changing, the staff is paid nothing and anyone can show there."[171] Under the once benevolent landlord Jerry Wolkoff, the warehouse building, which actively rented spaces for artist studios and garment warehousing, was transformed into an internationally renowned Mecca for curated aerosol art, with Jonathan "MERES" Cohen as its chief curator [II.015]. The decades-long love-affair between Wolkoff, MERES, and the 5Pointz artists continued until 2013 when Wolkoff decided to whitewash all the artwork, demolish the building, and build a new residential development. "I didn't whitewash it to be mean," claims Wolkoff. "I whitewashed it because I heard that they were going to put their hands together and stop the bulldozers from coming. Hell, they would be arrested. So I said, let me just get it over with, and that was the intent."[172] This sudden eradication of 5Pointz highlights some inherent incompatibilities between the viewpoints of traditional, profit-based real estate development and those held by hip-hop's faithful. The continuing saga of 5Pointz exposes similar incompatibilities that remain between hip-hop aspirations and even more progressively minded developments. The Museum of Street Art, which claims to have "[resurrected] a significant and beloved landmark of graffiti art in New York,"[173] now exists as a stairwell of a newly developed mixed-use tower on Bowery in Lower Manhattan with a single visible "graffiti wall" showcasing a piece by MERES [II.016]. The transition from a four-story Queens warehouse heralded as "world-class museum" where "the art is constantly changing" to a market-rate development where "20 graffiti artists collaborated in the painting of the staircase"[174] seems less of a resurrection than a relegation. These incompatibilities between two worlds with divergent intentions parallel the contradictions at the heart of our current discussions on hip-hop and architecture.

Having established the legitimate connections between the worlds of hip-hop and architecture—connected the history of hip-hop to a legacy of spatial practices negatively affecting Black bodies, connected contemporary urban environments to cultural practices informed by hip-hop, and outlined methods, techniques, and attitudes that bring the two disciplines into closer alignment—we must now face the contradictory nature of the term Hip-Hop Architecture. If architecture is indeed the slow-moving, conservative, elitist behemoth that it is here made out to be, then it will be equally slow to accept a phenomenon as progressive, multivalent, and malleable as hip-hop in its

II.015 | 5Pointz
Image courtesy of Ezmosis via Wikimedia Creative Commons. CC BY-SA 3.0. https://commons.wikimedia.org/wiki/File:View_of_5_Pointz,_January_20,_2013.jpg

II.016 | MERES mural at Museum of Street Art
© Sekou Cooke

canon. Conversely, a globally successful billion-dollar industry such as hip-hop, with its power to affect culture universally from fashion, to technology, to speech patterns, to politics, would be underselling itself in attempts to conform to the strictures of architectural practice. Put more simplistically, architecture doesn't want to be hip-hop, and hip-hop doesn't want to be architecture. So, is Hip-Hop Architecture a purely intellectual pursuit? In Volume III, I will explore the various ways hip-hop has expressed itself architecturally by practitioners, academics, and students attempting to define the movement in practical terms. The main question being posed will not be "Can hip-hop culture truly express itself within the built environment?" That much has already been made clear even without a deeper analysis of specific architectural products. Instead, the question that lingers on beyond this book will be "Do all these examples sufficiently define a legitimate architectural movement authentically emergent from hip-hop culture?" and further, "Is Hip-Hop Architecture a movement for architects or a movement for the people?"

A first step towards resolving these apparent contradictions might be to accept the contradictions endemic to hip-hop culture—contradictions Rose believes are "*central* to hip hop."[175] This brings us back to hip-hop's reputation for misogyny, homophobia, and violence. As we have established, this reputation is unfairly ascribed to hip-hop in exclusion of other forms of Black cultural production, contemporary popular culture in general, and all other forms of oppression from dominant societal forces. The hope here is not to promote the defeatist attitude that these will always be part of hip-hop, of other forms of popular culture, or of architecture. Instead, the goal is to recognize the successes hip-hop has realized in counteracting and disempowering these negative forces through unfiltered interrogation of urban realities regardless of their internal contradictions and to emulate this attitude within the architectural discipline. By acknowledging the presence of these same negative forces within architecture and promoting awareness of its own contradictions, architecture can begin to counteract and disempower its misogynistic, homophobic, and violent tendencies while leaving room for other contradictions including its seemingly irreconcilable incompatibility with hip-hop.

When considering architecture's history, stemming from loosely defined indigenous practices for creating shelter, then evolving to include higher forms of artistic expression and theoretical imperative, and now existing in its current form of technical expertise, legal responsibility, and narrow specialization, we can acknowledge a trend away from the speculative and towards the restrictive—the broadly defined to the narrowly defined, inclusive to exclusive. Hip-hop has realized the opposite trend having evolved from clearly defined forms connecting gang practices, technical formulations, and the Jamaican dancehall into loosely connected forms of expression recognizable in all aspects of contemporary culture—trending from the narrow to the broad, exclusive to inclusive. To find the sweet spot where these two trend lines intersect we may have to reverse each trend slightly to a place where architecture is more inclusive (the purely academic space of architectural speculation) and hip-hop is more exclusive (the nostalgic space where hip-hop exists in its purest form of clearly defined elements). Once that point is established, extrapolation into new territories of regional specificity, canonization, contemporary evolution, and universal application will become the logical next steps.

■ ■ ■

"I'm not switching between being a rapper and a designer. When I'm designing, I'm a rapper designing. And when I'm rapping, I'm a designer rapping. You know, it's not something that I'm conscious about. These are different lobes in my brain working. To me it all comes from that same place."

– *Tajai Massey*[176]

As I Manifest: Contemporary Speculations on Hip-Hop Architectural Education and Practice

VOLUME III

Track List	Page
01 FORM.	085
02 IMAGE.	097
03 PROCESS.	111
04 IDENTITY.	137
05 URBANISM.	159
06 SPACE.	177

01
FORM.

"So, I still don't get it."[1]

This was the response from an audience member after Lauren Halsey gave a riveting account of the Hip-Hop Architectural theories that ground her art practice. "Can you give me a scope of work for a hip-hop house?"[2] The rest of the audience had been captivated by her presentation at the panel discussion—one of many connected to the *Close to the Edge* exhibition[3]—but this one response reminded us all of the rampant conservatism in our profession and the incredible challenge of getting even the most visually gifted people to imagine the physical implications of this theoretical movement. Locating conversations about hip-hop, a progressive antiestablishment culture, at the AIA New York's Center for Architecture, the epicenter of organized architectural practice in America[4] was sure to elicit a few conservative comments. The exhibition itself was conceived as a way to challenge this conservatism and to answer the perpetual question: "What does Hip-Hop Architecture look like?" At the heart of this question are several formal concerns of primary interest to architects. "Can ideas gleaned from hip-hop culture be applied to a design process?" "Can it become legible in a building's form?" "If I see it will I recognize it?"

Close to the Edge: The Birth of Hip-Hop Architecture provided a platform for exploring these questions by showcasing various manifestations of Hip-Hop Architecture in both academic and professional arenas. [III.017] Examples of work included in the show came from twenty-one students, academics, and practitioners working in five different countries (Netherlands, Belgium, Nigeria, Australia, and the United States) with projects completed between 1992 and 2018.[5] Work ranged from undergraduate thesis projects to architecture studio courses taught explicitly about Hip-Hop Architecture; from landscape designs to artistic installations; and from building speculations and proposals to fully executed interiors, façades, and new constructions. The multivalent, cross-generational, and international collection of work underscored the broad reach of a movement intent on transforming the slow-moving discipline of architecture from the inside out. Though not organized chronologically, thematically, or methodologically, the work in the exhibition was identified and labeled using one of three characteristics: hip-hop image, hip-hop process, and hip-hop identity [III.018]. The first describes products whose image is recognizable as part of an established hip-hop aesthetic; the second evokes a method of production using specific hip-hop techniques or values; and the third includes authors who self-identify with the hip-hop community either by practicing one of the four elements or by general association [III.019].

III.017 | Exterior view of *Close to the Edge: The Birth of Hip Hop Architecture*
© Erik Bardin

III.018 | Interior view of *Close to the Edge: The Birth of Hip Hop Architecture*
© Erik Bardin

Beyond the primary work framed and hung in the main gallery, other sections of the show presented video [III.020], audio [III.021], and 3D content, along with expanded explanations and alternate narratives [III.022]. One such section of the show confronted the "What does it look like?" question head on. By reproducing three-dimensional models of several pieces included in the main exhibition and stripping them of color, material, and context, "On Form" created a mode of purely formal comparison between various Hip-Hop Architectural objects [III.023]. The new question posed was, "Is there a consistent formal language of Hip-Hop Architecture that can be easily discerned?" Though exhibition audiences were left to

III.019 | Detail view of *Close to the Edge: The Birth of Hip-Hop Architecture*
© Erik Bardin

formulate their own conclusions, my own reading of the objects as presented finds very little consistency in their formal language. *Third Space* by Scott Krabath and Renata Ramela shares almost no formal aspects with *Shanty Megastructures* by Olalekan Jeyifous; the three buildings by Maurer United Architects, each a collaboration with graffiti artists, are very formally different from each other; and *Amalgamated Cypher* by Rothelowman Architects bears very little resemblance to any other projects. What can be read in each project, however, is a unique relationship to "flow, layering, and ruptures in line,"[6] three concepts Rose uses to focus her arguments on hip-hop style.

In hip hop, visual, physical, musical, and lyrical lines are set in motion, broken abruptly with sharp angular breaks, yet they sustain motion and energy through fluidity and flow. In graffiti, long-winding, sweeping, and curving letters are broken and camouflaged by sudden breaks in line . . . Breakdancing moves highlight flow, layering, and ruptures in line. Popping and locking are moves in which the joints are snapped abruptly into angular positions. . . . The music and vocal rapping in rap music also privileges flow, layering, and ruptures in line. Rappers speak of flow explicitly in lyrics, referring to an ability to move easily and powerfully through complex lyrics as well as of the flow in the music.[7]

Flow, layering, and ruptures in line are the clearest criteria for discerning formal consistencies between musical composition, dance, and visual art in hip-hop. Other criteria, such as sampling, mixing, and improvisation, produce readings that are as varied as they are unique. Unlike typical architectural styles that produce consistent formal language, the products of Hip-Hop Architecture are only consistent in their flows, layers, and ruptures, but parallel all other hip-hop products in their inconsistency of form. Though Hip-Hop Architecture resists relegation to mere style, that resistance is consistent with the aspects of hip-hop culture that constitute hip-hop style. *How* Hip-Hop Architecture is produced is more easily described than *what* it looks like. The examples presented in this volume are some of the best that can be found.

■ ■ ■

III.020 | "I Know You Seen Me on Your Videos"
© Erik Bardin

III.021 | "Black Noise"
© Erik Bardin

III.022 | "B-Sides"
© Erik Bardin

"I'm Lauren Halsey. I'm from Los Angeles. My family's deeply from Los Angeles. They moved from the city via the great migration in the 30s, both sides. My maternal side to basically Watts, a mile west of Watts. My paternal side moved to downtown South Central and we're both there still. I practice and have studios in both areas in my Grandmothers' garages. What I think pushed me pretty forcefully into architecture was never going to school in my neighborhood and being this sort of insider-outsider every single day of my life, from elementary school to college. Also, never having a car in Los Angeles (still) and always being a passenger . . . seeing the city extremely slowly.

"As a kid I would have these very visceral emotional responses to the architectural boundaries along boulevards like Western Avenue or Western Crenshaw, and I would notice the hard, architectural materials, the soft materials, the cladding, the signage—all

Ill.023 | "On Form"
© Anthony Turner

these things that spoke to me about disempowerment or empowerment based on where I was.

"I went to community college in this area called Torrance and did the architecture program paralleled with art. I realized then I wasn't so much interested in "we are gonna do this add-on with a gabled roof," or whatever. It was more about how I could think about funkifying space though my lens. I was making these maps of my neighborhood. I made like a hundred of them until my dad's computer broke. The whole thing was about creating these like super-maximalist remixes of the neighborhood that were very concerned with who and what was already there. Then my own aspirational mapping and visioning through the lens of funk and hip hop. I'll show you a few.

"And then my collection. I'm a huge huge huge huge collector of anything people make or display in South Central and I use it for my own work. I was also employing a lot of that production in these maps. They were exercises. They were never meant to printed out or displayed. They were literally for me to imagine pretty radically the physical space that I was interested in and also the scale. I guess it's also important to say that I was also thinking along the lines of how I think architects operate as far as working from a point of research and then there is this 2D moment and then there some model or miniature and then you have the to-scale thing.

"I grew up with my father always having a building project. No matter what, there was always something to build or edit in the house, to work on. So, I was always going to Home Depot. This was the first time I started thinking of built materials as a surface which changed my scale. And while this was happening, I also started making these models, having made so much flat work. As a kid, I watched cartoons and stuff, but what really did it for me was Parliament Funkadelic. Being from LA, I inherited them via G-funk, which like Snoop Dog, Dr. Dre, and that whole thing, sampled Parliament. So, it was my father and my family members playing it in the backyard and my father disciplining me through Parliament lyrics, and while that was happening the internet came out and you could download music. I remember that I had Kazaa and Limewire so I downloaded Parliament Funkadelic. This really beautiful thing happened that empowered my imagination without having to ever leave my bedroom. When that happened,

Parliament gave me the conceit to think about fantastical scale and transcendence in a way that I'm still playing with.

"My first installation in 2013 was a breakthrough for me because I got to employ my father's building ethos and materials, which totally bumps up against the western way of building things, which says you have to have a stud 24" on center and there's code and blah blah blah blah, to sort of freestyle space, accumulate space on my own terms which was really great. And then also still sampling what I was collecting in the neighborhood, like literally. It was very important to me that it was structural, like it was a structure as well. This lasted like a year and then the fire marshal knocked on my door and was like, 'get rid of it.'

"All my work, no matter what it is, or what the form is, or medium is, is very much about living archives of Downtown, South Central, and Watts, because it's being deleted through oppressive forces and that was a thing for architects.

"I did this residency program at the Studio Museum in Harlem which was really great. I'm super obsessed with myths about ancient Egypt as far as origin for Black people. Of course, I know we weren't all kings and queens, but I'm still obsessed with what compels someone to move through that headspace as protections, as armor, as crown. I got a lot of that from Parliament, my father, and people freestyling history [about] who and what we were my whole life. So, I got to Harlem, 125th street and it took it to the next level where I was meeting these mythmakers. I was meeting for real pyramid builders who were doing this in 1990's Georgia and the FBI shut it down. I was going to the Met a lot and I started thinking about hieroglyphs as these document keepers of the Pharaoh's world. So, I thought how cool it would be to think about remixing the function of the hieroglyph for South Central since, as time is passing, it's becoming more and more under attack by various infrastructures.

"This was the first time that art handlers ever installed anything for me. It was really incredible to watch because they struggled because [the pieces] were so heavy. It was this breakthrough where I realized I had reached a point in my practice where I was actually creating wall—I was actually creating structure—and it didn't have to depend on the architecture of any other space. It was autonomous, it was fortified, it was strong, and it was a drawing.

"After that Studio Museum project of the hieroglyphs, I went back to LA. I wrote the council member, I emailed him, and I said, "Hey, we have like 10,000 empty lots in Los Angeles, can I use one?" I didn't get a response. Then I emailed like everyone on his website and I got a couple of responses and studio visits and really great conversations, but everything was really hypothetical. It was like it's gonna be this big and its gonna uhh and we're gonna uhh. And so, I had a project in this show at the Hammer Museum called "Made in LA" and the curators asked me what I wanted to do. I [told them] I had to build a prototype for this project for the city to actually believe it could happen, so I did the autonomous structure of those hieroglyphs. After five or six days, the city saw this (the tangible iteration) and they offered me a permanent city project.

"It's really exciting for me because it's the first time in my practice where I'm not just referencing architecture or animating my art with the discourse of architecture. It's an actual construction project. [Some] really great architects and firms in Los Angeles have been really generous in helping me articulate it. This will be the first time I actually have a budget, so I'm going to the Black Workers Center and using their resources to hire the contractors and the carpenters, to think about the docents, to think about who programs it. Going across the street to Nipsy Hustle who's the king of LA to think about who protects it, because gangs are real. Going to Spotify and getting a sponsor to have a festival and having the big names, [but] also making sure the marching bands are there, or that local talent is there, so that there aren't these hierarchies of presence. And really thinking about a building project as way of creating and sustaining energy, self-esteem, love, and all these ways for people to mobilize to think about neighborhoods. I call this project my FUBU architecture."

– Lauren Halsey[8]

■ "____"

– Lupe Fiasco[9]

02 IMAGE.

The image of hip-hop has been popularized and reified over its lifespan through album covers, music videos, clothing lines, and photo documentation of early hip-hop environments. Each graffiti-bombed abandoned building or subway car, each gold rope chain, do-rag, Kangol hat, pair of baggy denim jeans, or shell-top Adidas shoes frames the overall image of hip-hop culture and burns it into our collective consciousness. The easiest way for most outside the world of hip-hop to consume hip-hop products, regardless of their authenticity, is through its imagery. If it looks hip-hop, most assume it is hip-hop, and herein lies the problem of the image.

The drawbacks to this kind of thinking are multiple. First, the authority determining what is hip-hop and what isn't, from this perspective, are predominantly Western eyes. Volume II of this book discusses varying attitudes toward gatekeeping that are internal to hip-hop and the related dangers of insider-ism.[10] However, the instinct to categorize, classify, and name items is deeply connected to the instinct to consume (and not in the "consuming food for life" or "consuming knowledge for wisdom" sense, but in the manner of consuming a culture to feed off of its lifeforce). Second, it recasts the entirety of hip-hop culture, like most cultures that Western capitalist consumerists encounter, as an easily digestible set of Halloween-costume-friendly tropes. Again, the gate to appropriation is left wide open. Finally, and most significantly, what hip-hop looks like is ever changing. As a culture that is alive and evolving, hip-hop is constantly redefining its boundaries, annexing new elements, and experimenting with new modes of self-determination. Once the outside decides on a singular image for hip-hop a newer fresher image is waiting to take its place. (As soon as shell-tops get hot in the suburbs, Air Jordans start to rep the hip-hop heads. Once the reign of Jordans gets old, Chucks take over.) Hip-hop will decide what is hip-hop, not the casual observer. As such, most architecture interested in the image of hip-hop is relegated to reflection, interpretation, or mimicry rather than invention of its own hip-hop image. The following examples draw inspiration from iconic visualizations of hip-hop culture and convert them into their own proposals for Hip-Hop Architectural imagery.

Architecture professors Nathaniel Belcher and Stephen Slaughter came together under the collaborative name PHAT in 2003 for their participation in the *harlemworld: Metropolis as Metaphor* exhibition at the Studio Museum in Harlem. As they describe it, their project "*Harlem: The Ghetto Fabulous*, is both an action and reaction to the numerous failed strategies of urban renewal, the prevailing, inappropriate models of urban redevelopment, and the demographic and market pressures that are transforming Harlem, New York."[11] The bold imagery of this speculative penthouse

III.024 | *Harlem: the Ghetto Fabulous*
PHAT is: Nathaniel Q Belcher, Stephen M Slaughter, David Mesfin, and Adam Wheeler

space, including sharply-clad male hip-hop artists and scantily clad women occupying spaces decked out in glossy finishes, decadent furnishings, and luxurious adornments, projects the desired glamour associated with contemporary hip-hop lifestyles [III.024]. It is an unapologetic affirmation of a hip-hop-colored American Dream and an honest (though limited) reflection of a singular moment along hip-hop's timeline—one that is hyper-masculine and acutely misogynistic. This project suggests a new spatial paradigm steeped in bling. Without the proper contextualization as provided by the authors, however, misinterpretation and misappropriation are likely. "The installation was ultimately a critique of materialism, misogyny, and hypocrisy," says Slaughter of the original exhibition entry, "that ran and still runs rampant in both [hip-hop and architecture] cultures."[12]

Marc Maurer and Nicole Maurer of Maurer United Architects (MUA) have been experimenting with designs inspired by hip-hop culture since the mid-1990s. As Aaron Betsky writes, they "have been known to call themselves 'MC Architects'. Sampling and mixing elements from graffiti, video games, fashion, and hip-hop and working with 'kindred spirits' from all these fields, the two are indeed veritable architectural MCs."[13] The three projects described next, *Het Wilde Wonen*, *P2001*, and *Zedzbeton 3.0*, expand on some of those early experiments. Each was a collaboration between MUA and "the architect's most detested enemies,"[14] in this case, noted Dutch graff writers. Each preserves the visual language of graffiti, explores the potential inhabitation of letters constructed at human scale, and depicts both exterior formal massing and interior spatial environments as separate architectural experiences.

In the first example, *Het Wilde Wonen* (The Wild Life), MUA collaborates with DELTA to design a villa using "techniques culled from graffiti and dazzle painting."[15] The result is an intricate series of interlocking forms and spaces expressing the more vibrant aspects of wild style graffiti both internally and externally [Ill.025]. The next example, *P2001*, was an installation proposal for the "Rotterdam 2001" exhibition organized by MAMA (showroom for Media and Moving Art). It aimed to "confront visitors to the exhibition with the theme of identity"[16] using carefully positioned mirrored surface throughout its interior. Both the interior and exterior volumes are composed of three-dimensional graffiti pieces by ZEDZ and DELTA [Ill.026]. ZEDZ was once again the main collaborator with MUA for the *Zedzbeton 3.0* project, which the architects describe as "urban furniture... designed for a location in front of the main building"[17] at Eindhoven University of Technology Art Foundation. The overall piece comprises four concrete sections, each the extruded form in the x- and z-directions of the letters Z, E, D, and Z. The furniture scale at the lower edges of the piece is overwhelmed by its large size, with each letter measuring "five meters in width, fifteen meters in length, and four and a half meters in height"[18] [Ill.027].

In the design of *The Hive*, Zvi Belling of ITN Architects also collaborated with a noted graff writer. In this case, Belling called on PROWLA of the Melbourne-based RDC Crew to create 3D-relief *throw up*[19] letters "complete with arrows, swooshes and drips"[20] on the side of his new apartment building. Unlike the MUA projects, the graffiti here is extruded as a surface appliqué rather than a habitable volume. The arrow-shaped windows, also heavily identifiable with traditional graffiti, are used at key moments

III.025 | Poster for *Het Wilde Wonen*
Maurer United Architects

III.026 | Poster for *P2001*
Maurer United Architects

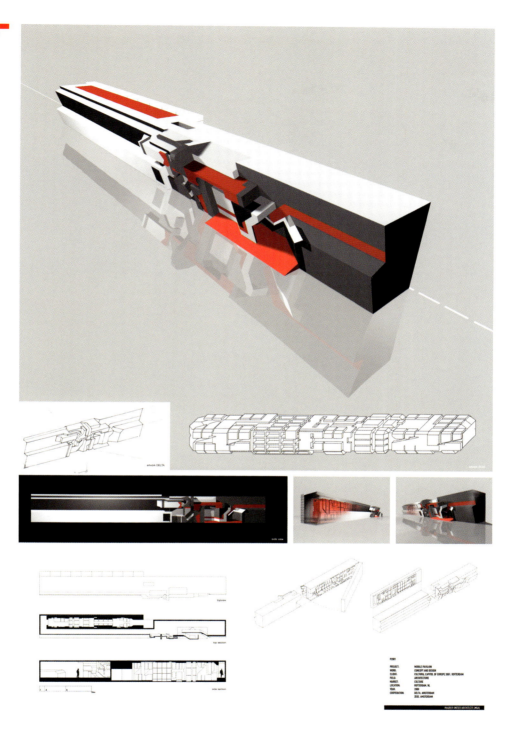

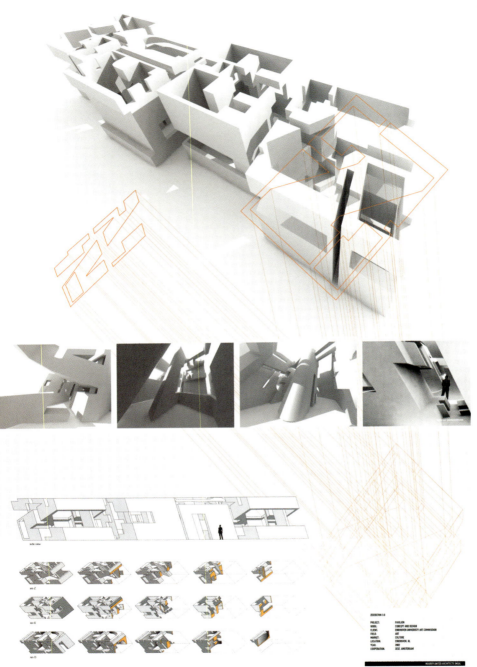

III.027 | **Poster for** *Zedzbeton 3.0*
Maurer United Architects

III.028 | "The Hive"
Zvi Belling

throughout the structure [III.028]. Though the building has been repeatedly cited in open conversation as a prime example of Hip-Hop Architecture, its remoteness from New York (hip-hop's birthplace) and its unfiltered translation of graffiti into structure has made its recurring inclusion controversial. The architect's statements that the building "is the first in a series of Hip Hop buildings"[21] and that "The urban street is celebrated by making permanent an ephemeral art"[22] clarify his intentions of solidifying a singly recognizable hip-hop image into built form.

Completed three years later, *The End to End Building* is Belling's "sequel"[23] to *The Hive*. The project's title refers to the "end to end" or "whole car" graffiti pieces done on the three decommissioned Melbourne Metro Train cars sitting atop a new office building. The "bombed-out" subway cars, iconic images of hip-hop culture present in cities across the globe, now house a rooftop restaurant [III.029]. Though the letters on *The Hive* and the graffiti-covered subway cars both create a visual link to graffiti culture the latter is read as being more authentic since each subway car lived real lives as moving canvases for Melbourne's graffiti crews as opposed to the former which casts a temporal art form in concrete. According to Belling, a third building is planned to complete his "trilogy."[24] The question of hip-hop authenticity will remain prevalent in this third effort as it has with the previous two.

Other projects by contemporary practitioners draw inspiration from the image of graffiti without explicit affiliation with the tenets of Hip-Hop Architecture or claim to hip-hop authenticity. Exemplary works include a recent

III.029 | "The End to End Building"
Zvi Belling

public infrastructure project by Molly Hunker and Greg Corso of SPORTS Collaborative and two speculative projects by John Szot of John Szot Studio. For *City Thread*, winner of the "Passageways 2.0" public space competition for the city of Chattanooga, Tennessee, SPORTS transforms an underused alley into a place for public gathering and recreational activity "including informal lounging/sitting, mini-stages, and movie screenings."[25] The competition organizers selected "graffiti alley" in downtown Chattanooga as the site for the second round of the public arts project, the first round of which saw five artist create a series of temporary installations around the city aimed at turning "auxiliary pedestrian spaces into engaging public areas full of life and possibility."[26] The primary formal gesture employed by SPORTS, "a continuous linear volume constructed from a series of large, simple steel tubes,"[27] implies the movement of a graff writer's arm with a three-dimensional aerosol can [III.030]. "I hadn't seen it until you talked about it that way," (as 3D graffiti) Corso admitted, "the three-dimensional element plays off of that."[28] Their intervention also includes 2D "shapes"[29] (large swaths of "aqua wish" blue paint) that complement the 3D "thread" ("limelight" yellow painted steel sections). These shapes are distributed along the alley walls and fold onto the ground surface, indiscriminately covering protruding building elements in their way. "There are so many different layers of paints and graphics," explains Hunker, "our added shape could just fall into that layering. If that got tagged or something happened on top of that, that would just be another layer. [The organizers] asked us 'do you want us to paint over all of the graffiti before you do your shapes?' and we were like, 'No. Our shapes are participating [with them]. We like that they are there and can be read against that'"[30] [III.031].

John Szot's recent drawings (listed on his website under various headings such as, "Drawing Code," "SXSW 18," "Matrix 1 & 2," in colorways including "Gold," "Copper," and "Red Series") deftly mix graffiti imagery with architectural drawings and other collage materials. His layering of multiple

III.030 | Detail view of "City Thread"
Photo by Justin Harris

III.031 | "City Thread"
Photo by Benjamin Chase

image types with technical drawings creates new dense readings of urban space, activity, and energy all reflective of core hip-hop attitudes [III.032]. This work is "not necessarily born out of hip-hop," claims Szot, "I'm not sure I have the cred. I identify with the irreverence of the culture [but] the work is more grounded in an interest in street art."[31] The short film *Architecture and the Unspeakable* (official selection of at least seven international film festivals[32]) tells "the story of three buildings, each with a pathological problem that contains the promise of a new cultural dialogue in architecture."[33] That dialog, in the first of the three buildings, is unmistakably fashioned by architecture's relationship with graffiti and street art. The film takes us through expertly rendered animations of a faceless concrete building on an unidentified block in SoHo that is soon subjected to a "commissioning of finishes"[34] as described by an architectural specification section spelled out in a spray-painted hand style by ELLIS G on one of its bare walls [III.033].

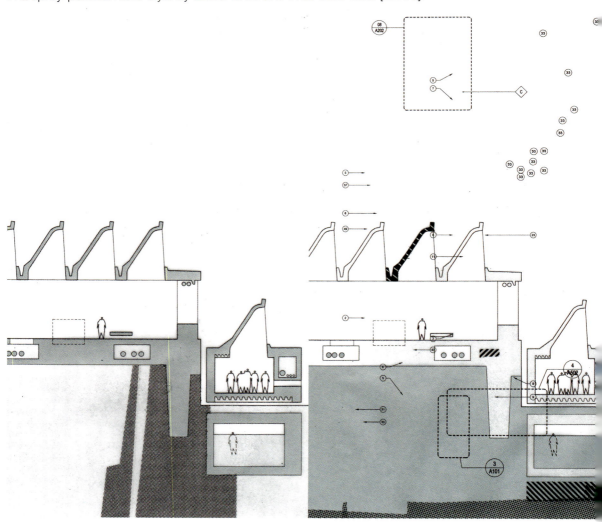

III.032 | Matrix 1 - Row F
John Szot

09 08 00 – Commissioning of Finishes
C. Definition of Steeping Period

1. Once the structural work is completed, the Job Site is to be subjected to a steeping period, during which time the Job Site will be considered to be in a state of "steeping".
2. To initiate the steeping period, the Job Site must be prepared as follows:
   a. evacuated by the Contractor and all tradesmen
   b. cleared of all surplus building material and construction equipment
   c. secured at ground (or street) level to prevent casual entry at all possible points of entry
   d. all other possible points of entry above ground (or street) level should be left unprotected

III.033 | Still from "Architecture and the Unspeakable – Part 1"
John Szot

III.034 | Still from "Architecture and the Unspeakable – Part 1"
John Szot

3. The Job Site will remain in a state of steeping for a period to be determined by the Architect, but not to exceed _____.
4. During the steeping period, the Contractor may not visit the Job Site.
5. Upon expiration of the steeping period, or upon notice from the Architect, the Contractor will return to the Job Site to resume work.
6. In resuming work, the Contractor:
    a. is permitted to remove any debris or obstructions that may have accumulated during the steeping period
    b. is not permitted to clean or parge any exposed concrete or masonry surfaces that were subject to vandalism during the steeping period unless expressly directed to do so by the Architect.[35]

After the specified "steeping period"[36] (which happens off camera), the next scene shows the building covered in graffiti and street art of all kinds. A new life and energy are added to the space rendered without human occupation. In this opening section of his film Szot suggests how buildings covered in street art can actually become more valuable to owners "despite the efforts of architects"[37] [III.034]. Through his films, his drawings, and the rest of his work Szot critically questions the relationship between architects, building owners, and street artists. "The profession needs humility," he claims. And, much like those more explicitly invested in practicing Hip-Hop Architecture, he is "interested in what makes architecture a more human discipline" and believes architects put "too much stock in controlling outcomes."[38] Regardless of his stated relationship with hip-hop culture, Szot is not only reflecting hip-hop's image in his work, but is also embodying many attitudes crucial for the definition of Hip-Hop Architecture.

Across each of the projects in this category there is a consistent reliance on predefined images of hip-hop culture to drive the aesthetic direction of the work. Since hip-hop process or hip-hop identity is not centrally at question in each case (included here in descending order of explicit claim to Hip-Hop Architecture), their authenticity as hip-hop architectural products is less important than their ability to exploit the architectural applicability of hip-hop image. Subsequent sections convey with increasing importance the ways designers, through the leveraging of process and identity, have produced more substantial Hip-Hop Architectural products that may not be easily associated with a singular image.

■ ■ ■

– Beyoncé[39]

03

PROCESS.

Each of the four elements expresses itself through a replicable set of techniques, methods, and processes. As detailed in Volume II,[40] DJs sample, scratch, and mix excerpts of prerecorded sounds, collaging contemporary references, rare musical discoveries, and long-forgotten standards. MCs deftly construct complex rhyme schemes and layer them over engineered beats. B-boys twist, contort, spin, pop, lock, and defy gravity in myriad bodily distortions, each following an established sequence from up-rock to down-rock to power move to freeze. Graff writers transform wall surfaces into canvases in obscure, forgotten, disregarded, and hard-to-reach locations using fluidly structured lines and dynamic color palettes. They layer paint, stencils, stickers, and tile onto any accessible face of buildings, bridges, and viaducts. For the creation of Hip-Hop Architecture, translating hip-hop processes into design processes may present the most direct route.

Examples included under this heading enlist processes extracted from one or more hip-hop elements or born out of hip-hop culture in general to guide architectural production.

Visual artists can often more easily test the precepts of a design movement than architects can since their processes require much less accountability to government agencies, clients' will, or public health, safety, and welfare. The two prominent Chicago-based artists profiled below employ hip-hop attitudes and processes in much of their work. In her widely exhibited and critically acclaimed *Color(ed) Theory* series, Amanda Williams "connect[s] culturally loaded colors with architectural space."[41] She selects houses slated for demolition in the Inglewood neighborhood on Chicago's Southside and paints them in a single hue from her predetermined palette—"Pink Oil Hair Moisturizer, Harold's Chicken, Flaming Red Hots, Crown Royal, Newports, Currency Exchange, all things that have a strong color signifier"[42] [III.035]. As she explains it, her process borrows tactics from graffiti artists to make a highly visible statement within the decaying community. "I can actually take the detritus and the used material and do something else with it," Williams states. "I find it to be a quiet exciting testimony . . . that you can do something that the community can just have as something to contemplate"[43] [III.036]. Due to the perceived disposable nature of the sites and structures on which she works, Williams, unlike graffiti artists, does not have to wait for cover of night or look for an obscure location in the city to complete her interventions. Her work elevates a simple graffiti tactic to a three-dimensionally significant operation capable of impacting large swaths of the city and impacting public perception of a community's built assets.

III.035 | *Color(ed) Theory*
Palette
Amanda Williams.
Courtesy of the artist

III.036 | *Color(ed) Theory:*
Pink Oil Moisturizer (fall)
Amanda Williams.
Courtesy of the artist

Another artist similarly invested in Chicago's Southside is Theaster Gates whose Rebuild Foundation (a nonprofit organization he created to administer the Dorchester Projects) has transformed one building at a time into local cultural institutions with programs that "support artists and strengthen communities by providing free arts programming, creating new cultural amenities, and developing affordable housing, studio, and live-work space."[44] Gates employs a similarly defiant attitude to Williams' in the development of these buildings, asking for forgiveness instead of permission. His process with Dorchester Projects involves the acquisition of properties, salvaging discarded building materials, and reusing these materials in the buildings' conversion or as artworks that help finance their development [III.037]. Legal processes requiring licensed architects or permits are circumvented in favor of progress and active change, which is later accepted and then celebrated by local officials. His 2015 *Sanctum* project, done in collaboration with Andrew T Cross of the UK–based An Architecture, brought similar techniques and processes to Bristol, UK in creating a temporary performance space to occupy the center of a bombed-out[45] church. The structure, described as "a rough-and-ready selection of rustic wood panels, bricks and windows from the Salvation Army and old Bristolian houses cobbled together in a manner that looks terrifically, effortlessly beautiful,"[46] resituates lessons learned from Dorchester [III.038]. Though Gates' closest relationship with architecture was his Loeb Fellowship at the Harvard Graduate School of Design (GSD), and he does not explicitly reference hip-hop in his descriptions, the processes and attitudes of his work bring him in unequivocal alignment with the movement of Hip-Hop Architecture.

Before these design processes and precepts can be tested professionally, even in art practices such as the ones mentioned earlier, they begin their lives in architecture schools. Since Nate Williams at Cornell, several other thesis projects have intentionally addressed hip-hop culture, beginning with Cornell, then spreading to other institutions on the East Coast and the West Coast, eventually covering the country and spreading to other universities around the world.[47] One of the earliest student projects interested in hip-hop processes, Nina Cooke John's 1995 undergraduate thesis, *The*

III.037 | Dorchester Projects
Courtesy of Rebuild Foundation

03 PROCESS.   113

III.038 | Sanctum
© Max McClure

Urban Porch, examined the linguistic patterns latent in Caribbean appropriations of Standard English to develop a mode of designing leftover spaces in New York City's Caribbean neighborhoods. "My aim was to steal space, ruffneck style," Cooke John claims in a clear callback to Wilkin's notion of stealing space[48] from his essay in *Ruffneck Constructivists*, "creating public spaces that members of the community could use for cultural enactment, mimicking strategies of appropriation practiced by marginalized people all over the world."[49] The result is a system for designing public spaces equally reminiscent of residential stoops across the city and porches across the American South—"prototypes for spaces throughout the neighborhoods adapting based on the local environment."[50] A narrow slot between two buildings on White Plains Road in The Bronx is one of several sites tested in her project. The various processes employed in her thesis highlight a few of the many resonances between Caribbean (particularly Jamaican) culture and the hip-hop community, especially that of finding creative value in the leftover or discarded (another example of "tun yu han' mek fashion") [III.039, III.040]. *The Urban Porch* "lies within this area of tactical appropriation," Cooke John explains, "exploring empowerment and urban public space.

III.039 | "The Urban Porch," collage and drawing
Nina Cooke John

III.040 | Model of "The Urban Porch"
Nina Cooke John

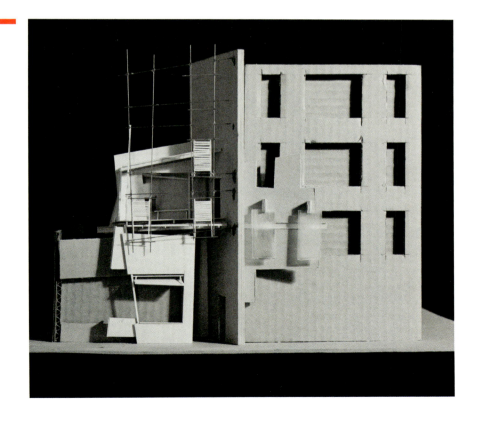

An architectural practice that deliberately carves out space for the disadvantaged, dispossessed and displaced."[51]

A contemporary international example comes from a pair of graduate students at the Politecnico di Milano who prepared the prize-winning[52] thesis "Remixing Architecture through urban culture: The Bronx revolution" in 2018. Andrea Bulloni and Marco Papagni, now able to build on academic theories of Hip-Hop Architecture including "The Fifth Pillar," proposed a new hip-hop cultural center between the Harlem River and Yankee Stadium in the Bronx, a comprehensive digestion of and reflection on traditional and contemporary hip-hop culture [III.041]. Their project "presents a main design intervention that embraces and represents past, present and future of the hip-hop experience."[53] The thoroughness of their research and high quality of their representations has gained them international social media attention (over 2,100 Instagram followers as of this writing) and multiple platforms for exhibiting their work. This is due mostly to the clarity of their translation of hip-hop cultural phenomena into distinct architectural processes.

Mauricio Zamora, at UC Berkeley, in 2019 produced the most recent example of a Hip-Hop Architecture thesis project with "Appropriated Teckniques: An Architectural Mixtape," which now exists as one of the more compelling student works. Like Bulloni and Papagni, Zamora was able to

III.041 | Model of "Remixing Architecture"— Main Hub
Andrea Bulloni, Marco Papagni

build on previous works of published theory. Also like the Italian project (and many other student theses), the program is predictably loose—a cultural center with performance spaces for entertainment and education on hip-hop culture. However, the design approach is exceptionally rich, beginning with a repurposed building shell and adding elements of three-dimensional graffiti and standard prefabricated components, all composed as if by a hip-hop DJ. As Zamora puts it, "Graffiti tekniques [sic] are used in form finding to house program or be adjacent to it, while the use of 'ready-made' architectural and construction elements allows for the over-writing of 'normative' occupancies."[54] The dynamic modeling and rendering style of the presentation further reinforces the lively spirit of the project [III.042, III.043].

A few pioneering professors, each having attended architecture school during the formative years of Hip-Hop Architectural thought, have conducted Hip-Hop Architecture studios courses of their own. Most projects produced in such courses will, by necessity, find themselves in the process category, primarily since the pedagogy and goals come directly from the instructors, not from students who don't necessarily identify with hip-hop culture. Even if the demographics of architecture schools were inclusive enough to increase the chances of having a largely hip-hop-identified cohort, most courses of this type don't allow students to self-select. As

III.042 | Appropriated Tekniques_Zamora
Copyright © 2019 Mauricio D. Zamora. All rights reserved

III.043 | Appropriated
Tekniques_Zamora
Copyright © 2019 Mauricio
D. Zamora. All rights
reserved

such, many of the culturally specific embedded attitudes necessary for producing authenticity within architectural products have to be stripped away, leaving process and technique as the main objectives of development. Nonetheless, the architectural design studio has proved to be a useful venue for incubating ideas yet to make their way in practice. Now that the pioneers of Hip-Hop Architectural thinking have come of age, they can test these ideas within dynamically discursive academic environments rather than confining them to idle discussion among peers.

Chris Cornelius, Associate Professor at the University of Wisconsin-Milwaukee School of Architecture & Urban Planning, has taught a data-mapping/representation seminar asking students to create visualizations of hip-hop music, has led two studios asking students to design a "Museum of Hip-Hop" in Brooklyn, NY, and is planning a third studio for fall 2019 on the same topic. Fourth-year undergraduates in 2015 and graduate students in 2017 created designs for the museum based on drawing and model studies they produced of various aspects of hip-hop culture. As Cornelius directs in his course syllabus, "We will do this by translating observations of the music, dance and graffiti into form."[55] Early phases of the courses expose students to the arc of hip-hop culture spanning from the early 1980s to the year 2000, highlighting its unique nature as "created at a specific time, in a specific place, under specific conditions"[56] and continually reflective of contemporary realities ("from hood to bling"[57]). Cornelius encourages students to "train subjectivity," drawing from their own experiences, in their design processes and to better align their work with hip-hop's legacy of "making something from nothing."[58] As he puts it, "I want students to ask themselves 'What do you like? And why do you like it?' Then I say, 'express it yourself. Draw the things that you like to draw, then think about it after the fact.'"[59] The resulting "found object" models and "S.N.A.F.U." drawings reflect each student's unique relationship with, and interpretation of, the hip-hop source material used [III.044, III.045]. The final museum designs remain consistent with the initial research and process, each a logical translation of the layered, ruptured, and colorful techniques observed [III.046].

Through the University of Cincinnati's community outreach program, MetroLAB, Stephen Slaughter conducted a design-build studio course at Elementz, a local urban arts center that uses hip-hop as its main vehicle for learning. Early in the process, readings of texts on Hip-Hop Architecture theory proved critical in the shaping of the students' design attitudes. The course included design charrettes between the school and the community, production of full-scale prototypes, and installation of finalized solutions in the space [III.047]. The studio was successful in exposing UC students to hip-hop culture while simultaneously exposing local high-school students of the *Elementz* program to modes of digital fabrication used in architecture schools. "The collaboration between MetroLAB and *Elementz*," states Slaughter, "was used . . . to foster a relationship that [would] allow each student group—the students of *Elementz* and my students—to learn and appreciate the training and talents of the other and hopefully form a bond that can forge community and sponsor change. The challenge though

III.044 | "Found Object Models"
Chris Cornelius, Associate Professor, University of Wisconsin-Milwaukee

III.045 | S.N.A.F.U drawing
Chris Cornelius, Associate Professor, University of Wisconsin-Milwaukee

was not just making the collaboration work but to have the artform of hip-hop play a central role in the pedagogy of the studio and serve as bridge between the predominantly White and affluent midwestern students of the school with predominantly Black and working class preteens and young adults of *Elementz*, who were ironically just as [un]familiar with Kool Herc as my UC students were"[60] [III.048]. Beyond its goals of interpreting hip-hop culture into tangible fabrication techniques, using these to teach students at both levels about hip-hop, and enacting effective community outreach, the project also confronted the lack of diversity within architecture programs across the US. "Through the process of the studio we were able to introduce, educate, and excite the students of the Urban Arts Center to the idea

III.046 | Museum design, final section drawing
Chris Cornelius, Associate Professor, University of Wisconsin-Milwaukee

of design as a career with the goal of increasing minority enrollment in university and ultimately the number of licensed practicing design professionals in the world. The collective experience of making, breaking, and making again, the rapid prototyping, allowed the students to develop a vested interest in the success of the studio and the well-being of those served."[61] The course, which ran in 2015 and 2017, continues to inform Slaughter's work on digital fabrication and hip-hop culture. Both Slaughter and Cornelius have found ways to essentialize hip-hop processes to make them relevant and applicable to students from varied backgrounds.

My own efforts to bring Hip-Hop Architectural thought into design education have resulted in five years of coursework developed in a series of seminars and studio courses taught at Syracuse Architecture. The studio courses (one discussed here in this section, the other in a subsequent section on urbanism) were taught two years apart and focused on hip-hop culture's potential impact on Washington and Chicago, while the seminars began with a single hip-hop element to frame its subject matter, one per year over a four-year period. The first seminar, entitled *Breaking Space*, began with b-boying, what I imagined at the time to be the most challenging of the four to express architecturally—quite literally "dancing about architecture,"[62] if you will. As detailed in the course syllabus, its intentions were to

III.047 | *Elementz* installation
Stephen Slaughter.
Reproduced with permission

III.048 | Stephen Slaughter with *Elementz* design team
Stephen Slaughter.
Reproduced with permission

"investigate the relationship between dance and architecture through the specific lens of hip-hop culture."[63] Students worked "collaboratively with hip-hop dance instructor, Tehmekah MacPherson, and a student-led hip-hop dance troupe to design, choreograph, construct and perform original pieces of hip-hop-based architecture and dance."[64] The resultant "constructed and choreographed interventions" provided "a means of coopting and redefining existing spaces around the Syracuse University campus, each designed to adapt and respond to their varying contexts and allow for ease of mobility."[65] During these design exercises, reading discussions, and lecture sessions the power of breaking to coopt, adapt, and reinterpret public space was more deeply understood. Other architectural parallels, as described in Volume II,[66] proved useful in diagramming dance moves and performances [III.049]. In decoding and evaluating subtler aspects of breaking—its roots in traditional gang dances; the importance of showing off, boasting, and showing each other up; and, as MacPherson notes, the parallels between breaking and "the expressive posture of graffiti"—students unearthed additional design potential for the construction of their final full-scale interventions [III.050].

III.049 | B-boy diagram
Stephanie White and Sabrina Reyes

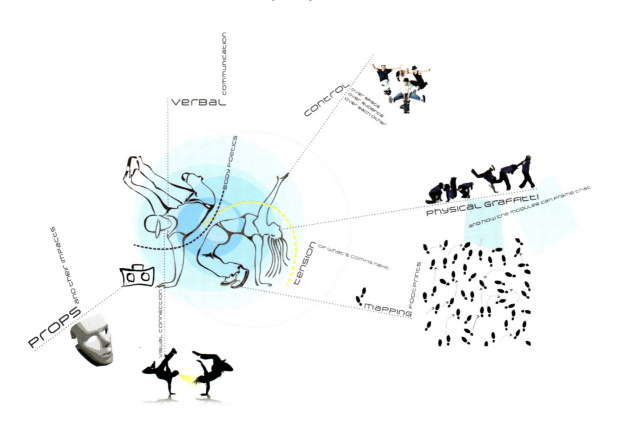

III.050 | Student installation in Slocum Hall
© Sekou Cooke

The second course, entitled *3D Turntables*, positioned hip-hop DJs as the original hackers of phonographic technology and paralleled their innovations with architecture's long-standing interest in "creating new modes of practice through the careful adaptation of available fabrication technology."[67] Students were tasked to use laser cutters, 3D printers and CNC mills to test attitudes arising from their analyses of DJ techniques. Each tackled questions similar to those confronted by early hip-hop DJs. What are the limits of this tool? What can it produce before it breaks? How can we use it in a way contradictory to the one intended? One example asked: "What happens if you minimize instead of maximize the efficiency of software-defined support structure generated during the 3D printing process?" Categorized as a "software hack," this approach resulted in a series of incomplete, erratic, and messy 3D solids [III.051]. Another example asked: "What happens if you laser cut a non-planar surface?" Since laser cutters are optimized to focus their cutting beams on a singular plane, the resultant "hardware hack" produces a variety of feathered, inconsistently cut, and incomplete textures on the reference surface [III.052]. The course mandate to explore the gap between the human and the digital required amplification rather than subjugation of these "errors." Other aspects of DJ culture—the collaging of multiple layers of preexisting material within a predetermined structure, the ability to read and affect the real-time responses of a crowd, and the elevation and amplification of lost or forgotten resources—provided a base point for further architectural analysis.

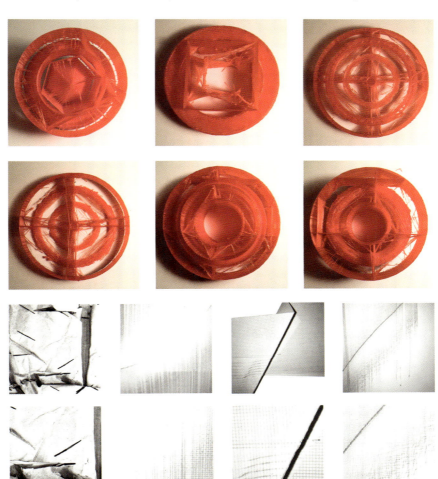

III.051 | 3D printer tests
Joshua Siev

III.052 | Catalog of laser cutter effects
Reide McClain

Third in the series was *Represent Represent*, an exploration of graffiti's relationship with architecture, focusing on its ability to "actively [transform] urban environments through simple repurposing of their 2D surfaces." In addition to graffiti, the course examined how "hip-hop fashion, party posters, magazine covers, album art, and music videos, helped shape the visual identity of the early counter-cultural movement."[68] Since graffiti is the element most easily associated with architecture, both in its artistic expression and its impact on public space, the range of ideas investigated here was markedly broader than the two previous seminars. The characteristics of graffiti used in course investigations (many already discussed in Volume II)[69] ranged from formal studies of graffiti letters, to temporal layering and surface transformation, to contemporary interpretations of graffiti's urban footprint through social media, and mappings of the ideal spaces for graffiti within the city based on accessibility and visibility [III.053]. Other studies focused on non-traditional categories of graffiti, such as stencils, stickers, and wheat pasting, as well as imagery from music videos and their collective impact on creating a recognizable identity for hip-hop culture. A series of temporary installations by student teams tested new understandings of graffiti-generated space. Here, graffiti was freed from its relegation to two-dimensional surfaces and allowed to interpret, appropriate, and transform spatial contexts [III.054].

III.053 | Graffiti in the city diagram
Nathaniel Banks

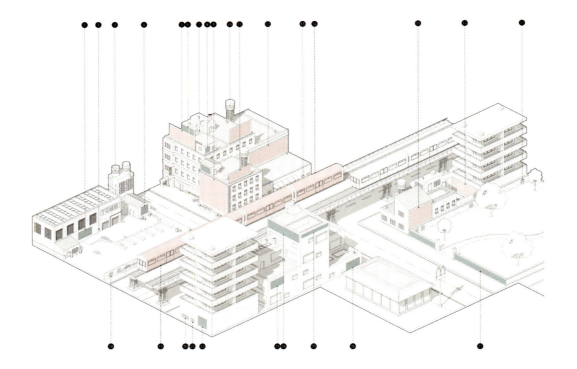

III.054 | Drawing study of graffiti installation
Noah Anderson
and Shao Li

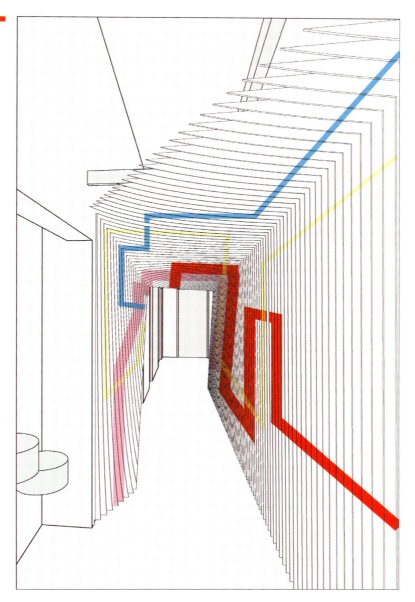

Spittin' Bars, the final seminar in the series, asked students to consider "the unique structure, syntax, grammar, rhyming schema, semiotics, and embedded references within the MC's lyrical flow."[70] Though it is unquestionably the most recognizable and consumed element of hip-hop culture, rap music was analyzed fourth in the sequence to normalize its relationship with the other three. Course assignments suggested four primary approaches to decoding rap and reframing it through an architectural lens. First, students evaluated and diagrammed the structure of various rhyming schema employed by several iconic MCs. Diagrams produced understood lyrical bars in relation to the underlying structure of beats and divided words into syllables in order to visualize rhyme frequency, density, intensity, and intonation [III.055]. Next, students investigated the semiotic structure of various lyrics. This study began with an understanding of syntactics, semantics, and pragmatics, the three components of semiotics, and their relationship to word arrangements, their meanings, and their contexts. The resultant diagrams aspired toward a thorough decoding of syntactic, semantic, and pragmatic references within selected rapper's lyrics. The final two suggested avenues for exploration—embedded architectural reference within rap lyrics and the concept of flow as discussed in Volume II—didn't make it into any particular student diagrams but were interrogated during class discussions.

Again, similar to the efforts of Slaughter and Cornelius, each seminar expanded the number of architectural processes that can be directly extracted from hip-hop elements or that are reflective of broader hip-hop culture. Building from a similar base, the studio courses explored the ability of these processes to more specifically shape the design of cities, neighborhoods, and buildings. In *New Chocolate City,* a third-year studio at Syracuse Architecture, students tested ideas within neighborhoods identified in Washington, DC's creative place-making initiative, *Crossing the Street: Building DC's Inclusive Future,* as prototypes for Hip-Hop Urbanism in other cities. Students immersed themselves in the theoretical framework of local hip-hop culture, researched each site's specific history, and explored the potential creation of new forms of architecture and urbanism. They subsequently used the specific lens of hip-hop to address urban planning, urban design, public programming, and architectural design within their selected neighborhoods. Three examples from the Southwest Waterfront, Adams Morgan, and Ivy City neighborhoods are described here in more detail.

Third Space
(Scott Krabath and Renata Ramela)

The deejay, the first player in the hip-hop opera and the first subject of diagrammatic analysis, uses a free-form assembly logic that is immediately applicable to

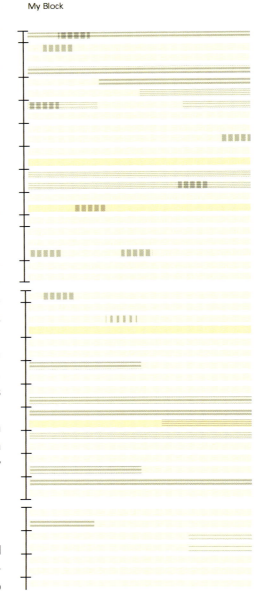

III.055 | Diagram of "My Block"
Elizabeth Mandato

III.056 | Diagram of "Planet Rock"
Scott Krabath

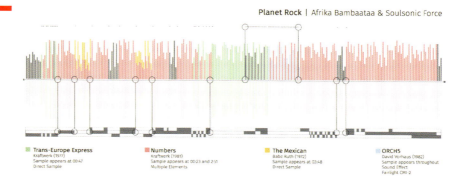

architectural production and suggestive of a new design methodology. Audio tracks, once only consumed through the phonograph, are now seen as a starting point for manipulation, fragmentation, and distortion. Each composition produced is a collage of diverse references from a multitude of musical genres and miscellaneous recordings. Through simple color-coding of waveforms representing each individual sound sample, a clear diagram of these multi-layered compositions is created for complex tracks such as "Planet Rock" by Afrika Bambaataa & Soulsonic Force [III.056] or "The Adventures of Grandmaster Flash on the Wheels of Steel" by Grandmaster Flash. Additional annotations indicating primary transitions, loops, and breaks are layered on as part of the rich indexical language of the diagram—a Rosetta Stone of sorts for translating the language of hip-hop to that of schematic design.

The techniques and attitudes of the deejay are brought to the Southwest DC Waterfront neighborhood, an area that has long occupied a privileged position just a few blocks south of the National Mall with its iconic memorials and monuments. What existed for over a century as slum settlements for poor Blacks was indiscriminately razed to make way for gridded modernist superblocks—a classic example of mid-century urban renewal hubris. Aerial photographs from the 1950s (informal era) through the 1960s (new urbanism era) to the 2010s (gentrification era) tell the story of the neighborhood's drastic transformation. Backyards, side yards and courtyards once used for informal collective street life make way for rational grids and I.M. Pei–designed residential monoliths. These, in turn, catalyze a series of high-end developments claiming waterfront territory once occupied by the fishing trade. The projected future of the area looks much like a continuation of the last few decades of high-density, low-risk, market-rate developments.

Referencing organizational techniques learned from the deejay, the new proposal samples 1950s-era conditions of Southwest DC and imprints itself between the high-rises, forming the blueprint for a new pedestrian

III.057 | **Axonometric view of "Third Space"**
Scott Krabath and Renata Ramela

promenade. Traces of former tenements, lean-tos, and outhouses mark the rise of permanently and temporarily programmed insertions paralleling the busy M Street throughway. A barbershop or a meeting hall creates a permanent anchor while transformable frames and planes allow for seasonal occupation of the throughway. The new path connects low-income housing to the east (slated for imminent demolition) with the waterfront to the west. Other traces simply mark the ground with grassy plots, variable pavement, or informal seating. A new mixed-use development, at the end of the promenade, grows out of the inscribed urban pattern and stands in contrast to the self-similar waterfront housing [III.057].

Adams Morgan Re-coded
(Evelyn Brooks and Richard Kim)

Whether using simple line work, bubble letters, or wild style, graffiti writers communicate in code. Decoding these various styles—understanding their varied patterns, geometry, and structure—was the first step in understanding its applicability within the architectural design process. The resultant process provides architects with a graphic means of understanding, and thus decoding, complex urban systems. Density mappings based on programmatic connections help decode the nightlife along 18th Street in the Adams Morgan neighborhood—bars and nightclubs, restaurants, and retail locations [III.058]. The three graphics intersect and interlock to generate a new coded identity for the popular strip, legible around the clock only to those with the master key. *Adams Morgan Re-Coded* marks place with colored surfaces weaving through and overlapping across the existing pavement. Proposed pedestrian amenities fold off the ground in the form of benches, tables, and tiered amphitheater seating. Each ground manipulation realizes graffiti's long-held aspiration of breaking away from the two-dimensional canvas. The outdoor life along 18th Street is now a programmatic extension of its indoor function, all connected through color [III.059].

The final phase of the proposal tests graffiti's ability to not only suggest space, but to inscribe space. Streetscape graphics, first imagined to re-code desire paths for commercial activity, fold and thicken to define places for human occupation and activity. The architectural object seamlessly integrates with its color-coordinated context [III.060]. The final presentation is not immune to this reconceptualization of graffiti's process and image. Drawings, renderings, and models recode themselves to seamlessly integrate the graphic backdrop that, in turn, is grafted onto an uneven surface [III.061]. Hip-Hop Architecture thus forces a reassessment of both product and process.

III.058 | Diagrams of "Adams Morgan Re-coded"
Evelyn Brooks

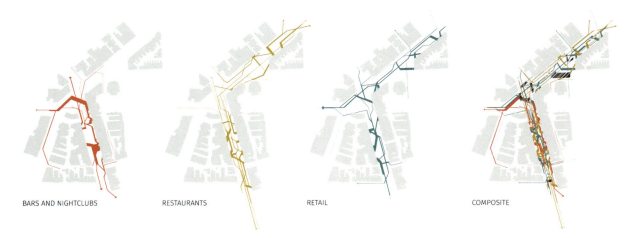

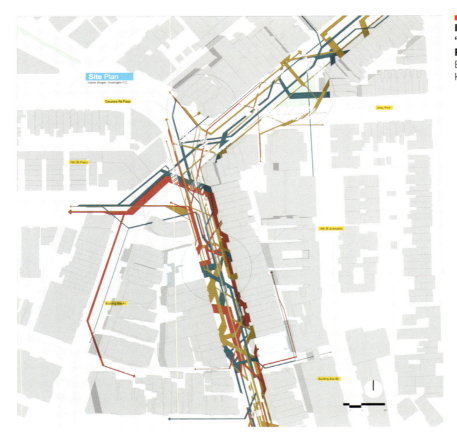

III.059 | Site plan of "Adams Morgan Re-coded"
Evelyn Brooks and Richard Kim

III.060 | Streetscape perspective views of "Adams Morgan Re-coded"
Evelyn Brooks

III.061 | Final presentation, "Adams Morgan Re-coded"
Evelyn Brooks © Sekou Cooke

Ivy City Redux
(Kyle Simmons and Clarissa Lee)

In addition to its coded organizational logic, graffiti culture maintains an unwritten code of conduct. Etiquette and respect are essential aspects of this society guided by territorialism and competition. Hierarchical structure within graffiti production (tag, throw up, burn, piece, mural) is determined by graphic complexity, color variety, and time commitment [III.062]. Each level supersedes the level below. (You don't piece a mural; you don't burn a piece; you don't tag anything you're not prepared to fight over.) A similar hierarchical structure is overlain onto one of DC's fastest transitioning neighborhoods as a tool for envisioning its imminent growth. The denizens

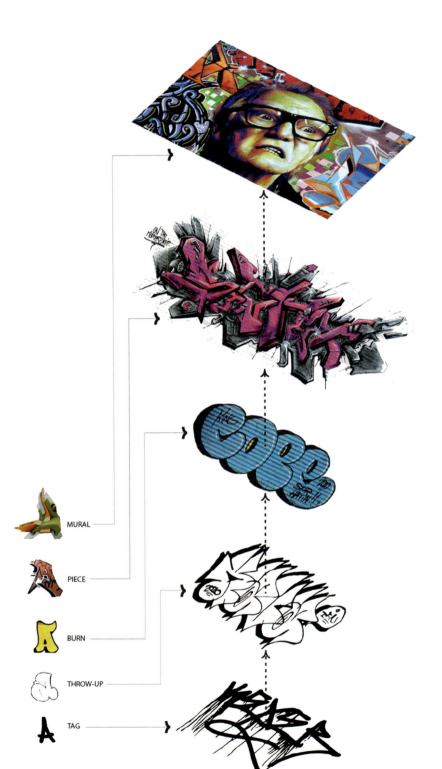

III.062 | Graffiti hierarchy diagram
Kyle Simmons

of Ivy City are first organized into four stereotype-dependent crews representing four distinct ways of life. Each is a metaphoric graff crew jacking territory and jockeying for supremacy. *Entrepreneurs*, the primary gentrifiers, provide the most revenue and contribute the most to rising property values. *Homo Ludens*, or hipsters, provide the necessary reference points for contemporary culture, lifestyle, and image. *Pupils*, the most transient and diverse group, operate in a world between the first two, bringing equal parts financial and cultural influence to the neighborhood while committing only year-to-year investment in its identity. *Proletarians*, the blue-collar residents, boast the longest tenure in the area and are the only ones who can remember "the good old days." Each crew is assigned a territory based on Yelp-rated locations typically frequented by its members. These territories consolidate themselves along a dense commercial strip requiring new rules of engagement and reconciliation.

The proposed new construction typology of Ivy City is one born out of claiming and reclaiming space. It begins with a semi-demolished structure as its foundation and builds itself gradually, as any marginal neighborhood might, on its way to becoming an artistic icon. Each crew has access to disparate resources ranging from custom-fabricated curtain wall systems (entrepreneurs) to crowd-funded materials (homo ludens) or from stolen shipping containers (pupils) to discarded delivery palettes (proletarians). Each has its own set of programmatic requirements and design agendas. All will have to collaborate to identify common circulation and support systems (stairs, elevators, lighting, plumbing, etc.) and to negotiate emergent spatial complexities. The final proposal is an ever-growing organism adherent only to rules set by its occupants. It has no identifiable genre or style, as it is never finished. Time is its only limitation [III.063]. The work as presented for review rejects the flat pinup surface and instead creates its own backdrop collaged from found and recycled materials—a prototype of the proposal itself [III.064].

III.063 | Building section, "Ivy City Redux"
Kyle Simmons

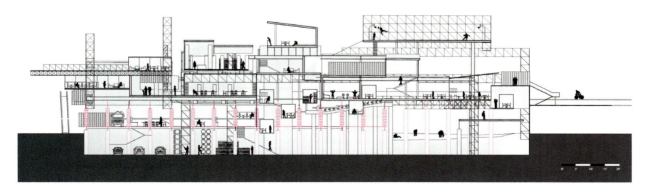

III.064 | **Final presentation, "Ivy City Redux"**
Kyle Simmons © Sekou Cooke

These three examples give us a glimpse at an architecture directly informed by hip-hop processes—an architecture expressive of freestyle composition and the improvisational spirit of hip-hop's pioneers. When combined with the examples from the four Hip-Hop Architecture seminars, the work from other students in Milwaukee and Cincinnati, and the progressive work of the visual artists Williams and Gates, the results of their similar attitudes toward process begins to become legible. Where the hip-hop triad of flow, layering, and ruptures in line can be intuited in each final product their image is far less attributable to a singular hip-hop-derived reference point as in the examples from the previous section. As we move forward with the work in subsequent sections, the relationship of each project to a clearly defined hip-hop image and/or hip-hop process will continue to expand our understanding of Hip-Hop Architecture.

■ ■ ■

" _____ "

– Cee-Lo Green[71]

04 IDENTITY.

Many authors who decide to add their voice to the expanding body of knowledge now known as hip-hop studies (especially those more easily assumed to be "outsiders"), begin with a clarification of how their identity aligns with that of hip-hop's core practitioners. For example, Rose, in her introduction to *Black Noise*, qualifies her opinions as coming from "a pro-black, biracial, ex-working-class, New York-based feminist, left cultural critic [which] adds even greater complexity to the way I negotiate and analyze the social world."[72] Similarly, before describing his own identity as "a Jew in America" in his introduction to *Making Beats*, Joseph Schloss argues for an ethnographic process that "requires researchers not only to examine their relationships to the phenomenon being studied, but also to speculate on the larger social forces to which they themselves are subject."[73] Though they don't make explicit statements about the relationship of their identities to their work, authors like Murray Forman and Roy Christopher (both White Americans), Dan Hancox (White British), and Jeff Chang (Chinese American), all referenced in this book, identify differently than their Black and Latino subjects. In each case, these authors include a thorough description of their appreciation for and deep study of all aspects of hip-hop culture for large portions of their lives.[74] Other authors like Hager have approached the study of hip-hop culture from a more distant anthropological perspective. In his prologue to *Hip Hop*, he readily admits that his first encounter with the culture came only two years before the publication of his book on the topic.[75] My own identity as a Black Jamaican man in America gives me almost immediate access to hip-hop credibility, even though I still consider myself an outsider. Being more embedded within the academic world than the hip-hop world, I may have more in common with Hager than Schloss. This is not to say I don't listen to or understand hip-hop music, or that I am only recently familiar with it. (In fact, I can distinctly remember jumping up and down on my uncle's bed in the Bronx with my sister and cousins to Kurtis Blow's "The Breaks" back in the early 80s.) The point is that I have not had to pay any dues other than Blackness or "drag [myself] in over the windowsill"[76] as have other authors with non-Black identities.

As in any culture, identity is a key feature of hip-hop. Having been stripped of their histories, names, language, and sense of self as African slaves, Caribbean immigrants, or recipients of public services (housing, schools, prisons), hip-hop pioneers invented a new identity as aggressive, defiant, and as flamboyant as anything New York and the rest of America had ever experienced. As Wilkins asserts, "Hip hop architecture is concerned primarily with identity."[77]

The work described in this section comes from practitioners who more explicitly identify with this fundamental understanding of hip-hop culture either by first being practitioners of one of the original four elements or by adopting hip-hop as their personal identity.

Tajai Massey of the 90s rap groups Hieroglyphics and Souls of Mischief is one such practitioner. Having spent most of his adult life as an MC, Massey made the decision to go back to grad school in his late 30s, receiving a Master of Architecture degree from UC Berkeley in 2014. "I learned early on," Massey explains, "that rap doesn't pay. I knew I didn't want to end up like 'The Wrestler,'" he continued, conjuring the image of a washed up, beaten, fifty-something Mickey Rourke character trying to get booked for one more fight so that he can pay the bills. "I was not about to hit a glass ceiling and get exploited. I learned how to make money first."[78] Despite the ironic move of pursuing an architectural career for financial stability, Massey continues to tour the world with Hieroglyphics and his new venture, Rap Noir. When he's not touring or recording, he is building his design practice working for an Oakland-based architecture firm, gaining architectural experience credits toward his imminent licensure. Though his work doesn't explicitly engage with hip-hop culture (yet), Massey is clear about how he wants to bridge the two halves of his persona. He describes practice that embraces a hip-hop attitude by reflecting its entrepreneurial spirit, taking space, while making it all look cool. He aspires to an architecture that brings the inclusion and opportunity that is native to hip-hop culture. He imagines art spaces, cultural spaces, and housing that embody these values. "Why are there shanty towns all over Oakland when we live in the richest city in the country? The technology is there for us to mass produce housing, faster and more efficiently, with style—personal style."[79]

Some of these ideas found grounding in Massey's master's thesis at UC Berkeley which proposed a playful organization of shipping container units converted and assembled to form expandable farming community spaces in San Francisco. The main project goal as described, "is to create a small-scale tool for neighborhood infill, re-use and development projects geared toward horticultural activity." The "game" comes complete with "game pieces," "mobile farm units that can be dropped on any site and immediately begin to produce fresh, nutritious food with minimal inputs"[80] [III.065].

As with most good architectural theses, its proposals aren't meant for immediate construction, but rather they form the philosophical basis for the author's continued research and practice. For future practice, Massey imagines spaces that can be easily malleable with programmatic flexibility—convertible spaces for performances that are performance pieces themselves. "I still run my own [recording] studio," he says. "When I build a new

III.065 | "The Growth Game"
© 2014 Tajai Massey

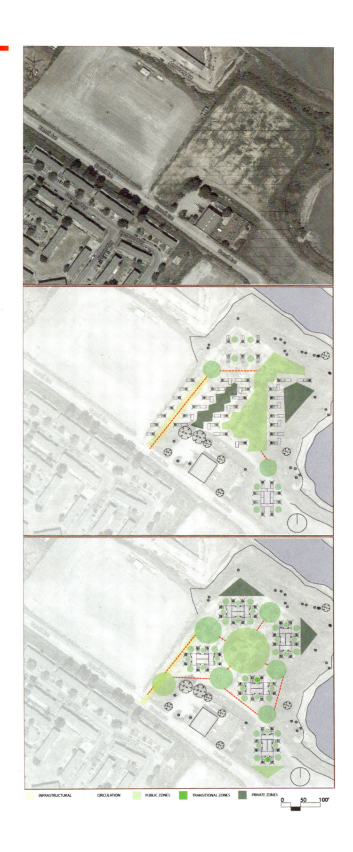

space, it will have a recording studio, conference rooms, manufacturing spaces, and mentoring spaces."[81] This project will present a prime opportunity to incorporate the hip-hip attitudes he describes into his own work. "I've been rapping since I was eight. I was part of a group that changed hip-hop when I was eighteen. I'm still figuring architecture out so it will take 10 or 20 years for me to reach personal mastery."[82]

Similar to Massey, b-boy and graff writer, Anthony "YNOT" DeNaro decided later in his hip-hop career to get his master's degree in industrial design from the University of Arizona. As a member of the Five-Percent Nation, YNOT has long believed in the spiritual resonance of physical spaces as reflected in the tenets of sacred geometry. His early interest in b-boy geometry and the mechanics of graff letters guided his design explorations. "Letters are done with real ideas of physics and constructability," he explains. "It's the same with b-boying. We are extending the limits of our bodies using balance and weight."[83] His 'S' Chair (a collaboration with recent architecture graduate, Van Escobar) is an attempt to "integrate hip-hop culture, architecture, and industrial design into one expressive art piece."[84] The prototype, fabricated using laminated sections of CNC milled plywood sheets, reflects the bold graphic qualities typical of graffiti lettering coupled with the anthropomorphic sensitivities of b-boy movements [III.066].

III.066 | 'S' Chair Iteration
Anthony "YNOT" Denaro and Van Escobar

Carlos "MARE 139" Rodriguez has leveraged his identity as a pioneering graff writer and b-boy into a successful career as a painter and sculptor. He has also been fascinated by the idea of graffiti architecture since his time at the High School of Art and Design. He has lectured about his work and his ideas about graffiti architecture at several art schools across the world and at least one architecture school, the School of Architecture, Design, and Urbanism at the University of the Republic in Uruguay. MARE believes that contemporary digital fabrication tools can bring a more democratic and accessible era to architecture. "The technology has caught up," he declares, "kids are seeing it in their sneakers and their clothes. With parametric design and Grasshopper and 3D printing, we're ready. We can start here. This fits the hip-hop model." He describes all his other encounters with contemporary architecture as "overly meticulous, dry, and lacking excitement."[85]

For his own work, he is inspired by Frank Gehry and believes Belling's "Hive" building in Melbourne is an exemplar of what he calls "graffiti architecture."[86] "It's one of the most innovative of this genre. It's a true collaboration with [PROWLA] someone from the culture. [It's lines and arrows are] consistent with the style of graffiti."[87] Though his sculptures have long been anthropomorphic in nature (many depict abstractions of b-boys in frozen power moves), MARE's later works have expanded into the human scale. His "Freestyle Archityper" series, first installed at Brighton University in the UK in 2008, is attributed to his affinity for Gehry's work[88] [III.067]. More recently, as of this writing, he is designing the interiors of a public lecture hall in Dubai as part of a collaboration with several famous rappers.

Boris "DELTA" Tellegen, another renowned graffiti artist, has similarly expanded his practice into the realm of full-scale three-dimensional interventions. Given DELTA's pedigree as one of Europe's earliest and most prolific graffiti writers his identity as a hip-hop pioneer is unquestioned. His 3D work and collaborations with architects (as previously discussed with MUA and further discussed ahead) makes him immediately relevant to any conversation about Hip-Hop Architecture. "Although I am not sure if hip-hop fits best with the description of my work," DELTA says of his sculpture, exhibitions, and installations, "I do understand what the connection is."[89] Similar in process to James Garrett, Jr.'s *SCHMO: stratum, surface, time* (discussed later), DELTA's *Exothermic* installation at the De Fabriek gallery in Eindhoven, Netherlands, imagines graffiti that exists not just as a surface application to existing walls, but as an agent for delaminating and deconstructing wall construction [III.068]. Though no legible lettering is used, the installation is stylistically consistent with his early graffiti art, here using wood framing, gypsum board, and various layers of insulation and wall paneling as his palette in lieu of colored cans of spray paint. His solo exhibition,

III.067 | "Freestyle Archityper" (Facing page)
Carlos "Mare139" Rodriguez

A Friendly Takeover, at the MIMA in Brussels, Belgium, features a series of large installations, each of which is a backdrop for smaller drawings, illustrations, and sculptures. The form of each installation, such as the one shown here, recalls the three-dimensional lettering style of his early graffiti work [III.069]. These tags are no longer flatly applied to walls but are rather habitable spaces in their own right, programmed to be full-scale displays. In 2011, Ymere, a social housing company in Haarlem, Netherlands, commissioned DELTA to design a brick façade pattern for one of their housing projects. The result is a warped, layered distortion of the base window pattern that suggests a deeper three-dimensional reading of the surface [III.070]. In this collaboration with Heren 5 Architecten, DELTA was able to go beyond mere wall painting to affect the wall construction itself. Each step in DELTA's evolution brings his work closer to a fully realized architectural product.

While Massey, YNOT, MARE, and DELTA have yet to realize work that is both recognizably architectural and reflective of their hip-hop identities, Stéphane Malka has successfully made the transition from full-time graff writer to prolific architect. In fact, according to Malka, there was no transition period whatsoever. Like any major ideology in architectural history, his hip-hop ideas simply required "many years of digestion."[90] The desire to produce Hip-Hop Architecture was always there. "I was the freak in my group," Malka admits; "all of my friends were DJs and MCs. I wanted to create architecture."[91] And not just any architecture, but architecture that is an extension of his hip-hop identity. "You don't need to say it. It's a lifestyle; it's just there. You just produce the work then you write and talk about it

III.068 | Exothermic
Boris Tellegen

04 IDENTITY.

III.069 | "Ego" installation, part of "A Friendly Takeover"
Boris Tellegen

III.070 | Berlaagen
Boris Tellegen

afterwards, and in some projects, it's more important for me to say publicly [that this is Hip-Hop Architecture]."[92]

Many of Malka's current projects reflect more than just his hip-hop identity. His desire to reflect a recognizable hip-hop image, for example, is evident in the Homecore clothing brand store's design [III.071]. Here, Malka draws inspiration from the iconic Krylon logo, a callback to the aerosol cans he used in his teenaged graff days while operating under the alias, RAYEM.[93] Each arch in the existing mall storefront creates the outline for a separate chromatic projection unto the store's interior. The overlapping and intersecting colors create a dynamically interlaced background for the clothing and accessories on display. The elegant simplicity of this project provides further evidence of the broad range of interpretations possible for hip-hop aesthetics.

Two other projects by Malka incorporate the hip-hop processes of sampling and layering. In *Bow-House,* described as a "graffitectural project,"[94] his intention to "reclaim neglected areas of the city to transform them, using existing objects just like a sampler to rebuild a whole new track"[95] is evident in his use of reclaimed doors and scaffolding to define the spaces of this parasitic pavilion [III.072]. For *A-Kampa47,* described as a "vertical camp"[96] in response to increased homelessness in Marseille and other French cities,

III.071 | Homecore
© Laurent Clement

III.072 | **Bow House (Facing page)**
© Laurent Clement

III.073 | **A-Kampa47**
Malka Architecture

Malka attaches a wall of tents to existing railway infrastructure, once again using a modular scaffolding system [III.073]. The project adapts graffiti strategies of grafting three-dimensional space unto flat surfaces to create a low-cost parasitic structure for housing multiple nomadic occupants. Both projects are physical representations of ideas posited in Malka's 2014 book *Le Petit Pari(s)*,[97] which explored the spatial impacts of graffiti on urban environments. "The book talks about the locations of graffiti pieces around the city," Malka explains, "typically in areas of neglect. It is not about replicating the style of graffiti, but about public ownership of space and the process of transforming from nothing to something."[98] Both the book and

his work are similarly interested in transposing the spirit of graffiti culture into architectural production. Malka envisions a practice that embraces "recycling, ready-made architecture, hijacking elements of other buildings, sustainability in the form of upcycling materials, not destroying them."[99]

James Garrett, Jr. of 4RM+ULA Architects has been intent on integrating his hip-hop identity into his successful architectural practice for several years. Winner of the 2019 AIA Young Architect's Award, Garrett's early association with the multi-faceted, Saint Paul-based, RHP cru, has guided the attitude behind several recent projects. First shown as *Sittin' on 24s* in the 2005 *Afrofuturism* exhibition at the Soap Factory in Minneapolis, the design for the *JXTA Arts Center* has evolved over time, taking new forms that continued to evolve until site clearing begun in 2018 [III.074]. The design for the center, which teaches art education through hip-hop ideology and methods, was first shown as a changing urban intervention revolving on the surface of 24" truck rims. The updated design draws on the dynamic nature of graffiti in its façade design.

> This building was essentially conceived as a space for hip-hop arts. Within it are spaces for photography, spaces for high school students to learn about urban design, to l earn about graphic are and a number of more traditional studio arts. But we looked at it as an opportunity to really explore hand styles. I was able to start to take my hand style and break it down into these geometric movements that started to move three-dimensionally and move through and around the building. Embracing the building and almost protecting the building. The system of these extruded polycarbonate pieces starts to create these frames for projections and other types of graphics designed with the color kinetic system in mind. The color kinetic system of lighting is able to change through all the different ranges of CMYK in real time. So, one minute this thing could be glowing blue, the next minute this thing could be red, the next minute it could be off. The idea was that we wanted to create a façade that began to actually express the energy and the movement of the inhabitants, of the students—how people were feeling. We wanted to have a dialogue with the community, to be able to let people know the creative things that were going on and what the temperature of the psychology of the people on the inside was. So, we try to communicate some of these things visually but also metaphysically.[100] [III.075]

The application of graffiti to any wall surface automatically affects the reading of the adjacent interior or exterior space. In his *SCHMO: stratum, surface, time* installation, Garrett transforms both space and surface by

Ill.074 | "Sittin' on 24s"
James Garrett Jr.

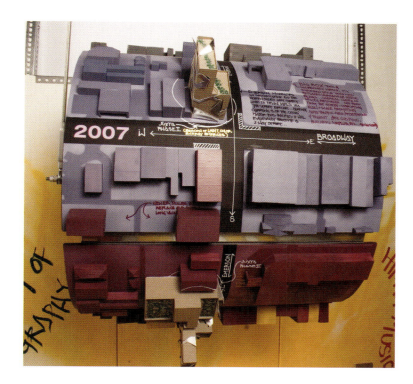

Ill.075 | Perspective view of "Juxtaposition Arts Center"
4RM+ULA, LLC

eroding, delaminating, and overlaying the existing gallery walls. "It is taking my tag, blowing it up, deconstructing a wall around it," Garrett explains, "and then creating a colored mask, and then projecting light through that mask to create a three-dimensional piece which is indecipherable from the wall"[101] [III.076]. Similar to *Exothermic* by DELTA, the project expands on graffiti's ability to represent three-dimensional space. It also reflects hip-hop's ability to uncover lost or hidden histories.

III.076 | *SCHMO 15: surface, stratum, time*
© Rik Sferra Photography

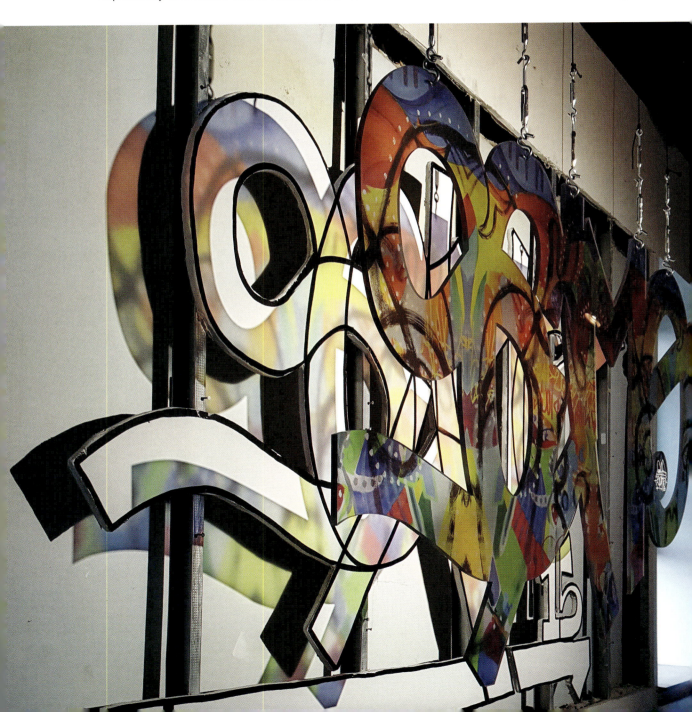

Others have taken their hip-hop identities into visual art practices. Here, their identities are primary to the work produced and their architectural training is subservient to larger project goals. For example, having briefly studied architecture during her undergraduate years, Lauren Halsey went on to complete her education in fine arts and now fuses her hip-hop identity with architecture in her installations. "I wasn't so much into 'we are gonna do this add on with a gable roof,' or whatever," she says of her early community college experience in Torrance, California, "it was more about how I could think about funkifying space through my lens."[102] Her recent exhibition at the Museum of Contemporary Art (MOCA) in Los Angeles, CA, entitled *Lauren Halsey: we still here, there* is a continually evolving installation featuring objects and spaces that reference Black culture and hip-hop processes. Of her design process for that show Halsey explains, "I was studying these Chinese grotto havens and I was super obsessed with myth. And the myth was that in the Mogao caves this Buddhist monk had this vision while he was walking along the mountainside and started carving onto this structure. . . . I remixed that with South Central. I did this concrete cave that me and my best friends and a lot of people on my street and in my life built in my grandmas backyard and we put it together at MOCA"[103] [III.077]. The work reflects several processes within hip-hop including sampling and coded references found in rap music, as well as the dynamically changing surfaces created by graffiti writers.

III.077 | *Lauren Halsey: we still here, there*
Installation view of *Lauren Halsey: we still here, there*, March 4–September 3, 2018 at MOCA Grand Avenue. Courtesy of The Museum of Contemporary Art, Los Angeles. Photo by Zak Kelley

For her upcoming *Crenshaw District Hieroglyph Project* Halsey continues the theme of carving culturally charged images onto 12" × 12" wall tiles used in previous installations. The new project is planned as a permanent structure embedded within the Crenshaw community with carved panels, or hieroglyphs, hand engraved by the local public. Halsey imagines these as "a medium to express narratives, honor community leaders, celebrate events, [and] leave memorials."[104] A full-scale prototype of this structure was created for display at the Hammer Museum in Los Angeles in 2018 with the final project expected to be completed in 2019 [III.078].

Another great example of a visual art practice heavily influenced by both hip-hop and architecture comes from Olalekan Jeyifous. Though emceeing in the amateur rap group Cornbread while in college is his only real foray into practicing one of the four elements, his work exudes more of the creative energy necessary for producing Hip-Hop Architecture than arguably any other contemporary practitioner. For instance, Jeyifous experiments

III.078 | Crenshaw District Hieroglyph Project (Prototype Architecture)
Photography: Brian Forrest; Courtesy of David Kordansky Gallery, Los Angeles and Hammer Museum, Los Angeles; © Lauren Halsey

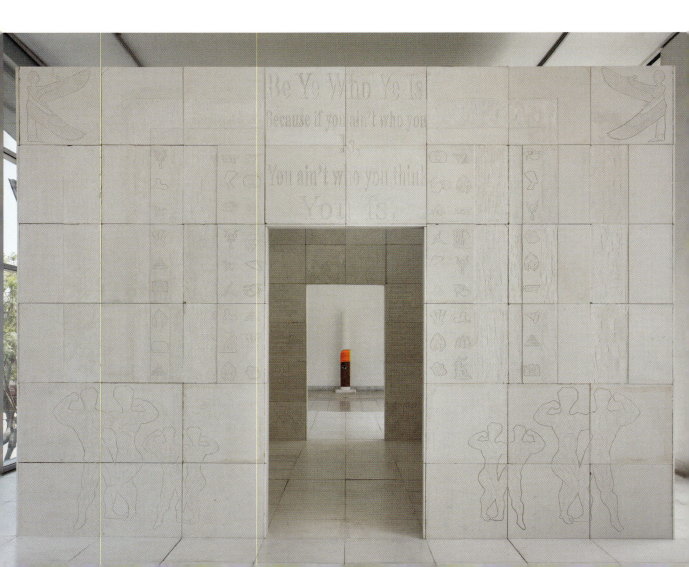

III.079 | *Surface Armatures*
Olalekan Jeyifous.
Reproduced with permission

with sampling and remix in multiple ways within the *Surface Armatures* series. "These are just kind of more fun exercises," he admits, "but they also reflect what's always been my particular style, my visual language, a blend of analog and digital and of remixing spaces and source imagery."[105] His visualization process itself begins with downloading, editing, and collaging existing digital models from open-source portals with his own photographic content. "I then put [the content] into the computer program, SketchUp, modeled over it, extruded the surfaces and then added these sci-fi, pod-like interventions that speak to society. A society in the future, and the past is no longer there."[106] These machine-like parasites that attach to the surface of the abandoned industrial buildings can also be interpreted as 3D graffiti *pieces* that allow informal human occupation. The "armatures" move across the surface of the host buildings, creating graffiti art of their own [III.079]. "This is very much my thinking about my process, which just lends itself to, and has always been rooted in, appropriating, re-appropriating, intentionally misappropriating, and remixing over and over again to create these layered works of mine."[107]

First exhibited at the 2015 Shenzhen Biennale of Architecture and Urbanism, *Shanty Mega-Structures* is another of Jeyifous' utopian/dystopian visions of urban environments, this one for Lagos, Nigeria. It imagines shantytowns that aggregate vertically into towers, drastically transforming the skyline of the city and elevating the vibrant and varied activity within. "It became much more about thinking about development and large-scale urban developments in Lagos, Nigeria," Jeyifous explains, "and literally throughout all of the world. And about the fact that a lot of the major developments don't take into account marginalized communities such as this, Makoko, which is a fishing village right outside of the third mainland bridge which connects Lagos island to the mainland."[108] Both the formal language and materiality of the towers employ improvisation and sampling, techniques commonly associated with hip-hop DJs and their live performances. "This was a blend of chopping up [not only] different photographs but also 3D models"[109] [III.080]. One of his more radical gambits during this project's development was executed in the production of a promo video for the project and deploys hip-hop attitudes as deftly as it deploys hip-hop techniques. "What I did was I went to YouTube and I found one of [a major Lagos development's] ten-minute long promo videos and then I found two- to five-second outtakes of different neighborhoods, downloaded it,

III.080 | *Shanty Mega-Structures*
Olalekan Jeyifous.
Reproduced with permission

chopped it up, put my Shanty Mega-Structures skyline into it, and then uploaded it back to YouTube with the same keywords. 'Come to Shanty Mega-Structures! Come see this new development!' It's kind of a fun guerilla sort of architectural move."[110]

In an earlier speculation, Jeyifous created a series of hand drawings exploring radical potentials in urban development and their resulting Deconstructivist dystopias. Titled *Political Impermanence of Place (P.I.M.P.)*, these pieces can also be read as historical reinterpretations of the built environments that incubated hip-hop's birth. In one particular instance, Jeyifous depicts a "faceless man mapping out the neighborhood and thinking about exactly how [he is] going to go in and intervene on this particular space"[111] [III.081]. He considers each drawing in this series "reflections on my experience" living as an architect in Brooklyn.[112] Overall, his identity as a member of both the hip-hop and architectural communities is evident in this and all his work.

The previously introduced thesis project by Nathan Williams, *Hip-Hop Ar(t)chitecture Signifyin'* (described here in more detail) translated the creative processes within hip-hop culture and the related histories of African

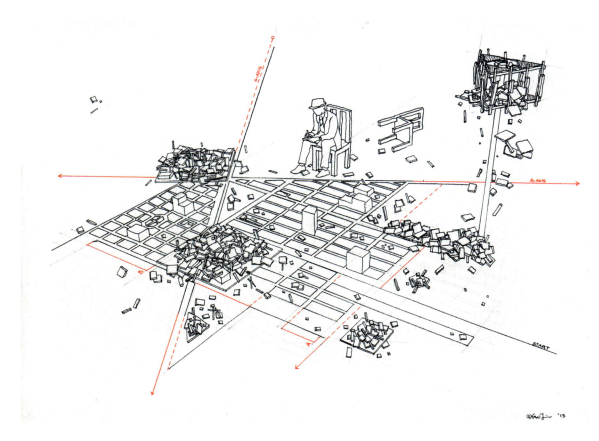

III.081 | "Political Impermanence of Place (P.I.M.P.)"
Olalekan Jeyifous.
Reproduced with permission

American peoples into new interventions for "underused spaces in underserved communities"[113] across New York City. The products of this research are presented as three investigations: "Hip-Hop Housing" (appropriations of abandoned buildings and empty lots for public housing), "Hip-Hop Sidewalk" (underground DJ booths buried below sidewalk grates), and "Hip-Hop Under and Over" (transient living units suspended below elevated train tracks). Each space was conceived, developed and presented as a series of dense collages extrapolated from several key hip-hop tenets: "Appropriation; Layering; Repetition and Rhythm; Call and Response; as well as Syncopation and Disruption; and Codification and Improvisation."[114] The thesis presentation was fully immersive,[115] reflecting the nature of the environments suggested in the design proposals. Though much of the original work has been lost, Williams recreated three collaged perspective drawings for the *Close to the Edge* exhibition in 2018 [III.082].

Though each of these examples may have some evidence of processes derived from hip-hop elements (Jeyifous samples like a veteran DJ; Garrett writes with building components as he would write with an aerosol can) the method of each project's development is more a reflection of each author's individual identity than a premeditated desire to translate hip-hop into architecture. Similarly, the image reflected by each of these products is not intentionally mimetic of predetermined hip-hop tropes. They are rather natural projections of the authors themselves. As such, identity-based examples of Hip-Hop Architecture are less dependent on predictably nostalgic notions of what hip-hop is or should be. Their ultimate authenticity as Hip-Hop Architectural products comes from a pure expression of hip-hop's embodied truth. If you are hip-hop, whatever you do will be hip-hop. By this logic, if you then produce architecture, it will be Hip-Hop Architecture, regardless of its legibility as connected to a specific set of processes or images.

■ ■ ■

– Kendrick Lamar[116]

III.082 | *Hip-Hop Ar(t)chitecture Signifyin'*
Nathan Williams.
Reproduced with permission

04 IDENTITY.

05

URBANISM.

Much like hip-hop architects, hip-hop urbanists must first ground themselves in the core concepts of Hip-Hop Architectural theory discussed in Volume II before proposing their own practical applications in urban contexts. When the logic of Hip-Hop Architectural thought is extended into the realm of urban design an intricate relationship between hip-hop and constructed environments becomes more immediately apparent. A respondent at one of my recent lectures put it this way: "There can be no urbanism without hip-hop and no hip-hop without urbanism."[117] Or, said less simplistically, the design of contemporary urban environments and the cultural narratives latent in hop-hop culture cannot and should not be understood independent of each other. The tenets of Hi-Hop Urbanism build on Wilkins' assertion that "the study of hip-hop culture in general and rap music in particular is essential to the new generation of urbanists."[118] Additionally, in explaining the spatial imperatives embedded within rap music and hip-hop culture, Murray Forman explains that "urban spaces and places have figured prominently in various studies of African-American culture."[119] To make this case he cites John Jefferies who declares, "The city is where black cultural styles are born," and Tricia Rose who states, "Hip Hop gives voice to the tensions and contradictions in the public urban landscape."[120] For example, when considering that residential playgrounds and school yards are as fenced in as prison yards, or that bars on residential balconies and classroom windows recall the bars on prison cells, the expressive nature of hip-hop form can be better understood and predicted.

This section presents projects that extend the ideas latent within Hip-Hop Urbanism to promote more inclusive narratives for architectural education and practice.

For Sara Zewde, Hip-Hop Architecture and Urbanism has existed for as long as hip-hop has existed. "The whole culture was architected," she proclaims. "The music and the lifestyle are all constructed; they are all about making."[121] In her master's thesis for MIT's Department of Urban Studies and Planning, Zewde created an idea framework and proposed a set of design principles for what she then called "Black Urbanism," of which she believes Hip-Hop Urbanism to be the most contemporary form. "It's interesting [that] while Black and 'design' are oppositional," she reflected during her presentation at the 2015 Black in Design conference at Harvard GSD, "Black and 'urban' are used interchangeably."[122] Her theories on the ways that the Black experience reshapes urban landscapes have the power to "shatter typologies of Western space."[123] Her current work as a landscape architect builds on the ideas from her thesis and projects her unapologetic hip-hop identity. ("Oh, I'm definitely a hip-hop head," she reminded me. "[Hip-hop] is not an object of study for me. It is me.") Her project for Genesee Street in the Freedman's Town neighborhood (constructed by freed slaves in 1866, it "became the civic heart of Black Houston,"[124] Texas) tests many of her design principles and theories. The proposed intervention envisions a series of urban stoops along the sidewalk edge of a series of empty lots, each stoop a recreation of demolished shotgun rowhouse from the neighborhood's rich past [III.083]. "The ubiquity of the porch," Zewde explains of the historic buildings, "created a gallery of spaces that punctured the streetscape, blurring the delineation between public and private."[125] Her proposed recreation of these narrow street side façades, to be formed in black concrete using boards from the demolished houses in the formwork, also recreates their unique urban experience. "We didn't want to just summarize the past on a plaque. African American philosophies of time are largely influenced by a circular notion of time. The future is the future, but it is composed of pieces of the immediate present and the past."[126] Similar philosophies of time now guide the production of rap music, hip-hop dance, and graffiti art.

III.083 | Genesee Street perspective view
Sara Zewde. Reproduced with permission

The next two examples continue this application and amplification of hip-hop attitudes within urban landscapes (Hip-Hop Landscape Urbanism?). Dating back to 1992, Craig Wilkins' proposal for a hip-hop park is the earliest documented example of hip-hop ideas being tested on an architectural scale. The project, later referenced in his 2000 essay *(W)rapped Space*,[127] is sited on a vacant lot in the Near Southside neighborhood of Chicago and is bordered by two partial facades of a faux Greco-Roman Coliseum. As Wilkins describes it, the design is informed by the "making do" ethos common in hip-hop culture.[128] By deploying found site materials—crumbling facades, bricks, poles, rods, wood planks, boards, and metal plates resulting from decades of neglect and decay—the design seeks to create a place that ultimately reaffirms the vibrancy of African American identities in the post-industrial city [III.084]. Wilkins tests his design against his own four criteria for Hip-Hop Architecture[129]: palimpsestic as "evidenced by the appropriation of space by the local youth as a place of recreation"; anthropomorphic in that "the spaces provide not only for the tangible interaction in various forms of creating and viewing the performance of everyday life . . . by people in motion, but also for the tactile interaction with (im)mobile objects"; performative when "viewed as one large stage, a stage for the performance of life for diasporic members . . . that recalls historical spatial practices that are specific to this particular location;" and adaptive in its construction "from wood, metal, wire, and canvas, they blend perfectly with the materials used in the park design, as the walls, flooring, and booths utilize the materials discarded in the neighborhood every day."[130]

In 2015, Detroit real estate developer, Jacobs Street, commissioned Ujijji Davis to convert a derelict structure in Detroit's Milwaukee Junction neighborhood into a fully functional neighborhood park. Her design envisions multiple public uses collaged against a backdrop of new and existing walls. *The Bottega*, still under development, will serve as a public amenity featuring commissioned artworks from local and international street artists. "The idea," Davis explains, "was that we wanted to anchor artists in this

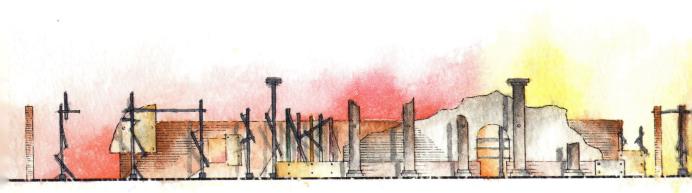

III.084 | Watercolor rendering of elevation view, "Hip-Hop Park"
Craig L. Wilkins.
Reproduced with permission

III.085 | The Bottega
Ujijji Davis. Reproduced with permission

outdoor amenity to consistently come, tag, be a part of this fluid space within some type of rigidity that would be the design"[131] [III.085].

The foundations of a Hip-Hop Urbanism will be rooted in similar approaches to landscape design as demonstrated in the preceding examples. However, the study of Hip-Hop Urbanism will first be expanded in academic arenas. As introduced in the section on process, this has been the subject of two of my own design studio courses. In contrast to the professional projects discussed thus far, the student considers a much larger area of operation and equally large contextual impacts. The work from both courses are discussed in further detail (the first in Section 3 and the second following) in order to illuminate the vast potential of hip-hop's application at the urban scale.

The previously discussed *New Chocolate City* design studio positions itself as the first true test of Wilkins' charge to "the new generation of urbanists."[132] To do so, the course cited excerpts of Kara Walker's manifesto[133] for "Ruffneck Constructivism," thus framing the main arguments for its own "Hip-Hop Urbanist Manifesto."[134] Two years later, *You Say Chi-City* became the second test of this manifesto. The new design studio course challenged students to image potential influences of hip-hop culture within Chicago's West Woodlawn neighborhood and to propose urban-scale design interventions that transform both public space and public perception. Woodlawn, the primary site of investigation, occupies an area south of The University of Chicago and Washington Park, site of the DuSable Museum of African American History, and west of Jackson Park, site of the proposed Obama Presidential Center. West Woodlawn's strategic location, surrounded by the aforementioned institutions, close to public transportation, and adjacent to the growing East Woodlawn neighborhood, makes it a prime candidate for impending gentrification. The primary area of interest for the studio, as targeted by development partner, Green Lining Realty, was the South West quadrant of West Woodlawn, an area defined by King Drive and South Chicago Avenue to the west, Cottage Grove Avenue to the east, and 63rd Street to the north. The high vacancy rates, large numbers of empty parcels of land, and relatively low property costs positions the area as a prime target for speculating developers while posing a threat to the sustainability of historically African American communities. A four-block strip along Cottage Grove, between 63rd and 67th Streets, was selected for closer study [III.086].

In early phases of project development, students simultaneously analyzed the existing context of the area (physical, historical, programmatic, socio-economic, etc.) and the architectural applicability of hip-hop processes. Marrying the two proved to be the most difficult yet revelatory step. This revealed a series of compelling analytical diagrams connecting

III.086 | Cottage Grove Strip
Rui Li

the techniques, formal languages, and attitudes extracted from DJs, MCs, b-boys, and graff writers with attributes observed on site. For instance, gaps in the vocal and musical layers of a typical hip-hop track create emphasis on important sections of words or sounds. These gaps echo the voids within the fabric of the urban strip and highlight moments of potential emphasis—ideal sites for new construction [III.087]. Loose, varied sampling techniques employed by DJs to assemble multiple reference tracks into a single composition suggest both a sampling of materials found in the surrounding built (and demolished) environment and a reclamation of undervalued spaces [III.088]. The tendency of b-boy battles and graffiti pieces to violate boundaries, either implicit or contextual, can be interpreted to mirror the various possible violations of boundaries within a cityscape [III.089].

Other mappings and analyses generated provocative interpretations of hip-hop phenomena and progressive attitudes towards urban design. One example understood the perceptual distortion legible in each hip-hop element as measured against an accepted norm [III.090]. Another connected the three musical elements into a mapping of interconnected response within a singular performance [III.091]. A third example reinterprets the flows and attitudes of hip-hop culture to propose a development strategy irreverent to zoning codes, street grids, or historical contexts [III.092]. This last example incited an unanticipated debate between the historic preservation of a given site and the scripting of new narratives boldly juxtaposed against old ones. Which is more authentically hip-hop?

III.087 | Strip Diagram
Angela Murano

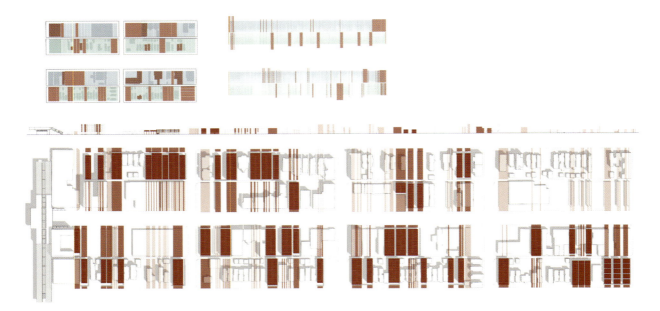

III.088 | Neighborhood Diagram and Precedents
Ashley Dunkwu

III.089 | Graffiti and B-Boy Diagram
Xinyao Wang

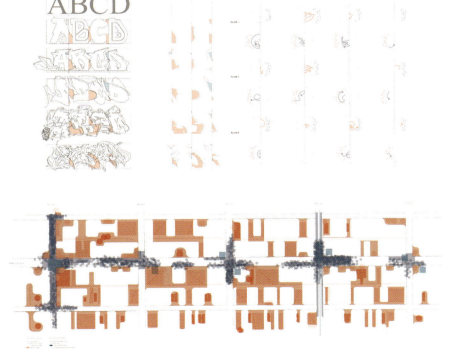

III.090 | Graffiti and B-Boy Diagram
Bohan Li

III.091 | Hip-Hop Call and Response Diagram
Elise Zilius

Three other approaches to densifying the Cottage Grove Avenue strip explored during the semester warrant more detailed description. Each leveraged both the formal techniques extracted from early hip-hop studies and the attitudes implicit within individual readings of hip-hop culture. These techniques and attitudes remained legible throughout each of the three processes all the way through more detailed housing strategies developed for individual blocks. Manifestos generated early in the process and refined throughout the semester served as guides for focusing each project's approach.

III.092 | Strip Diagram
Rui Li

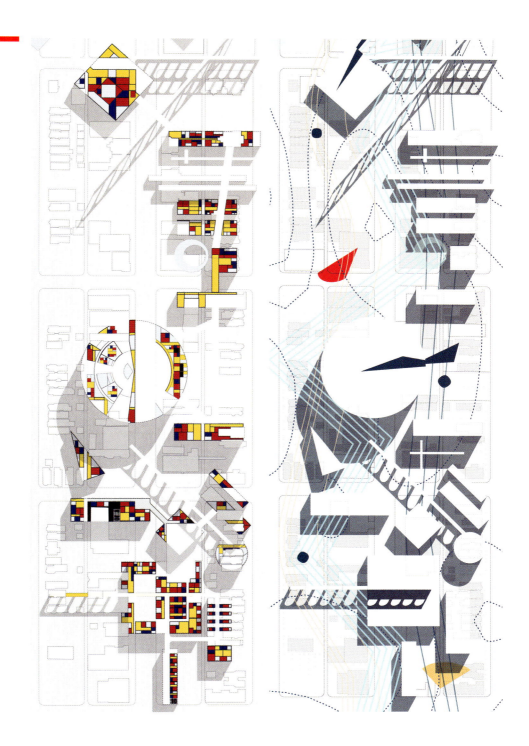

05 URBANISM.

Hip-Hop Architecture must commandeer the grid, appropriating it to remix the urban block into something equitable and just. The patterns that inhabit the rhyme schemes of hip-hop emcees must be employed on the community scale. We must learn from these emcees, who appropriate the negative, non-rhyming space within a song's measure and saturate it with rhymes, creating motifs of density, symmetry, and points of emphasis—and apply this strategy in furnishing neglected neighborhoods in a density which best suits their needs.[135]

In the first example, the structure of rhyming schemes within iconic rap lyrics is used as the primary framework for understanding the volumetric and programmatic makeup of the existing neighborhood. The grid was used to code each syllable within the chosen tracks—black representing non-rhyming syllables, other colors identifying sets of rhymes. Translated volumetrically, the grid is then grafted onto the strip suggesting new areas of densification within empty lots, between existing buildings, and atop others [III.093]. The final proposal recalls the baseline grid of the original

III.093 | Remixable Housing Modules for Southside Chicago
Alexander Sheremet

III.094 | Remixable Housing Modules for Southside Chicago
Alexander Sheremet

rap lyrics with new "rhyming" bathrooms, kitchens, bedrooms, and living rooms color-coded and dispersed across the development. The project also imagines a gridded ground surface modulating various hardscape and softscape patterns and creating a new publicly accessible realm connecting residential and commercial backyards across the existing alley [III.094].

> Hip-hop defies the indifference of its environment, reinvigorating the cityscape with the vitality of its anthropomorphic expression. It comprehends the movement of bodies in space—weaving, carving, and twisting through the boundaries of its environment. Hip-hop challenges the rigidity of the urban grid, establishing relationships that overlap, intersect, and intertwine, instead of segregating, designating, and marginalizing. The dynamic flow, energy, and composition of hip-hop introduce a new vocabulary to the environment. Thus, the neighborhood is recoded.[136]

Drawing inspiration from one of Wilkins' four criteria for producing Hip-Hop Architecture,[137] the next example exploits the anthropomorphic intersection of breakdancing and graffiti. Both forms share a language of continuously flowing, intersecting, and overlapping lines described by bodies in space. The deformation of b-boy appendages mimics the twisting of "wild style" letters. Informal lines of movement across the site's empty lots (desire lines) provide opportunities for locating new lines of movement, and existing areas of informal gathering suggest areas of new density. Various line colors and thicknesses representing distinct types of movement across the site intertwine three-dimensionally to outline the new proposal. The resultant housing development takes full advantage of the graphically powerful language used throughout the phases of design. A formally dynamic, volumetrically expressive, and materially diverse building and site strategy is the direct result of this process [III.095].

> Hip-hop artists are rebels who recognize that no boundary has ever restricted territories from self-expression. Such is the Woodlawn community, once covered in a delicate grid outlining every block and street. In its new revival, street conditions and activities penetrate bounded blocks, liberating the self-centered area with large-scale vacancies into a space of opportunity. Buildings, on the other hand, push the terrains beyond their walls, re-establishing connections with the streets. Mutually, the two juxtapositions are protruding their own territories into the other side. The boundary, therefore, has been shattered.[138]

III.095 | Cottage Grove streetscape perspective view
Timothy Mulhall

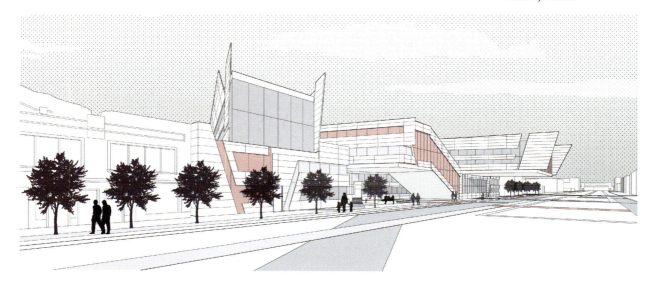

III.096 | Exploded axonometric view of "Intrusion"
Xiangyao Wang

The final example develops the violation of boundaries identified in the study of graffiti and b-boy battles previously mentioned. The proposal interprets the language of graffiti into an exoskeletal support structure that organizes the cladding materials. It imagines public movement transgressing the private realms of the development and private pathways connecting across public realms. Similar to the first example cited earlier, the territory between buildings connected across the alleyway is now reimagined as a public promenade consistent with the hip-hop attitudes gleaned from the first phase studies [III.096].

Both *New Chocolate City* and *You Say Chi-City* have positively influenced the thinking of their sponsors. Eric Shaw, former Washington, DC Planning Director credited work produced in the first studio course with bold decision making on subsequent public art projects. And, though it's too early to measure the results, the executives at Greenlining USA in Chicago have begun considering a few alternative models for developing large sets of empty lots in West Woodlawn based on student work in the second studio course. In many ways, Hip-Hop Architectural ideals and methodologies are more readily legible and actionable at the urban scale.

■ ■ ■

"Initially, the name of this conference seemed simple—Black in Design. As I reflected on it, I found the word 'in' to be the most compelling of the three. You see, Blackness and design are often presented in opposition to one another. 'Design should do this for us,' or 'Design did this to them.' Their mutual exclusivity prompted me to review the words of one notable Harvard alum, Du Bois, who states: 'It is a peculiar sensation, this double-consciousness, this sense of always looking at one's self through the eyes of others, of measuring one's soul by the tape of a world that looks on in amused contempt and pity.' He goes on to say that 'the end of the Negro's striving is this: 'To be a coworker in the kingdom of culture, to escape both death and isolation, to husband and use his best powers and his latent genius.' The breadth of the work in this conference speaks to each one of these aims. So, to declare that one is Black in design, we position ourselves in this space, in the chasm created by the double-self. We posit that there is, here, a latent genius untapped by contemporary design.

"I'd like to speak today towards a process to engage productively with spatial culture, especially those underrepresented in architecture's canon. I call this process 'interpretation.' Lefebvre, de Certeau, and their contemporaries declared that people experience space in a multitude of ways. However, design has not progressed much towards articulating what those experiences are and how interpreting them might be generative towards design. Interpretation is really an analysis process that's at the heart of the basic concept of design. We are supposed to consider the experiences of others as shape the spaces of their lives. But, inherent in the way we are trained to see space are cultural assumptions that silently guide our practice of architecture. An elaborated process of interpretation aims to step us outside of these bounds. I propose three departure points as a process of interpretation:

"Time. Lefebvre asserts that 'time is a critical fourth dimension for establishing place consciousness.' So, a redesigning of space with cultural relevance requires an intimate insertion of time.

"The arts. The arts, including the performance arts, have been historically very accessible with low barriers of entry. They also form the roots of many oral traditions. As such, cultural production should be considered a registration of spatial vernacular.

"Delineation. Different cultures delineate space in different ways. So, this is about looking at the distinct ways people negotiate between private and public, indoor and outdoor, and types of uses. Of the three, this is the one we're most trained to identify. So, this is set up to suggest that these three are both nested and recursive. . . .

"We can't ask that every designer be of the people they are designing for. But we can compel design to develop methods that allow designers to step outside of themselves. This is important for design itself to evolve. . . . The work displayed throughout the conference should not be considered self-referential but should be approached with intellectual seriousness from across design. It's interesting [that] while Black and 'design' are oppositional, Black and 'urban' are used interchangeably. You know, 'urban schools.' I don't doubt that this is related to the profound influence that Black people have had on the space and culture of cities. Architecture has largely failed to recognize that influence in a productive way. To this end, interpretation aims towards a productive resolution of the double-self, towards becoming what Du Bois calls 'coworkers in the kingdom of culture.' We otherwise remain suspended in the chasm between Black and design."

– *Sara Zewde*[139]

"So, one of the projects I worked on a couple of years ago is here. This is Milwaukee Junction, which is a neighborhood just north of the midtown area which is where Wayne State University is. It's further north of downtown. And there's not a lot there, as you can see. There's a gallery, which is cool. But, other than that, this is a postindustrial neighborhood which oddly lands itself in the middle of everything. It's really close to several highways. This is an active rail line for both freight and commercial. I think Amtrak comes here. So, there's not a lot here, however, there's a ton of murals. So, the developer I'm working with wanted to curate what we later called 'The Bottega,' which is an outdoor workshop/art gallery space.

"So, this is what the site looked like before. It was an assemblage of buildings that were for an auto service as most things in Detroit would be (the motor city). This is a local guy, he's a rapper, climbing the walls. But, as you can see, it's entirely tagged. It was made entirely of CMU blocks. People knocked the blocks down, so the blocks came down themselves, and they created these really cool interior spaces. And it was open, and it was visible. Some areas were not so visible. So, these are the kind of elements that we really wanted to emulate because they didn't wanna keep these. These are not structurally sound, even though the guy was on the walls.

"Part of the design intention—there is an organization in Detroit called Artist Village which is in the Old Redford community, northwest in Detroit—and what's special about them is that, as a group of artist, they purchased a commercial corridor, a [whole] block. They had about half a million dollars which, in Detroit at that time, went really far. And they were able to, more or less, stabilize their neighborhood by stabilizing this one commercial corridor, by developing an artist space that has this huge beautiful exterior outside, a coffee shop, local retail, affordable apartments on the top. And so, in them doing that, other small developments started to happen, epically. I think across the street is Sweet Potato Sensations, which is amazing. It's a small street, but it has a really big impact. So, the idea was that we wanted to anchor artists in this outdoor amenity to consistently come, tag, be a part of this fluid space within some type of rigidity that would be the design.

"So, this is what I proposed. I more or less followed the architecture of the auto service areas and created different rooms to really emulate what a gallery would look like. We wanted to incorporate different types of artists, not just visual, so there is a small amphitheater. But for the most part it was a maze. And so, there's a level of security and insecurity that you have in the space because the walls are high, but you're also looking at some very provocative pieces.

"These are some of the renderings that I've created in really thinking about 'what is identity?', 'what is territory?', 'how do people identify with the space as a turning point for the neighborhood, but also as a representation of what they've done and how they've contributed to this area over time?' I've rendered over an existing photo. So, these are forms that have yet to be poured but ideally the walls themselves will be really high and a little bit jarring, a little bit uneasy, to be very much in your face. I think they're 8 feet to 10 feet tall. And since were in a container, they also wanted to activate a container as a coffee shop or some type of gathering space, thinking about how the interior can change with different installations.

"So, this is what it looks like right now. The thing about doing creative stuff in Detroit is that it's really hard to do it. My developer partner is currently in litigation with the contractor. It's not my fault. We have a big shortage in construction, experts and personnel. So, the forms were ready, and then it rained, and then they didn't come back, and then it snowed, and they didn't come back, and this is what it looks like right now. So, one of the limitations with access to funds is that people don't understand why this is important. This is not a playground, this is not a green space, this is walls for graffiti. Our mayor right now is very anti-graffiti and calls it 'blight.' So why would we have a place where we do that on purpose? It's stupid! So, we're trying to figure out different ways around it right now.

"So not all the time does Hip-Hop Architecture manifest in the same ways, because there are some of the other social, equitable, cultural, and economic barriers that stop people from understanding what this is and what impact it could have. So when we think about the public realm, and we also think about people who occupy it, who are a part of hip-hop and occupy a space outside, there are still a lot of social conditions that limit the public realm to being expectant of them as just a presence in that space. The intentionality behind this project is really to embrace difference and what that means in Detroit, what that means behind art, and we'll see what happens from here."

– Ujijji Davis[140]

06

SPACE.

In attempting to isolate what exactly make hip-hop hip-hop, Harry Allen refers to a "superforce"—a fundamental force of the universe from which all other forces emanate. "It makes me wonder," says Allen, speculating on the applicability of this universal theory,

> when we say that b-boying is hip-hop, what is it that we're really saying? What is it we're saying that the b-boy does to dance, time, and space that is, in any form, hip-hop? And how is it related to what a DJ does to the surface of a record that makes his performance with that record hip-hop? And what is it that artists do with words, and semantics, and time, and inflection that makes that use of words hip-hop, but not John F. Kennedy using the same words hip-hop? What is it that the aerosol artist does with a spray can that makes that hip-hop and not Picasso or Eve Klein, hip-hop? What is the "superforce" that generates these four forms of practice? My argument is that whatever that superforce is, that superforce is what we mean by hip-hop. It's the thing that when you throw it against dance, or throw it against playing a record, or throw it against speaking or speaking in rhyme, or throw it against these other things, time then converts them into hip-hop. So, my argument, my initial impression, is that if one could define the characteristics of this superforce, then one could say that when you throw *that* against architecture it becomes hip-hop.[141]

Allen's assessment challenges any form of architectural production claiming to be hip-hop if it is only defined by the categorizations I've explored previously—image, process, identity. Wilkins' attitude toward space gives us further insight on what it might mean to define Hip-Hop Architecture beyond its physical manifestations. He refers to space as "the essential material of our profession."[142] "It is not so much the visible object," he explains, "—the museum, the concert hall, the gallery, or library, as stunning as any may be—but the not so visible, the space within."[143] Since the core of any discursive architectural practice is its attitude toward the production of space, the identification, qualification, and definition of hip-hop space becomes an invaluable pursuit for Hip-Hop Architects.

Attitudes towards space have also been critical in hip-hop's evolution. "The prioritization of spatial practices and spatial discourses underlying hip-hop culture," Murray Forman posits, "offers a means through which to view both the ways that spaces and places are constructed and the unique kinds of space or place that are constructed."[144] Later in his treatise on "Race,

Space, and Place in Rap and Hip-Hop" Forman more singularly states that "the spatial complexities of hip-hop, far from being incidental or insignificant, are central to all that emerges from it."[145] Whether read at the urban or building scale, interior or exterior, architecture or landscape architecture, Hip-Hop Architectural Space, if properly defined and understood, will prove to be the most transformative aspect of the burgeoning architectural movement. Beyond any specific form, process, or identity gleaned from studies of hip-hop culture, space and attitudes towards producing space will be the ultimate barometer of Hip-Hop Architecture's impact and importance. How can we then make manifest the sculpting of the invisible through a lens of the intangible? Further, how can we do this without a predefined image, process, or identity? I've had two recent experiences worth sharing, both of which I think come close to suggesting a clear way forward.

The first came in the early fall of 2018, when I was invited by CHINO to check out an event called "Rooftop Legends" at the New Design High School (NDHS) located on Manhattan's Lower East Side. Not knowing what to expect as I entered the school, walked its empty hallways, ascended the elevator, then took a stair to the roof, I was blown away by the atmosphere I encountered. The event, started in 2007 by the school's dean, Jesse Pais, and sponsored by Mass Appeal Records, is an annual fundraiser for NDHS bringing all the various elements of hip-hop culture together for a rooftop party. "Making money for the event is something that's a bonus," Pais clarifies, "But really it's kind of giving back to the culture is really what I'm trying to do."[146] The space itself is an outdoor recreation area, typical of New York high schools that don't have ground-level playgrounds and ball fields, with high protective walls, meshed-in canopy, and basketball and handball courts at the three tips of the E-shaped, full-block building. At each bulkhead and vertical wall surface there were legendary graff writers—a lineup including ALBERTUS JOSEPH, CES, CEY, CHINO, CLAW, CURVE, CYCLE, DETER, DMOTE, DOC, DONTAY, DRAGON 76, ENUE, HOST, GOREY, JAKE, MR. KAVES, KEO, KLASS, MAST, NOAH, PART, PURE, QUEEN ANDREA, RATH, REAS, REVOLT, RIBS, SP ONE, SPOT, STASH, TATS CRU, WANE, WEN, WOLF, and YES 2[147]—creating new pieces atop those from the previous year. At tables, other writers exchanged tags in each other's graffiti books or autographed books for fans. DJ Enuff and DJ DP One live mixed classic records throughout the event in front of a 12" by 12" linoleum mat that invited b-boys to get down at will [III.097, III.098].

The music, the dancing, the art, the smell of Jamaican food cooking on the grill all came together to transport visitors to a temporal hip-hop utopia. Even with its thick coating of nostalgia, it is difficult to define the event as anything but authentic hip-hop space. The varying timescales—one-day performance piece, periodically available event space, everyday high

III.097 | **Rooftop Legends (Facing page)**
© Sekou Cooke

III.098 | **Rooftop Legends (Facing page)**
© Sekou Cooke

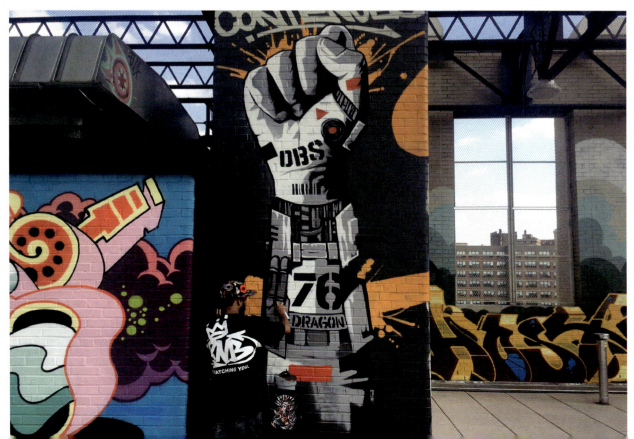

school playground, and annually updated art gallery—help construct the spatial dynamism necessary for realizing Hip-Hop Architecture. Just as with the early days of hip-hop, however, this event and others like it only happen within given spaces not designed by its constituents, though transformed by their activities. Translating these clearly legible hip-hop spaces into an intentionally designed architecture is the primary goal of the movement.

Though I rarely ever refer to myself as a hip-hop architect, the second example comes directly from a project that I designed—or, better said, orchestrated. With James Garrett, Jr.'s connections and influence with both the architecture and hip-hop communities in the Twin Cities, Saint Paul emerged as a likely second stop for the *Close to the Edge* exhibition. Instead of soliciting space in a formal gallery similar to the location of the first show at the Center for Architecture in New York (and since the primary sponsor, AIA Minnesota, doesn't yet have its own permanent center), the organizers and I opted for a temporary "pop-up" space run by Springboard Center for the Arts. The building, now known as SpringBOX, is a former car dealership along University Avenue that had been vacant for about ten years before Springboard's acquisition. James' firm, 4RM+ULA Architects, was commissioned to transform the building into a community arts space for Springboard and suggested a construction timeline that created a window of time for the exhibition to be installed, have a two month run, and then be taken down before the first days of demolition. The space selected for installing the exhibit was a vacant, unprogrammed, former garage at the back of the building. With the impending demolition, we had free reign to transform this space as aggressively as we thought necessary to produce the exhibition's desired effects.

The challenge of redesigning the exhibition to fit the new space's unique spatial conditions coupled with the reduction of many construction restrictions present at the New York space brought a new level of hip-hop authenticity to the project. We could now actively sample, scratch, and remix repurposed elements within a leftover space. The shipping container sections and original graffiti work on the walls, the primary improvisational elements of the original show, were now taken to a new level of effectiveness—the backs of the container were now fully legible and multiple graff artists created a more vibrant background for the main content. Events planned during the show's run by members of various local arts and hip-hop organizations added a more effective community engagement. The overall result was a complete programmatic and physical appropriation of space.

The most legitimate argument for the Saint Paul show's hip-hop purity came as a result of the installer's complete failure to carry out their contracted responsibilities. Unlike the New York Center for Architecture, which

III.099 | During and after, *Close to the Edge: The Birth of Hip-Hop Architecture*, Saint Paul
left: © Sekou Cooke,
right: © Chad Holder

has two full-time staff dedicated to exhibitions and programming, and access to installers who have completed multiple shows in their three galleries, the Saint Paul remix was a completely improvised undertaking involving volunteer help and a contractor more familiar with dimensional wood framing and drywall than metal strut channels and shipping containers. It did not become fully apparent that this contractor was incapable of completing the installation until two days before the opening. By that point, there was little more that could be done except fire the contractor and complete the installation myself with the help of about twenty-two volunteers (each with varying levels of skill and time availability) who showed up to help at various points during the weekend. The amount of improvisation and performative adaptation required to bring all aspects of the complex exhibition together was reminiscent of a DJ manipulating levels, controls, and sounds to create a musical masterpiece.

"If that is not Hip-Hop Architecture," I later noted, "I don't know what is"[148] [III.099].

■ ■ ■

– *RZA*[149]

Flipping to the B-Sides: Tangents to and Projections from Hip-Hop Architecture

VOLUME IV

Track List	Page
01 KANYE.	185
02 DECONSTRUCTIVISM.	191
03 AFROFUTURISM.	197
04 INFORMAL SETTLEMENTS.	201
05 ACTIVIST ARCHITECTURE.	207
06 NEO-POSTMODERNISM.	215
07 OUTRO.	223

01 KANYE.

As the black limo pulled up near the back entrance of Gund Hall on a rainy November evening in Cambridge, Massachusetts, the fourteen of us waited with quizzical anticipation. Virgil Abloh and two other members of Kanye's entourage had arrived a few minutes earlier to prepare us for what to expect for the evening. In truth, nothing can truly prepare you for meeting Kanye West and Kim Kardashian West in person, and very little about the evening went as expected.

There are several trivial connections that exist between famous personalities within hip-hop and architecture or design. From Ice Cube's viral video celebrating the forward-thinking virtues of the Eames' case study house ("This is going green 1949 style, bitch") to Pharrell Williams' and Zaha Hadid's collaboration on designs for new Adidas shell-tops to Jay-Z's involved role in the realization of Barclay's Center in Brooklyn, the architecture world has developed an increased appetite for hip-hop and architecture mash-ups. West has fueled more of this newfound interest than any other figure since his 2013 New York Times interview where he invokes Le Corbusier as one of his major creative influences. "Architecture," he says in response to a question asking what sparked the change at work in his *Yeezus* album, "you know, this one Corbusier lamp was like, my greatest inspiration."[1] He then reaffirms design as his inspiration in an impassioned interview with radio DJ Zane Lowe, where he characterizes the audible frustration on *Yeezus* to not being taken seriously as a designer. "It's just the way I was consuming information in my life at the time. Negative information to positive information, from the Internet, just going to the Louvre, going to furniture exhibits and understanding that, trying to open up and do interviews like this, learning more about architecture. Taking one thousand meetings, attempting to get backing to do clothing and different things like that. Getting no headway whatsoever. It was just that level of frustration. This is what frustration fucking sounds like."[2] He later drops bombs like "I'm working with five architects at a time," and "I hang around architects mostly,"[3] setting the architecture blogosphere abuzz.[4] This was the beginning of several public revelations about West's relationship with design (the existence of his active design practice, Donda, his collaborations with design firms OMA and 2x4, and the launch of his fashion line, Yeezy) including his now infamous visit to the Harvard Graduate School of Design.

We had expected a short conversation with Kanye about his general design interests and our desire to diversify architecture schools. What followed was an intimate 75-minute journey into the mind of a creative genius where he recapped the frustrations he expressed to Lowe and revealed his plans to open a Yeezy store in Soho. (I'm still not clear if he expected us at the time, a group of students, to deliver professional design services.) He and Kim were then given a tour of Gund's facilities beginning with the manual and digital fabrication shops in the basement and continuing through "the trays," the building's main studio spaces, from the fifth floor down to the first past unwitting students working on their projects for Monday's classes. By the end of his tour, having amassed a throng of giddy followers with phones at the ready to document each moment, Kanye was wearing an ear-to-ear grin and carried the aura of a kid in a candy store [IV.100]. He was so inspired that he decided to invite the entire building to his concert later that evening. To announce this offer, he hopped on a studio desk at the base of the trays and made a five-minute impromptu speech, two and a half minutes of which has now been enshrined in architecture history as Kanye West's Harvard lecture,[5] aided in no small way by Abloh's tweet, "Just gave a talk at Harvard GSD with Kanye. Super surreal. #DONDA design lecture series."[6]

Where West's interview with Lowe inspired me to write about the potential impact of having such a powerful mouthpiece for Black people in architecture, his subsequent visit to the GSD inspired me to write even more, this time reflecting on early conversations about Hip-Hop Architecture during my time at Cornell and taking a deeper dive into these underexplored ideas. From that first article about West to the first journal article on Hip-Hop Architecture through various lectures, presentations, symposia, exhibitions, and ultimately this book, those ideas have flourished into a fully rounded research agenda. Each step has been much less interested in such trivial intersections as that between famous people and design, but more interested in authentic hip-hop cultural expressions in the built environment. "Though it warrants inclusion in the conversation," I clarified in that first essay on Hip-Hop Architecture, "the orthographic projection of a basketball court as Lebron James's new logo does not exactly define hip-hop architecture. Artist Filip Dujardin remixing photographs of buildings comes close, but also does not define hip-hop architecture. The collaboration of rapper Pharrell Williams and architect Zaha Hadid, both of whom operate at the leading edge of their respective fields, on a design for prefab houses has a little hip-hop and a little architecture, but still does not define hip-hop architecture." Similarly, when West later declared his intentions to open an architecture firm of his own, my next article skeptically (and cynically) questioned: "If a hip-hop artist opens a design firm hiring architects to design high-end projects for himself and his peers does that constitute Hip-Hop Architecture?" Simply aligning "hip-hop thing A" with "architecture thing B" was not cutting it.

And yet, there is another way of positioning Kanye West within the larger Hip-Hop Architecture framework rather than adjacent to it. He may

IV.100 | **Kanye West at GSD (Facing page)**
© Noam Dvir

be the quintessential example of the Hip-Hop Architect. On the one hand, West may not fit into the classic stereotypes of rappers of his time having been raised by an English professor, not rapping about guns or bitches, and projecting an overall image that has always been antithetical to accepted gangsta imagery—while others wore hoodies and bubble jackets, West wore pink polo shirts and argyle sweater vests. He also used samples and beats early on that most producers wouldn't imagine touching. On the other, his willingness to constantly redefine himself, ability to push the edges of music, and his larger-than-life attitude and persona are all consistent with hip-hop's internal mandate for fluid definition. Even if he is just outside the bounds of hip-hop in its most limited definition, West is unquestionably hip-hop by the standard of its expanded definition as used in this book. In terms of his architectural credibility, the most limited definitions of the term architect would absolutely not apply. Even more liberal definitions that include those educated at schools of architecture but unlicensed or those actively involved in delivering building solutions to clients would be an unrealistic stretch. However, if we continue to work with the expansive definition or the term as used in Volume II, then we can recognize West's efforts in orchestrating all aspects of music production, fashion design, shoe design, stage sets, and indeed, space, in the same vein as starchitects like Rem Koohaas, Bjarke Ingles, Zaha Hadid, and Herzog & de Meuron.

"You can call him an architect in the sense that he orchestrates all these different worlds," admits Oana Stanescu, a New York-based practitioner and professor, at times referred to as "Kanye's architect." "He is like a conductor of sorts." Stanescu and former partner Dong-Ping Wong executed multiple projects for West as part of their collaborative practice, Family. I was privileged to witness one of the most impressive of these in action during West's *Yeezus* concert the night of his GSD visit. The dynamically transforming stage set created a continually changing and immersive experience for tens of thousands of fans at the TD Garden. Watching the single figure of Kanye West atop a volcano that turned into an iceberg floating slowly toward the crowd, as snowflakes fall from the sky, wintery images move across the three massive projection screens overhead, and he sings "Hey Momma," one gets the sense of a singular being manipulating the entire physical and sensorial environment [IV.101]. Though Stanescu herself or Family as a firm sometimes get singularly accredited with the design, she is quick to list the collaborators. "We were part of a team," she clarifies. "[W]e were extremely lucky to work alongside Virgil Abloh, S. Devlin was at one point involved, Vanessa Beecroft played a huge role, and John McGuinness who does all of Kanye's stages. Most credit in something like this goes to Kanye because he is able to orchestrate us in such a precise manner in order to achieve his vision." Given current modes of practice where singular authors get credit for design work that includes multiple collaborations at each level and phase of design and execution, often with that author being involved solely as the guide of the vision and orchestrator of the process, West appears to fit perfectly as an architect.

IV.101 | Yeezus Tour Stage
Image courtesy of ZiaLater via Wikimedia Creative Commons. CC BY-SA 3.0. https://commons.wikimedia.org/wiki/File:Yeezus_Tour_Stage.jpg

■ "So, after walking through here I decided that I wanted to make sure that for anyone who didn't have tickets tonight that you all could have tickets to the show. So, anybody that wants to come tonight, we're going to give tickets to the entire office. But I just wanted to tell you guys, I really do believe that the world can be saved through design and everything needs to actually be architected. And this is the reason that some of the first DONDA employees were architects that started designing T-shirts instead of buildings. But just to see their work actually come into- to be actualized. And if I sit down and I talk to Orpah for, you know, two hours the conversation is about realization—self-realization—and actually seeing your creativity happen in front of you. So, the reason why I turn up so much in interviews is because I've tasted what it means to create and be able to impact and affect in a positive way. And I know that there's more creativity to happen and I know that there's traditionalists that hold back the good thoughts and there's people in offices that stop the creative people and that are actually intimidated by good ideas. And I believe like Utopia is actually possible, but we're led by the least noble, the least dignified, the least tasteful, the dumbest, and the most political. So, in no way am I a politician, I'm usually and- at my best- politically incorrect. And very direct. I really appreciate you guys willingness to learn and hone your craft and not be lazy about creation. And I'm very inspired to be in this space. And tonight, the show, if you come see it, I'm a bit self-conscious because I'm showing it to architects. So, the stage does have flaws in it. It's an expression of emotion so give me a pass on that. And that's basically all I had to say. So, thank you very much."

– *Kanye West*[7]

■ "____"

– *Common*[8]

02 DECONSTRUCTIVISM.

In direct response to conversations about the forefathers of hip-hop and Hip-Hop Architecture from the previous day, Amanda Williams came up with a few hip-hop relatives of her own for her day-two presentation at *Towards a Hip-Hop Architecture*. The most notable examples include "Nate Williams is the godfather of Hip-Hop Architecture," "Kara Walker is the baby mama of Hip-Hop Architecture," and "Hype Williams is the great-grandfather of Hip-Hop Architecture."[9] Hype Williams is given the most senior role in the family presumably because of the role his music videos played in defining a universally discernable aesthetic for 1990s hip-hop and influencing aspiring architects of that era. "From coast to coast, from every facet in the way that hip-hop was being portrayed or projected to us, Hype Williams had a very integral role in doing that."[10] His extensive use of the fisheye lens (one of his early signatures), flashy colors, and provocative backdrops (stage sets and buildings) made his videos easily identifiable icons of the medium. Cyrus Peñarroyo points out a compelling contradiction in Hype William's treatment of the Guggenheim Bilbao as a backdrop to Mariah Carey and Jermaine Dupri's 1998 "Sweetheart" [IV.102]. Instead of distorting the building using his favorite lens, as he did for most rappers' backdrops, he allows the inherently distorted forms of Frank Gehry's Deconstructivist masterwork to stand in "as a proxy for his trademark suite of visual tricks."[11] Peñarroyo's argument that "This union of the avant-garde in design and hip-hop offered

IV.102 | Still from "Sweetheart" music video
"JD & Mariah Carey - Sweetheart" directed by Hype Williams © SME (on behalf of Columbia); LatinAutor - UMPG, Spirit Music Publishing, UMPG Publishing, LatinAutor - Warner Chappell, Warner Chappell, ASCAP, PEDL, LatinAutor, UMPI, UNIAO BRASILEIRA DE EDITORAS DE MUSICA - UBEM, and 14 music rights societies 1998. All rights reserved

a perfect window into this era of black pop and instrumentalized architecture as a visual effects apparatus,"[12] could be restructured to posit that William's visual effects apparatus is itself a way of architecturalizing backdrops, and the Guggenheim, already reflective of hip-hop and the avant-garde, required no further distortion. (Hype Williams and Frank Gehry both Hip-Hop Architects? Let's not get ahead of ourselves.)

For those who still desire to find a singular aesthetic for Hip-Hop Architecture (even after reviewing all the examples included in Volume III), Deconstructivism may present a plausible image alternative. The mid-1990s architectural movement marked by a disassociation of a building's surfaces from its structure, is an almost perfect formal interpretation of flow, layering, and rupture of line. As previously discussed, MARE 139 is a huge fan of Gehry and believes his work shares more affinity with the language of graffiti and b-boying than anything done by DELTA which, he claims, "is built around soulless, old-school, Bauhaus, European ideas."[13] It is difficult to characterize Gehry's contemporary work as anything but exuberant, expressive, and dynamic. His Dancing House, for example, is a remarkable expression of anthropomorphic movements in built form. Harry Allen, in his own musings on Hip-Hop Architecture, finds similar correlations between the architecture of Zaha Hadid and graff writing. "That's one thing I've been thinking of, this question of whether the ways that hip-hop artists generate forms themselves could be corollaries to the things that Zaha Hadid is or was doing—she spoke of calligraphy. And when I think of a piece by PHASE 2, for example, I'm wondering: 'are there architectural beginnings in something as possibly cacophonous or unified (depending on how you're looking at it) as a tag by this great artist?'"[14] These aesthetic parallels could continue to include those between Jeyifous' visualizations and those of noted Deconstructivist, Lebbeus Woods; between *3D Turntables* and Gehry's Stata Center at MIT; or between the shifted, delaminated forms and spaces in Eric Owen Moss' Culver City projects or the Capital City Towers by NBBJ, and the scratches, loops, and cuts of a hip-hop DJ [IV.103].

On the surface, none of the preceding examples of Deconstructivist works or practitioners appear to be coming from the specific cultural, political, or economic conditions that birthed hip-hop. The connection between the two architectural movements—Deconstructivism and Hip-Hop Architecture—would therefore be best described as an aesthetic one. However, beyond its formal readings, Deconstructivism embodies an attitude of defiance. The Deconstructivists, like the Postmodernists before them, challenged the Modernist notions of clear structural logic, buildings as machines, or form following function. In formulating an argument for Hip-Hop Architecture connecting to histories of cultural expression, Wilkins places Deconstructivism within an expanded lineage of twentieth-century

IV.103 | Capital City Towers
Image courtesy of IndexxRus via Wikimedia Creative Commons. CC BY-SA 3.0. https://commons.wikimedia.org/wiki/File:Capital-city-towers-moscow-indexxrus.JPG

movements. "Out of the communist manifesto comes an architecture designed to bring about and create a new and just egalitarian social order with the emphasis on the people—a classless society. Out of the ideas of the enlightenment comes Modernism, man being able to know himself, and an attempt to create a new and just democratic order with an emphasis on the common man—a universal society. Deconstructivism, a critique of our ability to know anything with certainty—a decentered society—of course, develops its own architecture."[15] It may not be too far-fetched to imagine Hip-Hop Architecture as a continuation of that same lineage.

■ ■ ■

■ "Thinking about matters like this—like how hip-hop could work in terms of a source of architecture—I began to think: 'What are the gestures that are important to hip-hop?' So, for example, and this again is from Joe Schloss' book, *Making Beats*, quoted again on Wikipedia (or, as I wrote, 'what are the languages of hip-hop processes?'). It says: 'In hip-hop music sampling, "chopping" is the altering of a sampled phrase or break by dividing it into smaller segments and reconfiguring them in a different order.' So, here's the question: 'What is this equivalent of a "chop" in architecture?' If you were to chop, architecturally speaking, how would you apply that? How would you make that work?

"And we're just talking about hip-hop production in terms of sampling. There's chopping. There's looping. There's EQ-ing. There's filtering. There's quantizing. These are all terms, or transformative approaches to sonic materials, that producers use. Like 'digging in the crates.' That's another way of organizing materials. Could these forms be the beginnings of architectural forms, or form generators? I know professor Cooke has looked at, for example, how the shapes that b-boys make when dancing can generate forms that might be of architectural interest, and these would come directly from hip-hop.

"That's one thing I've been thinking of: this question of whether the ways that hip-hop artists generate forms themselves could be corollaries to the things that Zaha Hadid is or was doing—she spoke of calligraphy. And when I think of a piece by PHASE 2, for example, I'm wondering: 'are there architectural beginnings in something as possibly cacophonous—or unified, depending on how you're looking at it—as a tag by this great artist?' (That's actually one of his pieces that I rendered on a hoodie. I've always been amazed and overwhelmed by this graphic, and so I just had to put it on my clothes.) I guess you might say this is calligraphy on steroids, calligraphy cubed. These are applications of hip-hop thinking that might themselves be the generators of forms, or approaches to making forms.

"I just wanna close by again talking about this idea of interpolation, of having something between forms, between a viewer and that original form, something that translates the form, something that shapes it. Mondrian uses intellect to translate Broadway boogie-woogie, the boogie-woogie music that he loved, into a painting. I'm wondering if we were listening to the music, or the way the Invisibl Scratch Piklz approach sound or approach a scratched surface, is there a way to interpolate that and to use those forms, the sonic forms they generate and find, if you will, a form, a material analog. . . .

"There's an incredibly wide-ranging set of forms that Qbert is generating with his hands. His hands are actually making a multitude of forms to make these sounds. And then you have the forms which result from changing the sound of the record into the sound that's coming out of the speaker. Now what does that look like? What do these sonic forms look like when you visualize them? I don't know, but as Corbu said, 'it would have to be something quite amazing and magnificent.'"

– Harry Allen[16]

03 AFROFUTURISM.

The 2005 *Afrofuturism* exhibition at The Soapbox Factory in Minneapolis was ahead of its time in unexpected ways. It was not the first time that artists had been gathered to exhibit work related to an Afrofuturist theme, and certainly not the first time the term Afrofuturism had been used to describe works of art. Most unique to the 2005 show was the inclusion of three artists who ground most of their work in architecture: Amanda Williams, Olalekan Jeyifous, and James Garrett, Jr. It is difficult to find any significant reference to Afrofuturism applied to architecture before the release of the 2018 film, *Black Panther*. Since then, however, many have been interrogating the applicability and relevance of Afrofuturist thought within architectural theory and practice. These include articles in the architecture blogosphere (Curbed[17], ArchDaily[18], Dezeen[19]), an essay by noted British writer and curator, Ekow Eshun, who believes, "Afrofuturism has particular relevance when it comes to questions of architecture and urbanism,"[20] and another recent article in the *Financial Times*[21] with interviews from Nigerian American architect Mariam Kamara, Ghanaian Scottish architect and newly appointed Dean of the Spitzer School of Architecture at The City College of New York Lesley Lokko, and Jeyifous. Each piece traces the term back to a 1993 essay by Mark Dery[22] and grounds Afrofuturism in other creative outputs of literature, art, and music in the 1960s and '70s, including works by Octavia Butler, George Clinton, Rammellzee, and the "germinal deity in the pantheon of Afrofuturist gods,"[23] Sun Ra. Lisa Yaszek traces the Afrofuturist legacy much further back as "an extension of the historical recovery projects that black Atlantic intellectuals have engaged in for well over 200 years."[24] Going back even further, Baltimore MC Labtekwon notes, "the legacy of Black people envisioning the future is ancient itself. When we see Dogon people predicting the return of Nibiru for thousands of years of the nature of the Nile Valley civilization and interdimensional relationships, this idea of imagining and projecting into the future existed long before the term 'Afrofuturism.'"[25] Here again, western architectural thought has been slow on the uptake of an idea that has existed for millennia—that Black people can define the image of the future.

This is the true power of *Black Panther*: its ability to visualize for us what might be if the architecture community were only able to be more inclusive in its composition. As Eshun puts it, "The make-believe Wakanda prompts an existential question that also haunts Africa in real life: what would the continent be like without the legacy of colonialism?"[26] [IV.104]. The majestic image of the fictional city constructed by production designer Hannah Beachler, collaged from multiple historical images of African buildings and futuristic structures from Deconstuctivist and Metabolists, won her an Oscar and the hearts of Black architects. She partially credits some of this imagery to "walking through Zaha's buildings"[27] (and not to renderings from Jeyifous, much to the disbelief of many familiar with his work). Beachler's Wakanda stands in stark contrast with the Eurocentric, post-colonial edifices featured in the book *African Modernism*,[28] using Afrodiasporic imagery and sensibilities to define its aesthetic rather than Corbusian principles. In "blending things that were existing in a lot of different African cultures and then creating them as if they had evolved over time"[29] Beachler aligns her work with the tenets of Hip-Hop Architecture. Models of fantastical cityscapes designed and built by Congolese artist Bodys Isek Kingelez share similar affinities with the movement. Each is built from scraps and appropriated materials by an artist who spent most of his life as a school teacher and had no formal training in architecture[30] [IV.105]. These "something from nothing" constructs, inherently Afrofuturistic given their content and aspiration, are directly reminiscent of the models made in Chris Cornelius' studio courses described in Volume III.[31]

Akin to Christopher's assertion that "hip-hop is inherently futuristic,"[32] for Garrett, Afrofuturism and Hip-Hop Architecture have always been mutually aligned. He, more so than Williams or Jeyifous, used the Soapbox exhibition as a way of exploring the potential architectural expression of Afrofuturism and its connection to his nascent idea of "Hip-Hop + Architecture." His entry was also a catalyst in the early phases of his design for the Juxtaposition Arts Center discussed in Volume III. As described in his artist statement for the exhibition, the center was "designed to represent the infinite transformative possibility of hip-hop culture when applied to the discipline of architecture."[33] With George Clinton and Parliament Funkadelic serving as her primary aesthetic influences, Lauren Halsey's work exudes Afrofuturism. The spaces in the grotto-like installation for her show at MOCA are filled with selections from her ongoing collection of Black Power paraphernalia, depicting ankhs, pyramids, and other Egyptian, Nubian, and Kemetic symbols. She continues to use this imagery in newer installations, whether by including items from her collection or by imprinting them on the surfaces as in the *Crenshaw Hieroglyph* project. Dan Hancox also calls grime (a British derivative of rap) a "unique incarnation of Afrofuturism"[34] and connects much of the form's evolution to the futuristic architecture of the Canary Wharf building complex in London. "You can hear this Afrofuturism most of all in the sonics of grime production—the stark, unfiltered minimalism of the kick drums, the interplanetary weight of the baseline, the sleek raygun zaps and zips of the synth, the way the whole edifice shines sleekly like a spacesuit."[35]

The two movements—Hip-Hop Architecture and Afrofuturism—certainly share affinities, either in the ways described by Garrett, Halsey, or Hancox, or via other modes of alignment. Imagining futures and fictions that include

IV.104 | Screenshot from "Black Panther" (Facing page)
"Black Panther" directed by Ryan Coogler © Marvel Studios; Walt Disney Pictures 2018. All rights reserved

IV.105 | City model from "Art and Society: Bodys Isek Kingelez: City Dreams" (Facing page)
Digital Image © The Museum of Modern Art/ Licensed by SCALA / Art Resource, NY

technologically advanced African peoples requires uncovering lost histories and collaging various Afrodiasporic cultures. A parallel process occurred at the birth of hip-hop culture when, deprived of any authentic representation of self within the city, Black and Latino youth referenced several disparate cultures in the creation of a new identity. The Universal Zulu Nation, a hip-hop cultural organization formed in the early 1970s by legendary DJ Afrika Bambaataa, was essentially an Afrofuturist project. Contemporary hip-hop artists such as Andre 3000, Erykah Badu, and Janelle Monáe have continued in Bambaataa's Afrofuturist tradition. Also similar to Hip-Hop Architecture, Afrofuturism's architectural impact has thus far been primarily theoretical and visual rather than constructed. "My sense is that in 10 or 15 years you're going to see the beginning of something," says Lokko. "Any attempt to build it before that would be pastiche—it's not mature enough yet."

■ ■ ■

"Shanty Mega-Structures for Lagos, Nigeria. This is a project that started back in about 2005, and it's been ongoing for me now. It's gonna continue for as long as I can continue to develop iterations. It initially started (actually it was an AIA competition I didn't finish), it started off as a skyscraper competition. So, it had ideas rooted in alleviating certain issues, right? But I abandoned it and I came back to it for the 2015 Shenzhen biennial . . .

"This was a blend of [not only] chopping up different photographs but also 3D models. The idea behind this was to extend hyper-visibility to communities that are often overlooked and projecting them into the future, diverging from a Western typology that confers a sense validity and luxury—developments in places like West Africa [where] Modernist architecture dominated much of the state and institutional buildings—to make this very organic sci-fi world where these communities now begin to meander through and overtake sites of privileged real estate throughout Lagos, Nigeria. So again, this is very much about reimagining certain communities in two ways: hypervisibility, but also sci-fi context.

"The most popular work I've ever done was these series of images that just juxtaposed an informal market culture of Nigeria with spaceships, because people just hadn't seen that kind of imagery. At the time, my collaborator and I, we didn't think it was radical at all. But it propelled us in so many different ways just [by] individuals seeing that kind of imagery."

– Olalekan Jeyifous[36]

04 INFORMAL SETTLEMENTS.

During my first semester of grad school I got a job helping to build a large-scale model for Christian Kerez. The Swiss architect who was teaching that year at the GSD is well known for creating massive beautifully crafted models of his most notable buildings, so it was a privilege for me to be on this team of about 15 building the latest one for an exhibition at the Druker Gallery in Gund Hall[37] [IV.106]. Though it was the newest, largest, and most complex model in the show, what truly set this model apart from the others was its content. Whereas the others represented singular structures, this model depicted an entire section of his favela-inspired design for social housing in São Paolo, Brazil. The desire for architects to intervene in such a context is understandable. As Louis Rice cites in his essay *Informal Architecture/s*, "at the turn of the millennium one billion people occupied these urban spaces [favelas and other informal settlements]. Within the next decade this will rise to two billion."[38] The idea of *designing* a favela, however, seemed oxymoronic. Surely, favelas were conditions that just happened, that didn't involve designers or planning agencies, at least not in their inception. Having watched the 2002 film *City of God* and all four seasons of *City of Men*, I was not convinced that what was being modeled had any resemblance to the conditions portrayed on screen.

IV.106 | Model of "Porto Seguro Social Housing, Brazil"
Courtesy Christian Kerez GmbH

Architects have a natural desire to bring under control those forces of man or nature that are uncontrollable and unpredictable. What essentially connects favelas to other forms of informal settlement is their universal rejection of this propensity for top-down planning common to architects and urbanists. The bottom-up informality of favelas, shanty towns, disaster relief communities, refugee camps, or even events like Burning Man is central to the development of Hip-Hop Architecture. Finding a balance between loose, unpredictable whims of individuals and the singular visions of individual authors is one of its primary challenges. Where in the process do architects have full agency? Over how much of the design process should architects continue to exercise control? Each type of settlement mentioned earlier by necessity involves some kind of top-down planning. Favelas and shanties often have government-installed stormwater and sewerage systems, or electrical grids and cellphone towers maintained by utilities; disaster relief communities and refugee camps begin with structures and infrastructure centrally designed for temporary occupation; and Burning Man, though completely wild and exuberant in its annual composition, is one of the mostly tightly planned events on the planet, housing several thousand people for two weeks then leaving virtually no mark on the desert landscape upon its departure. In the case of the favelas and shanties, support systems are typically added after the fact as a part of governmental responsibilities to its populace. And though occupants tend to personalize their living spaces in temporary communities, especially when these communities are occupied for much longer and for many more people than they were designed for, design and planning of these communities don't anticipate bottom-up agency over spatial definition.

Squatting, another means of informal occupation, shares additional affinities with hip-hop sensibilities and processes. "Invaders 'hack' into existing buildings," Rice notes, "to gain unauthorized access and make *ad hoc* modifications."[39] He further cites "The Tower of David" in Caracas as a particularly "startling illustration."[40] This forty-five-story office tower in the center of the city was only partially completed by its developers before being taken over by squatters who have appropriated it as a residential tower and vertical community center [IV.107]. Similar appropriations took place over time at Le Corbusier's Cité Frugés. Unlike "The Tower of David," this social housing development was originally intended for residential occupation. Much like the Caracas tower, Frugés is a great example of human desire for individual design agency. In designing the Cité Frugés in 1924 with his cousin, Pierre Jeanneret, Corbusier tested his purist ideal for low-income living in repetitive, machinic, concrete structures. These ideals were quickly challenged and transformed by the first occupants who added awnings, flower boxes, and shutters to the ribbon windows, added decorative doors,

IV.107 | Torre de Davide
Image courtesy of EneasMx via Wikimedia Creative Commons. CC BY-SA 4.0. https://commons.wikimedia.org/wiki/File:Torre_de_David_-_Centro_Financiero_Confinanzas.jpg

and individualized the exterior color schemes. The struggle between preserving the architectural vision and expressing individual modifications continued for most of the project's life until restoration efforts began in 1974 with a single rehabilitation to the original Corbusian vision.

Shanty Mega-Structures, by Olalekan Jeyifous (discussed in Volume III)[41] deserves further consideration within the context of informal settlements. The project visualizes a futuristic elevation (literally and figuratively) of informal developments above the Modernist fabric of a rapidly growing Lagos. His description of the project also illustrates the progressive attitude Hip-Hop Architecture can bring to urban developments—seeing informalities as assets rather than liabilities. "I was thinking first about different sustainability practices that occur not just as a function of necessity," he explains, "but out of genuine ingenuity and creativity—the idea that these communities are not things that we always need to go in and be patronizing and paternalistic and design for, but that they have an enormous amount to contribute to the way their cities may evolve (if there becomes a conversation around that)."[42]

A similar elevation of informalities is embodied in the Chicano aesthetic of Rasquache, where everyday items, styles, and attitudes expressing the shared values of the Mexican-American working class challenge the standards of Western taste. As Robert Bedoya describes it, "Rasquachification messes with the white spatial imaginary and offers up another symbolic culture—combinatory, used and reused. The Rasquache spatial imaginary is the culture of lowriders who embrace the street in a tempo parade of coolness; it's the roaming dog that marks its territory; it's the defiance signified by a bright, bright, bright house; it's the fountain of the peeing boy in the front yard; it's the DIY car mechanic, leather upholsterer or wedding-dress maker working out of his or her garage with the door open to the street; it's the porch where the elders watch; and it's the respected neighborhood watch program."[43] Bedoya later uses more language derived from hip-hop culture in stating that "The Rasquache spatial imaginary is a composition, a resourceful admixture, a mash-up imagination that through objects and places says, *I'm here*."[44]

In a stroke of genius, Alejandro Aravena anticipates this basic human desire for individual expression in his Quinta Monroy project in Chile. Aravena received a similar commission to Kerez for creating formal housing to house families on the same site they previously occupied informally and illegally. Instead of recreating the existing density or rationalizing every aspect of the previous settlements, Aravena's design recreates and rationalizes only 50 percent of the original density allowing the residents to reconstruct the rest based their own aesthetic desires. The result is a perfect blend of the rational and informal—leveraging the creative resources of the architect without subjugating its residents to his singular vision, will, and ego [IV.108].

There are several lessons for Hip-Hop Architects to be gleaned from each aspect of informal settlements described previously—ground-up rather than top-down development; use of found materials and non-traditional construction techniques; an aesthetic rooted in dynamic temporality; and accommodating the unpredictable, improvisational, and freestyle desires of human occupants. Indeed, all architects must heed these lessons since "Informal architecture will be the *de facto* mode of inhabitation for the majority of humanity this century."[45] One of the most pertinent of these lessons may be the one Le Corbusier learned later in his life when he admitted, "you know, it's life that's always right and the architect who's wrong."[46]

■ ■ ■

IV.108 | Quinta Monroy before and after
© Cristóbal Palma

■ "... attendant in this clip is this contradiction that permeates culture: On the one hand, you have this historical DIY ethos that professor Wilkins is speaking about, and then you have the contradiction that this DIY ethos is being promoted by a star. I think that it's these polarities that are constantly in contradiction, not just in hip-hop but in architecture as well."

– Lawrence Chua[47]

04 INFORMAL SETTLEMENTS.   205

05 ACTIVIST ARCHITECTURE.

Hip-hop culture has several enduring images that reinforce its position as a voice of activism. These include those painted by hip-hop icons NWA (Niggas With Attitudes) having their 1989 concert in Detroit shut down for performing their anthem, "Fuck tha Police"; the rise of Public Enemy's profile after "Fight the Power" also became an anthem; Kendrick Lamar's "We 'Gon Be Alright" becoming the soundtrack for the protests in Ferguson; the enduring notion of b-boys dancing instead of fighting;[48] Radio Raheem being choked to death by cops for defiantly blasting his boom box in Spike Lee's *Do the Right Thing* [IV.109]; virtually every public utterance by KRS One; and Melle Mel describing the abhorrent living conditions in New York on Grandmaster Flash's epic, "The Message." Tying hip-hop to activism can typically be considered a virtually seamless process, even though hip-hop, in its original form, lacks any true activist roots. As Jeyifous speculates, "I've always been interested in this narrative that hip-hop came out of this 'rage'—this response to the environment. For me personally, that has always sounded like an outsider journalist packaging it for SoHo or the West Village. A lot of it was party music."[49] Jeyifous' views are echoed by Robin Kelley who highlights the dominant academic view of hip-hop in that "most reduce it to expressions of pathology, compensatory behavior, or creative 'coping mechanisms' to deal with racism and poverty. Few scholars'" he continues, "acknowledge that what might also be at stake here are aesthetics, style, and pleasure."[50] Hip-hop artists themselves have also reinforced the anti-revolutionary aspects of hip-hop's origins. "We didn't actually want to do 'The Message,'" Melle Mel admitted back in 1992, "because we was used to doing party raps and boasting how good we are and all that."[51] In fact, Mel wasn't convinced anyone at the time would accept anything but party music. "When they played 'The Message' in the club and the people liked it I was shocked, 'cause I didn't think that coming from 'Planet Rock' to a serious record like 'The Message' I thought there would be a lapse in the level of the crowd, the intensity of the crowd. But it wasn't."[52] Ice Cube similarly reminisces with Eazy-E in the film, *Straight Outta Compton* that "In the beginning we were so young and ferocious, doing music straight for the hood,"[53] and not for any particular cause.

However, in its current manifestation, hip-hop is a "[movement] of malcontents replacing what they see with ever-new visions of how things should be."[54] Many of hip-hop's core activities—graffiti (vandalism), b-boying (unlawful assembly), hip-hop parties (public disturbance), etc.—have been deemed illegal. Thus, willfully engaging in such activities is both a matter of cultural preservation and political dissent. Similarly, the act of deejaying

IV.109 | Still from *Do the Right Thing*
"Do the Right Thing" directed by Spike Lee © 40 Acres & A Mule Filmworks 1989. All rights reserved

itself, Schloss believes, is politically charged. "[T]here is clearly political valence," he states, "to the act of taking a record that was created according to European musical standards and . . . physically forcing it to conform to an African American compositional aesthetic."[55] Additionally, with collective political will also come political power. "Do we realize," DJ Kool Herc asks, "how much power hip-hop has? The hip-hop generation can take a stand collectively and make a statement."[56]

Despite its original impetus, hip-hop's adaptability to political activism brings it into close alignment with political activists causes in architecture. Several special interest groups have found activist voices within architecture including spatial justice advocates Toni Griffin (Design for the Just City) and Brian C. Lee, Jr. (Colloqate Design), feminist collaboratives, F-architecture and Architexx, queer space advocates like Aaron Betsky, Julius Gavroche, and Éloise Choquette, and political border activists Eyal Weisman (Forensic Architecture), Ronald Rael (Rael San Fratello), and Teddy Cruz (Estudio Teddy Cruz + Fonna Forman) [IV.110]. (In reading Teddy Cruz, we can conclude that the last section and this one overlap since informal settlements are also forms of architectural activism in that "they are the product of resistance and transgression."[57]) Each of these movements is in some way focused on challenging the dominance of the global patriarchy and providing architectural solutions for rampant injustices.

Hip-Hop Architecture shares many affinities with each of the preceding, especially in their quest "to challenge, or go beyond, architectural codes, expectations and values," which the editors of *Transgression: Towards an Expanded Field of Architecture* believe "is to challenge society itself."[58] However, they each operate inside the same disciplinary boundaries of the elitist profession in which they hope to instigate institutional change. This may prove to be problematic itself, since "Architecture," as Ana María León notes, "a discipline dependent on power and capital, has traditionally

IV.110 | Cross-Border Community Station—Tijuana
Estudio Teddy Cruz + Fonna Forman. Reproduced with permission

served the master and remains beholden to its existential impasse."⁵⁹ And later: "Architects have a fraught relationship with communities struggling against exclusion."⁶⁰ Architecture and architects, then, may not be the most welcomed voices of activism, since they inherently speak the language of oppression. "Architecture is a symbol of power and a symbol of oppression," states Britt Eversole. "Architecture is the site of protest and the target of protest. Architecture is what fucks up your neighborhood."⁶¹

As discussed in Volume II, Hip-Hop Architecture (and its inherent griot attitude) operates outside of the professional strictures of architecture and resists its most oppressive tendencies.[62] More in keeping with hip-hop's origins and unbeholden to architecture's "existential impasse," Hip-Hop Architecture does not explicitly seek to solve problems or fix any existing condition. It is instead a reflection, a commentary, and a measure of contemporary cultural realities. Within Hip-Hop Architecture lies a legitimate opportunity for designers to engage in true acts of dissention and activism.

■ ■ ■

"In her text 'Art to Architecture: A Place Between,' architectural designer, historian and theorist, Jane Rendell, defines critical spatial practice as 'a term which serves to describe both everyday activities and creative practices which seek to resist the dominant social order of global corporate capitalism.' Brother Chua mentioned this earlier in talking about being embedded [in the culture], and at the same time, trying to break free from it as a utopian vision. Stephen Haymes, in his book 'Race, Culture and the City,' says, 'in the contemporary city, the urban has become a metaphor for race, for black people.' Not only in its physical form but also representations of the urban become a metaphor for hood or ghetto. 'The urban form, particularly its representation through the image of redevelopment or gentrification, is understood in relation to a politics of racial difference. That is to say, the urban spaces of black Americans in a white supremacist urban culture are racialized by constructing binary oppositions, contrasting black spaces with white ones.' What Rendell and Haymes create for us is are metrics for which spaces become legitimized and which don't—which practices become legitimized and which don't.

"The way I've constructed this keeps in mind that I'm not a theorist on this topic. A lot of other folks have a stake in the game. But in thinking about this topic and my work I'm now trying to combine and connect ideas that I have floating in my head as both a provocation to this audience and a provocation to myself. I have to now think through what this means in terms of an actual practice. So, let's get to Spatial Injustice. Complementing Rendell's spatial perspective on hybrid art and architecture practices in the public realm is the concept of spatial injustice as articulated by cultural geographer and theorist Edward Soja. In his text 'Seeking Spatial Justice,' Soja defines spatial injustice as, 'how space is actively involved in generating and sustaining inequality, injustice, economic exploitation, racism, sexism, and other forms of oppression and discrimination.' One of the things we want to take up is that if we are designing 'hip-hop inspired' spaces do we replicate what's outside that world? Do we take on the oppressions and isms of that world, along race or gender lines, within these spaces?

"Sekou asked me to mention this: my school, the School of the Art Institute of Chicago, has honored Kanye West with an honorary doctorate degree. He will be bestowed with that in May. There is a huge outcry from alums, particularly female alums, because of the misogyny both in his lyrics and in his visual practice. His video for 'Monster' shows parts of female bodies being hung [in the background]. That's problematic. My concern is that if we bring in the music industry into the culture—I'm not saying that hip-hop is completely rooted in that, but it is a part of the culture—what does it mean to bring that into these new spaces? What exactly happens in these spaces?

"In the city of Chicago (which is my city), spatial injustice has often played out in the physical and social terrain of communities of color, most notably through historical codes and municipal laws that unfairly governed the inhabitation, use, and ownership of space based on race and ethnicity. This form of spatial inequity also took shape through spatial markers and signage in the built environment that demarcated who should be where, when and for how long. We need only to look back to the segregated lakefront beach context that sparked the 1919 Chicago Race Riots as one example. We can think of other examples in urban areas over the last hundred plus years (Tulsa, for example, with Black Wall Street) where segregation of space has had a similar impact.

"In this instance, as in other historical examples of racialized control of space, transgressions within the built environment by minority groups were often met with severe punitive actions, whether sanctioned or unsanctioned, such as mass arrests, evictions, tar-and-feathering, lynchings, bombings, etc. All of these forms of spatial regulation amounted to actual assaults on the bodies and psyches of racialized 'others,' effectively demonstrating the consequences of stepping outside one's place and into unwelcome territory. Contemporary forms of racial profiling and spatial regulation within public contexts, whether occurring as a result of 'stop and frisk,' 'mob action,' or loitering laws, continue this legacy and defend it as justified and sanctioned activity by police and everyday citizens alike, most often at the expense of people of color. What we know is that through the music of hip-hop there is a critical response to this spatial regulation and how people are considered to be 'out of place' in some spaces and 'in place' in others. We also know that through our occupation of space—whether through graffiti, occupying the corner or other public urban spaces—these are reactions and responses to the notion of where one should be and what type of activity should happen in those places.

"This quote has stuck with me since I wrote it down when I was an undergrad. I wrote it on a piece of paper, and I found it while going through boxes looking at my notes, scrambling to get up to par with these brothers here. I found it and thought that this was such a great quote from bell hooks, in her book 'Love as the Practice of Freedom.' 'Wounded in that space where we would know love, black people collectively experienced intense pain and anguish about our future. The absence of public spaces where that pain could be articulated, expressed, and shared meant that it was held in—festering, suppressing the possibility that this collective grief would be reconciled in community even as ways to move beyond it and continue resistance struggle would be envisioned.' She identifies an absence of public space where Black expression can happen.

"This is a painting by William Walker who is an African American painter in Chicago, one of the founders on of the Chicago mural movement. This is a painting titled "A Drive Called King" of a public forum in Washington Park, potentially soon to be the site of the Presidential Library. This public forum has been around since the turn of the twentieth century. These were spaces dedicated for African Americans to do some politicizing and thinking about how to deal with what was happening around them, whether it was oppression, drug-use in the community, politics, etc. You had folks like Elijah Muhammad who were involved in this moment in the early days of The Nation of Islam organizing folks. You had people who were bible enthusiasts. You had Sun Ra who was there. All this amazing activity in this one designated area, and this still exists today. So, if hooks talks about the absence of public spaces what happens when hip-hop informed design creates more spaces like this? Will we be able to have these conversations out in the public? Also, what happens when we involve these other folks who are the other within the other? What does it mean to be a gang member inside a community of color? How can we embrace these others and their ideas of community? Here is an old image published in 1967 in an African-American newspaper in Chicago, called 'Pride at Work.' Here you can see members of the Blackstone Rangers and the Conservative Vice Lords (two of the most notorious Black gangs) creating a billboard image that reads, 'we want grass, not glass.' What's missing from the history is the revolution of pride in the community. When republished in 'The Chicago Defender in 1968 it prompted a truce between these long-time rivals, and 'we want grass not glass' became a rallying cry for the community redevelopment."

– *Andrés Hernandez*[63]

" ____ "

– *André 3000*[64]

06

NEO-POSTMODERNISM.

As discussed in Volume II, hip-hop itself has been classified as a postmodern product and may evoke many aspects and sensibilities typical of postmodern thinking, from its rejection of Modernist ideals to its widespread use of embedded references and codes.[65] Though Postmodernism as an architectural movement is primarily associated with the last quarter of the twentieth century, there has been a recent resurgence of Postmodernist design thinking, which architectural theorist Charles Jencks has dubbed PM2.[66] In his essay, *Contextual Counterpoint in Architecture*, Jencks uses two twenty-first-century buildings to illustrate his theory—Édouard François' Hotel Fouquet in Paris and Herzog & de Meuron's CaixaForum in Madrid [IV.111, IV.112]. Both buildings incorporate restored elements of existing buildings then violate their classical ordering systems with minimalist punctures ("violent disjunctions"[67]) on their façades. Jencks diagrammatically analyzes both façade strategies using musical analogy—"horizontal melodies contrast with vertical harmonies."[68] The syncopated pattern of the new windows in both cases is reminiscent of J Dilla's non-quantized drums.[69]

Jencks later discusses these same two buildings in his updated foreword to his 1972 book, *Adhocism*, as examples of what he calls "the timecity," a subset of contemporary adhocist architecture. As Jencks describes it, Adhocism is "a mongrel term [he] first used in 1968" with "[p]erhaps 90 percent of adhocist concoctions [being] old systems with a *few* supplementary clip-ons."[70] In architecture, the idea shares many overlapping attitudes with Postmodernism and with his newly identified PM2. The subtitle of his book, *The Case for Improvisation*, also suggests an overlap with hip-hop's proclivity for improvised performances. We can find other shared values of Adhocism and Hip-Hop Architecture in Jencks' descriptions of adhocist origins ("the surprising moments when a new idea or invention results from the sudden and successful conjunction of old ones"[71]); of James Stirling's bias toward mixing ("Stirling was thus the occasional adhocist, *simulating bricolage* . . . as part of his taste for the hybrid"[72]); of the palimpsestic "timecity" ("The reverse of the modernist *tabula rasa* is the *tabula scripta*, an urban landscape that keeps rewriting its memories the more it ages"[73]); and of Modernist and Classicist rejection of the ad hoc ("adhocism is a minority affar . . . the contradictions forcefully expressed may offend urban coherence"[74]). The most direct points of connection between the two movements is evident in Jencks' summary statement about the Hotel Fouquet and CaixaForum. "Both the French hotel and the Spanish cultural center are more than collage, or mere assembly of parts," he claims. "What gives them greater resonance is the careful contrasts of fabric, the functional motive

IV.111 | Hotel Fouquet Barrière
© Laurian Ghinitoiu.

IV.112 | CaixaForum
Image courtesy of Luis García via Wikimedia Creative Commons. CC BY-SA 3.0.
https://commons.wikimedia.org/wiki/File:CaixaForum_Madrid_(Espa%C3%B1a)_01.jpg

of each part, and the reconciliation of themes as a form of visual music."[75] Here, Jencks echoes many of the sentiments expressed in earlier volumes of this book regarding Hip-Hop Architecture's ultimate aspirations.

Though some may disagree with the existence of a Postmodernism 2,[76] there are several contemporary practices (many much younger than François or HdM) that reinterpret Postmodernist ideas and methods using new digital representation and fabrication tools. I refer here to such practices as Neo-Postmodernist. Kyle Miller, in his presentation on precedents, discusses a few of these practices and categorizes their primary methodologies using decidedly hip-hop-derived language: "techniques of appropriation: the cover, the sample, the remix, and the mashup."[77] For "the cover" he cites the various copies of Le Corbusier's Villa Savoye that exist around the world and admits that, as a type, covers offer "nothing new."[78] Bureau Spectacular's competition entry for the Louisville Children's Museum is cited as a contemporary example of a sample that borrows not only image but spatial strategies from OMA's Agadir Convention Center competition entry. "'The sample' pays homage and repositions."[79] Norman Kelley's "Seeing Doubles" is positioned as a remix of John Hejduk's "House of the Suicide" and "House of the Mother of Suicide." "'The remix' reinvents."[80] Miller uses OMA's Villa dall'Ava as a prime example of mashing up two previous works (Villa Savoye above and Farnsworth House below) before referencing the more contemporary example of Andrew Kovacs' work ("House Addition," for example) as a mashup of various housing elements. "'The mashup' brings two or more things together."[81] Beyond the blatant appropriation of hip-hop terminology to describe these contemporary design processes Miller discusses one of their core motivations that also shares some of hip-hop's intentionality. "We can turn to history and return to precedent as a driving medium for the production of architecture. What this does is it ensures the development and longevity of our discipline by picking up things that one may identify as native to the discipline and making sure that they are carefully and rigorously evolved through the work of things legible as architecture."[82] Miller's own work follow these basic guidelines. His series, "The Plan is the Generator,"[83] remixes precedents to generate new three-dimensional models for concept houses. [IV.113, IV.114] This consistent reference to historical and existing material in the production of new work is also critical in all forms of hip-hop production.

Jennifer Bonner, a contemporary of Miller, Kelley, Kovacs, and Bureau Spectacular's Jimenez Lai, can also be considered a Neo-Postmodernist as evidenced by the use of sampled commercial towers to create a new tower mashup in her "Best Sandwiches" project [IV.115]. Her "Haus Gables" project similarly mixes several common residential gable forms and collages laminate surfaces in the design of an Atlanta home [IV.116].

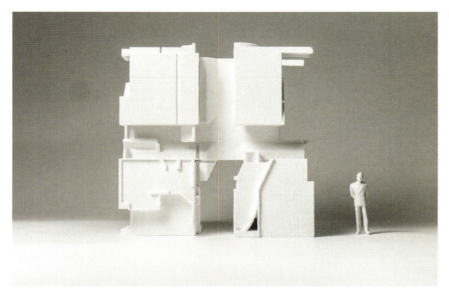

IV.113 | Model of "House No. 64"
Kyle Miller

IV.114 | Model of "House No. 77"
Kyle Miller

A more direct hip-hop influence can be found in her book, *A Guide to the Dirty South—Atlanta*, a compilation of work done in one of her architectural design studio courses of the same name. Beyond the mere use of hip-hop language in the book's title, Bonner explains the connections between her reading of mid-90s "east coast-west coast" hip-hop rivalries, contemporary parallels in east coast versus west coast architectural ideologies, and new readings of the city. "Paralleling the hip-hop industry, within the discipline of architecture," she writes in the book's introduction, "we find a similar geographic and stylistic divide. With all eyes on the NY-LA battle down south in Atlanta, hip-hop collectives Goodie Mob and Outcast formed the Dirty South."[84] Though the politics connecting the three hip-hop scenes has been simplified, Bonner shows clear interest in the applicability of hip-hop lenses in viewing the city. She introduces the book's contributors as "a group of thinkers, writers, misbehaving makers, and storytellers [who] borrow from the Dirty South hip-hop artists before them to produce an outcast architecture."[85]

For these gen-X Neo-Postmodernists, conscious or subconscious tendencies to use hip-hop techniques (mashups, remixes, samples) may be a direct result of hip-hop culture's prominence during their formative years, even though they may not personally identify with hip-hop culture. Other more established practitioners with less clear hip-hop connections show similar formal and graphic tendencies to their younger counterparts. The 2007 "Housewarming" exhibition by Jürgen Mayer H. at the Vitra Design

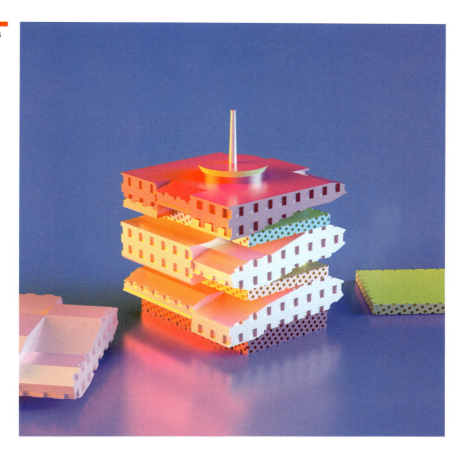

IV.115 | Best Sandwiches study model
Jennifer Bonner/MALL

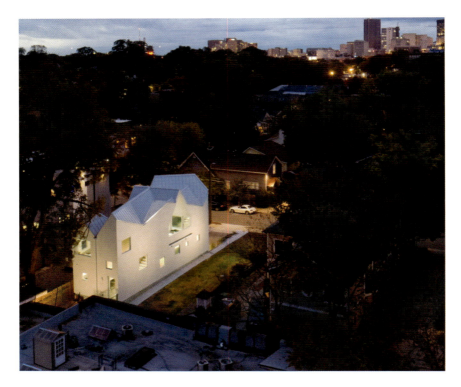

IV.116 | Haus Gables
Jennifer Bonner/MALL,
photo by Tim Hursley

IV.117 | Roy and Diana Vagelos Education Center
© Sekou Cooke

Museum bears strong resemblance to graffiti-derived building proposals by students, Evelyn Brooks and Timothy Mulhall described in Volume III. Diller Scofidio + Renfro's Roy and Diana Vagelos Education Center completed in 2016 in Manhattan displays the kind of distortions and flows that one could ascribe to the anthropomorphic lines of wild style graffiti or b-boys in motion [IV.117]. Hip-hop culture may have already been appropriated into contemporary architecture under other labels and headings than Hip-Hop Architecture.

■ ■ ■

■ "_____"

— *Goodie Mob*[86]

■ "When I started writing [*Brick Body Kids Still Daydream*], it was because . . . I had a memory of those buildings. And because those buildings got demolished while I was away in college, I wasn't able to take that moment to process it when it happened. And so, I was on a flight somewhere like two years ago when I thought about it. I was like, 'I don't even know what's in that spot right now?' I imagined that there were these condos or some redevelopment or something that was there, like in a lot of places where buildings like that got torn down. So, I researched it (I had the Wi-Fi on the plane) and I was looking it up and I was like 'Oh my God! There's nothing!' These vast expanses of buildings that housed like 30,000 people across 12 buildings. They knocked all that down and there's nothing there. Just the thought of that sort of erasure really impacted me and made me want to do the audio equivalent of a mural for what it was like to live there."

— *Open Mike Eagle*[87]

07

OUTRO.

Regardless of how far this book has gone in convincing anyone of the legitimacy of Hip-Hop Architecture as a bona fide architectural pursuit, my own belief in the power of the topic to positively affect the architectural discipline has increased exponentially. What began for me as an exercise in giving academic weight to a seemingly benign provocation has blossomed into a six-year quest "in search of a movement."[88] In fact, my original intent was to have "The Fifth Pillar" be my first and last statement on the topic. Only after receiving widespread feedback on the essay, mostly from minority students, practitioners, and academics (including my first introduction to Craig Wilkins who gently asked, "have you read some of this other work on the subject?") did I decide that the topic required some deeper interrogation. My next step was to invite as many thought leaders in this area as I could imagine into the same room to have as in-depth a conversation as I could imagine (at the time) about Hip-Hop Architecture. *Towards a Hip-Hop Architecture* was, again, intended to be the final word on the topic. The list of presenters and moderators included Ford, Wilkins, Hernandez, Laurence Chua, who admits Hip-Hop Architecture is a tertiary interest of his but wrote a book chapter connecting early hip-hop Utopianism to Modernist Utopian ideals, Amanda Williams, Jeyifous, Rashida Bumbray, exhibition coordinator for the *harlemworld* exhibition (who could not attend), Travis Gosa, professor of hip-hop studies at Cornell, Héctor Tarrido-Picart, former president of the Harvard GSD African American Student Union who helped bring Kanye West to the GSD, Jack Travis, Shawn Rickenbacker, then architecture professor at the University of Pennsylvania, and Garrett, Jr. Dr. Ray Dalton, former director of minority affairs for Cornell University, College of Architecture, Art, and Planning,[89] was also in attendance for the first evening. Instead of relegating the symposium to a series of panel discussions, the event was opened and closed with "provocation sessions" where panelists formed a cypher in the atrium of Slocum Hall to have open conversation in response to several image and text prompts. By the end of the final session two things became clear to me. First, the conversation about Hip-Hop Architecture needed to continue and be disseminated to as wide an audience as possible. Second, that dissemination needed to emerge from more detailed study of the many overlapping aspects of hip-hop and architecture. Where I first saw the symposium as an opportunity to compile various thoughts on Hip-Hop Architecture into an academic publication, I later realized it was a mandate for further investigation.

The ensuing journey has taken me in many unanticipated directions through a series of challenges and fortunate circumstances. The first major challenge coming from a mentor who helped me craft my first research statement. He warned that "the overall idea of Hip-hop Architecture is interesting however it is not an academic topic," and added that he "would not recommend such a controversial subject as this to a person trying to get into an all-white field."[90] I stubbornly ignored his warnings and resolved to develop an academic study where there was little to build on and to structure my academic case around this premise knowing its power beyond mere interest could be more fully realized outside academia. This obstinance lead to lectures at the AIA New York Center for Architecture, various universities in the US, a series of lectures and workshops at the Universidad del Istmo in Guatemala; panel discussions and presentations at various institutions; research activities funded by Autodesk, Washington, DC Office of Planning, New York State Council on the Arts, The Graham Foundation, The Knight Foundation, and a private developer; three design studios and four seminar courses; and a traveling exhibition. The work has also made its way into my practice, where I am currently designing two projects in Syracuse for different clients, both intent on prioritizing Hip-Hop Architectural design methodologies and spatial imperatives.

It would be nice to think that this book is the culmination of that study and the end of that journey—my final "final statement" on the matter. In truth, it is more of a beginning than an end. The work that comes hereafter to reify the movement in built form will be much more important to future engagement between underrepresented peoples and architecture. Also, though it has only done so in small pockets, the research itself may have had more lasting effects outside of any academic settings. The Saint Paul edition of the *Close to the Edge* exhibition, which I position in Volume III as an exemplar of Hip-Hop Architectural practice,[91] has touched more lives outside of the architecture community than any writing on the topic has had up to this point. Garrett, Jr., who did more to bring the exhibition to his hometown of Saint Paul than anyone else, helped organize a series of "takeover" events by community organizations during an extended run of the show. These included an event organized by Orko Eloheim, where DJs taught people to mix beats, one organized by Juxtaposition Arts Center, where students preformed poetry and freestyle emceeing, and a closing event that overlapped with the "Twin Cities Kinship Night" block party for the Free Minds, Free People organization, "a national gathering that brings together teachers, high school and college students, community activists, academics and parents from across the country to build a movement to develop and promote education as a tool for liberation."[92] All told, over 1,000 visitors made their way to the garage of a former used-car lot to view an exhibition about architecture having almost no idea what to expect [IV.118–120]. A few anecdotes of their responses have been summarized here by Mary-Margaret Zindren, executive director of AIA Saint Paul, AIA

IV.118 | Community "takeover" event at *Close to the Edge* exhibition
Aaron Price for NetWirth Ent.

IV.119 | Community "takeover" event at *Close to the Edge* exhibition
© Carl Atiya Swanson

IV.120 | Community "takeover" event at *Close to the Edge* exhibition
© Carl Atiya Swanson

Minneapolis, AIA Northern Minnesota, AIA Minnesota, and the Minnesota Architectural Foundation, and local logistics wizard for the exhibition and all related events:

> [The final event] brought in 230 people in one night, 95% of them people of color. When people entered the exhibit space – where every inch of every wall, two stories high, was covered with graffiti art of hip-hop lyrics – you witnessed the impact. They said, "Wow." Often repeating it. Once they looked at the Close to the Edge exhibits, the "Wow" moments kept coming. I started a tally sheet of Wow's and stopped keeping track after ten. (I should have tallied the number of Black men who said, "Dope!" and "This is so dope!" – it rivaled the "Wow's".) A woman at the event approached [Jeyifous'] work—the huge, futuristic images of Brooklyn—and she literally did a double take. She moved toward it, as if from a gravitational pull, and then shocked back a few inches before approaching it even closer. "Damn!", she said. She didn't take her eyes off of it for several minutes.
>
> A Black woman attended the opening event. She was looking at Amanda Williams' piece titled "Pink Oil Moisturizer." At first, she didn't read the label and was just mesmerized. I saw her then look over to read the label and she laughed out loud. "Pink Oil Moisturizer! Yes it is!" She then called her friend over and pointed it out.

They started to talk about how that color was exactly right, and did she use it too? Did she remember the smell? And they still sell it, right?

A Black woman approached the piece with the hieroglyphs of Black figures. She put her hand on her chest, took a step back, and seemed to tear up. She said, "I need a minute. It's a lot. It's just a lot." Later she said to me, "You just don't see yourself, your people, in this way."

A white woman who had seen the exhibit said, encouraging others to see it, "You have to go. You have to understand what the world would be like if we had more Black architects. It is vibrant, full of color and energy. We need more people to see this and to understand why the work of growing diversity in architecture is so important."

"Is this real?", a white teenager visiting the exhibit said. I responded that many of the items exhibited are indeed real, and many others were in the process of being built. She responded, "They should all be real."

When people exited the exhibit, they invariably thanked us. Not a polite, Minnesotan "Thank you," with no real emotion or intention; they said "Thank you" like they meant it. Often adding "This is amazing" or "this is so important."

Several people said things like, "How did this happen?" "Who did this?" "How did you get someone to let you do this?" in reference to the graffiti-covered walls. It resonated so much with them.

Every Friday for five weeks—the last five weeks of the school year—a teacher brought a different group of four or five teens to the exhibit space to view the exhibit and to take photographs. They always did a posed, group shot somewhere in the exhibit. One Saturday afternoon, a group of teens showed up, dressed up for their prom. They were some of the kids who had taken photos in the space for school. This is where they wanted to take their prom photos.

Nearly 50 members of the local AIA St. Paul and AIA Minneapolis chapters volunteered their time staffing the exhibit, each of them taking at least one of the four-hour shifts, most taking several. One member volunteered every Thursday afternoon for a four-hour shift—that's 32 hours volunteering in the garage of a building during the nicest weather Minnesota gets. Sometimes as many as 20 people would come through on one of his shifts. Sometimes only one or two people. He said no matter how many people came through, he always felt good about playing his part to make sure as many people as possible got to see the exhibit.[93]

My own reaction to the various responses relayed to me in these and other anecdotes and those I witnessed in person was a feeling of humility. I was humbled to see demonstrated in front of me how much larger this work is than I am as a curator, or any of the academics who've written about Hip-Hop Architecture, or any of the practitioners who have attempted to produce works of Hip-Hop Architecture. The power of this work to change people's perceptions about hip-hop, or more importantly, their perceptions about architecture, and the newfound ability for young Black people to see themselves and their lives reflected in contemporary built environments is a complete game changer. If anything has the power to shift the needle toward greater inclusion of Black voices in architecture this movement does. I will not go as far as Wilkins has to say that "Hip-Hop Architecture should be a model for architectural practice, period," but I do agree that expanding the issues, methods, and participants of architectural production to include hip-hop cultural inputs has the power to fundamentally transform the discipline, profession, and practice. More importantly, Hip-Hop Architecture's ability to shift power and control within the architectural realm from white-haired, White men, in black suits and black horn-rimmed glasses to colorful, young, ungendered masses, makes it potentially more democratic and progressive than any preceding architectural movement. For those willing to take on that challenge to ensure that this is not the final statement on the subject, this book is for you.

■ ■ ■

Craig Wilkins: We had this thing in New York and there was a panel associated with that. And we had this discussion, so this is going to be a kind of continuation of that. There was a sort a throw away comment that I made towards the end of this panel discussion that someone said something that I can't exactly remember, but my response was something like. . .

Sekou Cooke: Hip-Hop Architecture should be a model for architectural practice, period.

CW: Ok. I imagine that sounds better than what I actually said. But anyways, we all left, and we had dinner, and Sekou brought that point up and said, "What do you mean by that?" So, I want to return to that for my moment here because I want to kind of lob some . . . they're not really bombs . . . but I'm going to make some declarative statements that you can agree with, not agree with, debate. But it comes from that particular statement. And I want to tell you why I believe it should be our motto.[94]

▬ "Architecture as a profession is currently divided into several camps: the tired starchitects, the uninspired practitioners, the verbose academics, the vintage postmodernists, and the digital masturbators. But a new group is emerging—the strategic entrepreneurs. This group is starting to address the world's issues— beyond architecture—in meaningful ways, not the superficial gestures we've seen in the past. They find opportunities and are able to initiate projects instead of react to client demands. They don't feign expertise, but are able to assemble teams that can turn ambitions into concrete. They're scrappy, intelligent, and determined. And they don't care about the way things are typically done."

– Kyle May[95]

▬ "____"

– Lauryn Hill[96]

APPENDIX.

The following is a list of students who have completed architectural thesis projects (or equivalent) explicitly related to hip-hop (compiled based solely on direct knowledge of these projects with the help of Craig Wilkins and James Garrett, Jr.):

- Jeremy Sims, Texas A&M, College Station, Texas (2020)
- Demar Matthews, Woodbury University, Burbank, California (2020)
- Mauricio Zamora, University of California, Berkeley, California (2019)
- Nick Tettero, Rotterdam Academy of Architecture, Rotterdam, Netherlands (2019)
- Emily Fielder, University of Virginia, Charlottesville, Virginia (2019)
- Niels Matitawaer, ArtEZ Institute of the Arts, Zwolle, Netherlands (2018)
- Andrea Bulloni and Marco Papagni, Politecnico di Milano, Milan, Italy (2018)
- Ethan Miller, Washington University, St. Louis, Missouri (2017)
- Ade "Sonny" Joy-Hogg, Virginia Polytechnic, Blacksburg, Virginia (2016)
- DeShawn Jackson, School of the Art Institute of Chicago, Chicago, Illinois (2015)
- Tajai Massey, University of California Berkeley, Berkeley, California (2014)
- Edward Glover, Hampton University, Hampton, Virgina (2014)
- Sarah Courtney, Victoria University, Wellington, New Zealand (2012)
- Kouyate Toure, New School of Architecture and Design, San Diego, California (2012)
- Michael Coyler, Catholic University, Washington, DC (2011)
- Vanessa Daniel, University of New Mexico (2010)
- Dawn Hicks, University of NC-Charlotte, Charlotte, North Carolina (2010)
- Michael Ford, University of Detroit, Mercy, Detroit, Michigan (2010)
- Dina Soliman, Sheridan College, Oakville, Ontario, Canada (2010)
- Kendal Bowman, University of Michigan, Ann Arbor, Michigan (2009)
- Arendse Paige, City College of New York, New York (2009)
- Jabari Garland, Miami University, Miami, Ohio (2006)
- James Garrett, Jr., Parsons School of Design, New York, New York (2004)

- Sean Mauricette, University of Toronto, Ontario, Canada (2002)
- Amanda M. Faehnle, University of Cincinnati, Ohio (2002)
- Pat White, Dalhousie University, Halifax, Nova Scotia (2001)
- André Gould, Cornell University, Ithaca, New York (1997)
- Nathan Williams, Cornell University, Ithaca, New York (1993)

NOTES.

Portions of the following previously published essays were sampled and remixed for this text:

Sekou Cooke, "What's My Name? Defining Hip-Hop Architecture" in *Lunch*, Vol. 14, 2020

Sekou Cooke, "3D Turntables: Humanizing Architectural Technology Through Hip-Hop," in *Technology Architecture and Design: OPEN*, Vol. 3:2, 2019

Sekou Cooke, "(L)earning from Sellouts" in *Avery Shorts S01 E03*, Columbia Books on Architecture and the City, 2018

Sekou Cooke, Nadia M. Anderson, "Jefferson, Hip-Hop, and the Oppressive Grid" in *106th ACSA Annual Meeting Proceedings*, 2018

VOLUME I

1. Nas, "Simple Things," 00:45 to 00:51 on *NASIR* (Mass Appeal Records, 2018).
2. An idea first promoted by George Lipsitz in "The Racialization of Space and the Spatialization of Race: Theorizing the Hidden Architecture of Landscape," *Landscape Journal*, Vol. 26, No. 1 (University of Wisconsin Press, 2007), pp. 10–23.
3. Roy Christopher, *Dead Precedents: How Hip-Hop Defines the Future* (London: Repeater Books, 2018): 13.
4. Andrés L. Hernandez, *Towards a Hip-Hop Architecture* symposium, Syracuse, NY, March 19, 2015, transcribed January 25, 2016.
5. Drake, "Survival," 01:30 to 01:33 on *Scorpion* (Cash Money Records, 2018).
6. The exhibition, *Close to the Edge: The Birth of Hip-Hop Architecture*, curated by the author, debuted at the AIANY Center for Architecture in New York, NY on October 1, 2018 and ran through January 19, 2019. It later reopened at SpringBOX in Saint Paul, MN. As of this writing, the exhibition is being planned for a third opening at the a+d museum in Los Angeles, CA.
7. You will notice that many of these quotations have been removed from the manuscript. This is a consequence of the complex and fuzzy legality of quoting song lyrics in academic texts. Copyright laws and royalty structures that protect the intellectual property of everyone involved in producing a song prevent many forms of academic quotation that would have been useful to this text. Please refer to the timecodes in the end notes for selected excerpts of each song quoted.
8. *The Matrix*, motion picture, directed by the Wachowskis (Warner Bros., 1999).
9. Common, "They Say" 00:31 to 00:33 on *Be* (Geffen Records, 2005).

VOLUME II

1. Jay-Z, in Michael Eric Dyson, *Know What I Mean? Reflections on Hip Hop* (New York: Basic Civitas Books, 2007): x.
2. Dyson, xv.

3. Ibid., xv.
4. Full dissertation available online at https://phd.aydeethegreat.com accessed July 4, 2019.
5. Roy Christopher, *Dead Precedents: How Hip-Hop Defines the Future* (London: Repeater Books, 2018): 20.
6. Ibid.
7. Tricia Rose, *Black Noise: Rap Music and Black Culture in Contemporary America* (Hanover, N.H.: University Press of New England, 1994): xiii.
8. David Albert Mhadi Goldberg, "The Scratch Is Hip-Hop: Appropriating the Phonographic Medium," in *Appropriating Technology: Vernacular Science and Social Power*, eds. Ron Eglash, Jennifer L. Croissant, Giovanni Di Chiro, and Rayvon Fouché (Minneapolis: University of Minnesota Press, 2004): 108.
9. Ibid., 109.
10. In the TV series, *Seinfeld*, season 8, episode 13, "The Comeback," George Costanza was mocked for stuffing his face with shrimp during an office meeting with the quip: "Hey George, the ocean just called. They're running out of shrimp." As he was driving home that evening his witty comeback finally came to him. "Jerk store!"
11. Dan Hancox, *Inner City Pressure: The Story of Grime* (London: William Collins, 2018): 227–228.
12. Christopher, *Dead Precedents*: 15.
13. Travis Gosa, *Towards a Hip-Hop Architecture* symposium, Syracuse, NY, March 19, 2015, transcribed January 25, 2016.
14. Rose, *Black Noise:* 196.
15. Ibid.
16. Steven Hager, *Hip Hop: The Illustrated History of Breakdancing, Rap Music, and Graffiti* (New York: St. Martin's Press, 1984): 49–50.
17. Sekou Cooke, "The Fifth Pillar: A Case for Hip-Hop Architecture" in *Harvard Journal of African American Public Policy*, 2014: 18.
18. Ibid.
19. Ibid. Note here that I no longer define hip-hop culture as a subculture, though it may have begun as such. As defined in Volume I, Section 2, "MANIFESTO." hip-hop is *the* dominant cultural force of our time. Christopher also quotes Rammellzee in *Dead Precedents* (p. 15) as saying "I didn't see a subculture . . . I saw a culture in development." Also note the expanded definition of "Black" in Volume II, Section 4, "RACE." to be inclusive, in most cases, or Latino.
20. Christopher, *Dead Precedents*: 87.
21. Ibid., 101.
22. Joseph G. Schloss, *Making Beats: The Art of Sample-Based Hip-Hop* (Middletown, Wesleyan University Press: 2004): 32
23. Mos Def, "Fear Not of Man" on *Black on Both Sides*, Priority Records/Rawkus Records (1999), lyrics as transcribed on https://genius.com/Yasiin-bey-fear-not-of-man-lyrics, accessed March 21, 2019.
24. Ibid.
25. Jim Walsh, "What's Hip-Hop Architecture? Hip-Hop Culture in Built Form," MinnPost, April 11, 2019.

26. "I Had a Paper Route Too," *My Next Guest Needs No Introduction with David Letterman*, season 1, episode 4, *Netflix*, April 6, 2018.
27. Lupe Fiasco, "Dumb It Down," 01:05 to 01:25 on *Lupe Fiasco's The Cool*, Atlantic Records, 2007.
28. Nathan Williams, interview with author, February 28, 2019.
29. Ibid.
30. Ibid.
31. We may consider this date and the narrative around the birthdate of hip-hop as one of the "interesting and necessary fictions" described by Jeff Chang. "The act of determining a group of people by placing a beginning and ending date," Chang states, "is a way to impose a narrative." *Can't Stop Won't Stop: A History of the Hip-Hop Generation* (New York: St. Martin's Press, 2005): 1.
32. Cooke, *The Fifth Pillar*: 15.
33. Michael Ford, "What is Hip-Hop Architecture?" in *Platform 2017, Convergent Voices*, eds. Nichole Wiedemann, Charlton Lewis, The University of Texas at Austin: 16–19.
34. Schloss, *Making Beats*: 21
35. Stéphane Malka, interview with author, March 12, 2019.
36. Carlos "MARE 139" Rodriguez, interview with author, March 8, 2019.
37. Amanda Williams, "Red on the Wall: Basquiat When I Paint," at *Towards a Hip-Hop Architecture*.
38. Nathan Williams, interview with author, February 28, 2019.
39. Michael Ford, "Hip-Hop Inspired Architecture and Design," at 2014 NOMA Conference, Philadelphia, PA, October 4, 2014.
40. *Towards a Hip-Hop Architecture*.
41. Hancox, *Inner City Pressure:* 40.
42. Rose, *Black Noise:* 11.
43. Ibid., 2.
44. Schloss, *Making Beats*: 3.
45. Ibid.
46. Hancox, *Inner City Pressure*: 33.
47. Jeff Chang, *Can't Stop Won't Stop: A History of the Hip-Hop Culture* (New York: Picador, 2005): 2 (quoting Bakari Kitwana, *The Hip-Hop Generation: Young Blacks and The Crisis in African American Culture*, 2002).
48. Chang, *Can't Stop Won't Stop*: 2.
49. "Double-consciousness" is a term coined by W.E.B. Du Bois to describe the dualism required to exist as both Black and American.
50. W.E.B. Du Bois, *The Souls of Black Folk* (New York: Dover Publications, 1903): 2–3.
51. A simple calculation using the number collected on "The Directory of African American Architects" by Prof. Dennis Mann at the University of Cincinnati (2,286) and dividing it by the number listed on the NCARB website (113,554) results in a 2.013 percentage. http://blackarch.uc.edu/ and https://www.ncarb.org/press/number-of-us-architects-the-rise accessed July 23, 2019.

52. Whitney M. Young Jr., transcript of keynote speech from 1968 AIA Convention in Portland, Oregon.
53. Joseph Godlewski, *Introduction to Architecture* (Cognella Academic Publishing, 2019): xiv. Godlewski discusses here in general terms "the dissemination of disciplinary knowledge. . . ."
54. Lowery Stokes Sims, "Director's Foreword" in *harlemworld: Metropolis as Metaphor*, ed. Thelma Golden (New York: The Studio Museum in Harlem, 2003): 7.
55. Thelma Golden, "of Harlem: an introduction," Ibid., 11.
56. Greg Tate, "The Harlem Mystery School," Ibid., 59.
57. Ibid., 63.
58. Milton S. F. Curry, "Black Futurism: Architecture as Signifier," Ibid., 74.
59. Darell Wayne Fields, "House for Josephine Baker (Parody Series)," Ibid., 93.
60. Derek Thompson's article, "The 33 Whitest Jobs in America," cites 2013 figures from the Bureau of Labor Statistics that list architecture as a profession that is 91.3 percent White. *The Atlantic*, Business section, November 6, 2013 https://www.theatlantic.com/business/archive/2013/11/the-33-whitest-jobs-in-america/281180/ accessed August 12, 2019.
61. Mabel O. Wilson, "White by Design," in *Among Others: Blackness at MoMA*, eds. Charlotte Barat and Darby English (New York: The Museum of Modern Art, 2019): 104.
62. Ibid., 109. Wilson continues her note by pointing out that "Who identifies as African American or black can be complex and often reflects the legacy of racism."
63. Jack Travis, profile on *Afritecture* website, "Jack Travis: Notes on a Black Architectural Aesthetic," August 27, 2015 http://www.afritecture.org/profiles/jack-travis-notes-on-a-black-architectural-aesthetic accessed August 12, 2019.
64. Wilson, "White by Design": 107
65. Mario Gooden, *Dark Space: Architecture, Representation, Black Identity* (New York: Columbia Books of Architecture and the City, 2016): 13.
66. Ibid., 14.
67. *Towards a Hip-Hop Architecture*.
68. Women in Design online petition, "The Pritzker Architecture Prize Committee: Recognize Denise Scott Brown for her work in Robert Venturi's 1991 Prize" on change.org, posted April 2013, https://www.change.org/p/the-pritzker-architecture-prize-committee-recognize-denise-scott-brown-for-her-work-in-robert-venturi-s-1991-prize, accessed March 31, 2019.
69. Denise Scott Brown, as quoted by Alan G. Brake, "Zaha Hadid: Barrier Breaker, Conversation Starter" in *Architectural Record*, 192, no. 5 (May 2004): 25.
70. A cursory review of the Pritzker web page showing images of each laureate quickly reveals its extreme race and gender imbalance. I requested permission to publish a screenshot of their current website, but that request was declined.

71. Many feminist architectural theorists such as Diana Agrest, Hilde Heynen, Leslie Lokko, Bridget Fowler, Fiona M. Wilson, and Lori Brown have published notable works on women in architecture. Heynen has also written extensively on Scott Brown in particular.
72. "Women in Architecture and Engineering Occupations in 2016," U.S. Bureau of Labor Statistics website, March 10, 2017, https://www.bls.gov/opub/ted/2017/women-in-architecture-and-engineering-occupations-in-2016.htm accessed July 6, 2019.
73. "Demographics," National Council of Architectural Review Boards (NCARB) website, https://www.ncarb.org/nbtn2017/demographics accessed July 6, 2019.
74. "The Directory of African American Architects," website updated July 3, 2019, http://blackarch.uc.edu/.
75. Rose, *Black Noise:* xiii
76. Bettina L. Love, *Hip Hop's Li'l Sistas Speak: Negotiating Hip Hop Identities and Politics in the New South* (New York: Peter Lang Publishing, 2012): 20.
77. bell hooks, *Outlaw Culture: Resisting Representation* (Boston: South End Press, 1994): 2.
78. Love, 23.
79. Gwendolyn Pough, "Love Feminism but Where's My Hip-Hop? Shaping a Black Feminist Identity," in *Colonize This! Young Women of Color on Today's Feminism*, eds. D. Hernandez and B. Rehman (New York: Seal Press, 2002): 86.
80. Whitney A. Peoples, "Under Construction: Identifying Foundations of Hip-Hop Feminism and Exploring Bridges Between Black Second-Wave and Hip-Hop Feminism," in *Meridians*, volume 8, no. 1 (Duke University Press, 2008): 21.
81. Dyson, *Holler If You Hear Me: Searching For Tupac Shakur* (New York: Basic Civitas Books, 2001): 176.
82. Rashad Shabazz, *Spatializing Blackness: Architectures of Confinement and Black Masculinity in Chicago* (Urbana, Chicago, and Springfield: University of Illinois Press, 2015): Shabazz discusses many aspects of Black masculine identity and its formation on pages 1–2, 7–9, 32, 45–46, 52, 94–95.
83. I have published two essays on ArchDaily describing Kaye West's connection with architecture. The first, "Keep Talking Kanye: An Architect's Defense of Kanye West," discusses the importance of having a public hip-hop figure talk about architecture. (Sekou Cooke. "Keep Talking Kanye: An Architect's Defense of Kanye West" 10 Oct 2013, ArchDaily, https://www.archdaily.com/435952/keep-talking-kanye-an-architect-s-defense-of-kanye-west/ accessed 31 Mar 2019.) The second, "Stop Talking Kanye: No More Defense for Kanye West," seeks absolution from the position of apologizing for West. (Sekou Cooke. "Stop Talking Kanye: No More Defense for Kanye West" 22 May 2018, ArchDaily, https://www.archdaily.com/894887/stop-talking-kanye-no-more-defense-for-kanye-west/ accessed 31 Mar 2019.)
84. Dyson, *Holler If You Hear Me*: 177.

85. Statements made on her tumblr account have since been removed. They were reprinted by Andrew Martin in "Dream Hampton Says She's Done with Hip-Hop," August 12, 2012, Complex, https://www.complex.com/music/2012/08/dream-hampton-says-shes-done-with-hip-hop accessed Jan 13, 2020.
86. After her 2012 statement, Hampton continues to write about hip-hop artists and hip-hop related topics in several newspapers and magazines.
87. Hampton was an executive producer of the documentary series which aired on Lifetime in 2019. She chronicles her nineteen-year pursuit of the recording artist in "How I Took Down the Incarcerated Singer," 2 Aug 2019, The Hollywood Reporter, https://www.hollywoodreporter.com/news/surviving-r-kelly-filmmaker-how-i-took-down-r-kelly-guest-column-1227905 accessed Jan 2, 2020.
88. Gosa, *Towards a Hip-Hop Architecture*.
89. A. Williams, *Towards a Hip-Hop Architecture*.
90. Accounts from the 1998 NOMA Conference come from author's interviews with Amanda Williams and Andrés L. Hernandez, and from author's own recollection of events.
91. National Organization of Minority Architects, "History" page from organization website, https://noma.net/history/ accessed March 31, 2019.
92. Hernandez, *Towards a Hip-Hop Architecture*.
93. Craig L. Wilkins, "(W)rapped Space: The Architecture of Hip Hop," *Journal of Architectural Education*, 54:1, 2000: 11.
94. Ibid., 11–13.
95. Jabari Garland, "Flow Tektonics: Re-mixing Architecture to a Hip Hop Beat" in 93rd ACSA Annual Meeting Proceedings, 2005: 39-41
96. James Garrett, Jr., "Resonant Spaces/Dynamic Flows: Hip-Hop + Architecture," in *Reading Room* on Community Arts Network website, 2003 http://www.communityarts.net/readingroom/archive/56hiphop.php, accessed January 20, 2005.
97. Ibid.
98. Cooke, *The Fifth Pillar*: 16.
99. DJ Kool Herc in Chang, *Can't Stop Won't Stop*: 22.
100. Chang, *Can't Stop Won't Stop*: 79.
101. David A. M. Goldberg provides an insightful set of technological explanations and interpretations of these and other DJ techniques in "The Scratch Is Hip-Hop," 111–128
102. Christopher, *Dead Precedents*: 40.
103. See Volume II, Section 9: "TECHNOLOGY." and Volume III, Section 3: "PROCESS."
104. Christopher, *Dead Precedents*: 72.
105. Schloss, *Making Beats*: 6.
106. Garland, "Flow Tektonics": 39.
107. Murray Forman, *The 'Hood Comes First: Race, Space, and Place in Rap and Hip-Hop* (Middletown: Wesleyan University Press, 2002): 11.
108. Hager, *Hip Hop*: 89.
109. Chang, *Can't Stop Won't Stop*: 118.

110. Rammellzee, as quoted in Sonaike & Goetz, "Ramm:ell:zee," in *Guerilla Art*, Peiter Sebastian (ed.) (London: Lawrence King Publishing, 2009): 8–13, states that, "The graffiti artists of the 1970s in the tunnels of New York continued where the monks of the fourteenth century had left off with their illuminated letters."
111. KRS-One, "Out for Fame," on *KRS-One*, Jive Records (1995), asserts, "The first graffiti artists in the world were the Egyptians, writing on walls, mixing characters with letters."
112. Chang, *Can't Stop Won't Stop*: 74 (additional quote from Greg Tate, "Graf Rulers/Graf UnTrained," *One Planet Under a Groove: Hip Hop and Contemporary Art* (New York: Bronx Museum of Arts, 2001): 38).
113. Christopher, *Dead Precedents*: 15.
114. Wilkins, "Cuirass Architecture" in *Ruffneck Constructivists*, Institute of Contemporary Art, University of Pennsylvania, ed. Kara Walker (Brooklyn: Dancing Foxes Press, 2014): 18.
115. Ibid., 20–21.
116. Kara Walker, "Ruffneck Constructivism," in *Ruffneck Constructivists:* 9.
117. Ibid.
118. Wilkins, *Close to the Edge Symposium*, Saint Paul, Minnesota, April 17, 2019, transcribed August 8, 2019.
119. Dyson, *Know What I Mean?*: 156
120. Jeff "Chairman" Mao, with Afrika Bambaataa, "You Spin Me Round (Like a Record, Baby)" in *Vibe History of Hip Hop*, ed. Alan Light (New York: Three Rivers, 1999): 74.
121. Russell A. Potter, *Spectacular Vernaculars* (New York: State University of New York Press, 1995): 46.
122. Christopher, *Dead Precedents*: 133.
123. Mark Fisher, "It's Easier to Imagine the End of the World Than the End of Capitalism." *The Visual Culture Reader*, ed. Nicholas Mirzoeff, (Routledge, 2013): 312.
124. Hager, *Hip Hop*: 62–63.
125. Rose, *Black Noise:* 36.
126. Hernandez, *Towards a Hip-Hop Architecture*.
127. Sahra Sulaiman, "Nipsey Hussle Understood Cities Better than You. Why Didn't You Know Who He Was?" *Streetsblog Los Angeles* website, August 15, 2019, https://la.streetsblog.org/2019/08/15/nipsey-hussle-understood-cities-better-than-you-why-didnt-you-know-who-he-was/?utm_campaign=citylab-navigator&utm_me%E2%80%A6 accessed August 31, 2019.
128. A. Williams, *Towards a Hip-Hop Architecture*.
129. T.I., "Whatever You Like," 00:11 to 00:38 on *Paper Trail* (Atlantic Records, 2008).
130. A. Williams, interview with author, February 11, 2019.
131. Emanuela Guidice, "L'architettura tra 'Whites' e 'Grays.' Strumenti, metodi e applicazioni compositive," in *FAmagazine* 30, (November-December 2014): 24–25
132. A. Williams, *Towards a Hip-Hop Architecture*
133. Wilson, "White by Design": 106
134. Ibid.

135. Mos Def, "A Soldier's Dream" (2002), lyrics as transcribed on www.genius.com.
136. Wilson, "White by Design": 108.
137. Michael Brown, Jr. was shot in the street of Ferguson, Missouri on August 9, 2014 by police officer, Darren Wilson, sparking a series of riots, military interventions, and social unrest for several weeks thereafter.
138. Lawrence Chua, "Life in Marvelous Times: Hip-hop, Housing, and Utopia," *Archi.pop: Mediating Architecture and Culture*, ed. D. Medina Lasansky, (New York: Bloomsbury Academic, 2015), 205.
139. Victoria and Albert Museum, "What is Postmodernism?" Vimeo video, posted November 16, 2011, https://vimeo.com/32207784.
140. Rose, *Black Noise:* 23–24.
141. Ibid., 24.
142. Ibid., 25.
143. Paul D. Miller, *Rhythm Science* (Cambridge: Mediawork/The MIT Press, 2004): 21.
144. Ibid.
145. Adam J. Banks, *Digital Griots: African American Rhetoric in a Multimedia Age* (Carbondale and Edwardsville: Southern Illinois University Press, 2011): 25.
146. Ibid., 26.
147. Ibid.
148. *Towards a Hip-Hop Architecture*.
149. J Dilla (aka Jay Dee), born James Dewitt Yancey, produced 10 hip-hop albums between 1997 and his death in 2006.
150. Vox, "How J Dilla humanized his MPC3000," YouTube video, posted December 6, 2017, https://www.youtube.com/watch?v=SENzTt3ftiU.
151. Ibid.
152. Ibid.
153. Rayvon Fouché, "Say It Loud, I'm Black and I'm Proud: African Americans, American Artifactual Culture, and Black Vernacular Technological Creativity," *American Quarterly* 58, no. 3 (2006): 653.
154. Imamu Amiri Baraka, "Technology & Ethos: Vol. 2 Book of Life," in *Raise, Race, Rays, Raze: Essays Since 1965* (New York: Random House, 1971): 157.
155. Ibid., 157.
156. The title "media assassin" is used by Allen in all of his work and is also the title of his blog found at http://harryallen.info/.
157. Harry Allen, "Hip-Hop Hi-Tech," in *Step into a World: A Global Anthology of the New Black Literature*, ed. Kevin Powell (New York: Wiley, 2000): 91.
158. DJ Kool Herc, quoted in Chang, *Can't Stop Won't Stop*: 69.
159. Rose, *Black Noise:* 63.
160. Ibid., 64.
161. Anthropomorphism here is used in the sense described by Wilkins when he states: "The anthropomorphism in hip hop space is not concerned with typical Western understandings of the concept that focuses centrally on the physical attributes or appendages of the body. It is

instead concerned with a holistic understanding of the place the body inhabits." Wilkins, *(W)rapped Space*: 11.
162. Baraka, "Technology & Ethos," 157.
163. Fouché, "Say It Loud," 655.
164. Ibid., 656.
165. Ibid., 656.
166. Phillip Anzalone, Marcella Del Signore, Andrew John Wit, "Notes on Imprecision and Infidelity," in *ACADIA 2018 Recalibration: On Imprecision and Infidelity Proceedings of the 38th Annual Conference of the Association for Computer Aided Design in Architecture,* Mexico City (Mexico), October 2018: 16–17. The two main themes of this conference were: "Computational Infidelities," which are described as "the misuse, glitching, reconfiguring, and/or non-standard programming of both computational systems and production machines," and "Imprecision in Materials and Production," which "looks at the redefining of aesthetics and processes through the use of imprecise materials, tools, and computation techniques as a means of design." The attitudes implicit within these chosen themes reflect the growing interest within the academic community for more humanistic aspects of architectural technology.
167. Eglash, "Appropriating Technology: An Introduction," in *Appropriating Technology*: xiv.
168. Fouché, "Say It Loud," 655.
169. Jack Travis, *Towards a Hip-Hop Architecture*.
170. Wilkins, *Towards a Hip-Hop Architecture*.
171. Sarah Bayliss, "ART/ARCHITECTURE: Museum With (Only) Walls," *The New York Times*, National edition, August 8, 2004, Section 2, page 26.
172. "The Closing: Jerry Wolkoff," The Real Deal: New York Real Estate News website, December 1, 2018, https://therealdeal.com/issues_articles/the-closing-jerry-wolkoff/ accessed August 15, 2019. As further detailed in this article, the whitewashing and demolition of Wolkoff's building without proper notification of the 5Pointz artists resulted in a $6.7 million ruling in the artists favor.
173. Museum of Street Art website, https://www.citizenm.com/mosa accessed August 15, 2019.
174. Ibid.
175. Rose, *Black Noise:* 24 (emphasis in original text)
176. Tajai Massey, "The Birth—Part 1," *Close to the Edge: The Birth of Hip-Hop Architecture*, public lecture, New York, NY, November 26, 2018, transcribed May 27, 2019.

VOLUME III

1. Anonymous, "The Birth—Part 2," AIANY Center for Architecture, December 5, 2018, transcribed May 25, 2019.
2. Ibid.
3. *Close to the Edge: The Birth of Hip-Hop Architecture* was exhibited at the AIA NY Center for Architecture from October 1, 2018 to January 15, 2019.

4. The American Institute of Architects (AIA) is the primary governing body for architects in the United States. Its oldest and largest chapter is located in New York. The Center for Architecture is the headquarters of the AIA New York. www.aiany.org/about/aiany-chapter/ accessed May 28, 2019.
5. The second iteration of the exhibition, installed at SpringBOX in Saint Paul, MN, expanded to include work from four additional participants from two new countries, France and Italy.
6. Rose, *Black Noise*: 38.
7. Ibid., 38, 39.
8. Lauren Halsey, "The Birth—Part 2."
9. Lupe Fiasco, "Form Follows Function," 03:53 to 04:14 on *Food & Liquor II: The Great American Rap Album, Pt. 1* (Atlantic Records, 2012)
10. See Volume II, Section 2: "AUTHENTICITY."
11. Nathaniel Belcher and Stephen Slaughter, "Harlem: The Ghetto Fabulous," in *harlemworld*: 67.
12. Stephen Slaughter, "The Birth—Part 2."
13. Aaron Betsky and Adam Eeuwens, *False Flat: Why Dutch design is so good*, (New York, London: Phaidon Press Limited, 2004)
14. Marc Maurer and Nicole Maurer, "PLAY Design Approach," in *The Architecture Co-Laboratory: Game Set and Match II: On Computer Games, Advanced Geometries, and Digital Technologies*, eds. Kas Oosterhuis and Lukas Feireiss (Rotterdam, Episode Publishers: 2006): 145.
15. Ibid., 146.
16. Ibid.
17. Ibid.
18. Ibid.
19. Graffiti nomenclature includes four basic levels of aerosol-based work: "tag," "throw-up," "burn," and "piece/mural." Each level is typically marked by an increase in detail and expressiveness.
20. Zvi Belling, project statement sent to author by email, February 7, 2018.
21. Ibid.
22. Ibid.
23. Ibid.
24. Ibid.
25. Molly Hunker, Greg Corso, "City Thread" project statement, http://www.sportscollaborative.com/#/city-thread/ accessed June 10, 2019.
26. "About Passageways," *Passageways 1.0*, http://www.passagewayschattanooga.com/passageways/2.0/about accessed June 10, 2019.
27. Hunker and Corso, "City Thread."
28. Greg Corso, interview with author, April 29, 2019.
29. Hunker and Corso, "City Thread."
30. Molly Hunker, interview with author, April 29, 2019.
31. John Szot, interview with author, April 9, 2019.

32. Film festival listings included on *Architecture and the Unspeakable* website, http://johnszot.com/archandtheunspeakable/ accessed June 10, 2019.
33. John Szot, "Architecture and the Unspeakable," online video, Vimeo, https://vimeo.com/123460109 accessed June 10, 2019.
34. Ibid.
35. Szot, partial specification contained in video, full specification from email sent to author April 26, 2019.
36. Szot, "Architecture and the Unspeakable."
37. Ibid.
38. Szot, interview.
39. Beyoncé, "Partition," 00:21 to 00:42 on *Beyoncé* (Columbia Records, 2013).
40. See Volume II, Section 6: "NOSTALGIA."
41. Amanda Williams, "Red on the Wall: Basquiat When I Paint," at *Towards a Hip-Hop Architecture* symposium, March 20, 2015, transcribed January 24, 2016.
42. Ibid.
43. Ibid.
44. Rebuild Foundation, "About Rebuild," https://rebuild-foundation.org/our-story/ accessed June 10, 2019.
45. The fourteenth-century Temple Church was literally bombed by the German forces in World War II, not figuratively "bombed-out" as one might say of a graffiti-covered space.
46. Emily Steer, "Theaster Gates: Who Are the Builders?" in *Elephant*, Issue 26, Spring 2016: 170
47. For a list of all the Hip-Hop Architecture thesis projects known to the author, see "APPENDIX."
48. Craig L. Wilkins, "Cuirass Architecture," in *Ruffneck Constructivists*, ed. Kara Walker (Brooklyn, Dancing Foxes Press: 2014): 21.
49. Nina Cooke John, *Close to the Edge: The Birth of Hip-Hop Architecture*, symposium, October 6, 2018, transcribed June 11, 2019.
50. Ibid.
51. Ibid.
52. "Remixing Architecture" was the Politecnico di Milano's selection for the Schools of Architecture Prize at the 2018 Barcelona International Biennal of Landscape Architecture and the 2018 RIBA (Royal Institute of British Architects) President's Medal Prize.
53. Andrea Bulloni and Marco Papagni, "Remixing Architecture through urban culture: The Bronx Revolution," self-published thesis book, 2018. The original Italian reads: "propone un intervento progettuale primario che racchiude e rappresenta passato, presente e futuro dell'esperienza hip hop."
54. Mauricio Zamora, "Appropriated Tekniques: An Architectural Mixtape," thesis statement, 2019.
55. Chris Cornelius, "Wildstyle: Museum of Hip Hop (MoHipHop)," ARCH 850: Graduate Elective Studio syllabus, Fall 2017.
56. Cornelius, interview with author, May 8, 2019.

57. Ibid.
58. Ibid.
59. Ibid.
60. Stephen Slaughter, "The Birth—Part 2," *Close to the Edge: The Birth of Hip-Hop Architecture*, public lecture, December 5, 2018, transcribed May 27, 2019.
61. Ibid.
62. The famous quote "Writing about music is like dancing about architecture" has been attributed to various people from Frank Zappa and Elvis Costello to Martin Mull.
63. Cooke, syllabus for *Breaking Space: The Architecture of Hip-Hop Dance,* Syracuse Architecture, Fall 2015
64. Ibid.
65. Ibid.
66. See Volume II, Section 6: "NOSTALGIA."
67. Cooke, syllabus for *3D Turntables: Hip-Hop Architectural Technology,* Syracuse Architecture, Fall 2016.
68. Cooke, syllabus for *Represent Represent: Hip-Hop Architecture in 2D,* Syracuse Architecture, Fall 2017.
69. See Volume II, Section 6: "NOSTALGIA."
70. Cooke, syllabus for *Spittin' Bars: Hip-Hop, Architecture, and Semiotics,* Syracuse Architecture, Fall 2018
71. Goodie Mob, "Thought Process," 03:16 to 04:05 on *Soul Food* (LaFace Records, 1995)
72. Rose, *Black Noise*: xiii.
73. Joseph G. Schloss, *Making Beats: The Art of Sample-Based Hip-Hop* (Middletown, Wesleyan University Press: 2004): 15.
74. Schloss outwardly declares his love for hip-hop (*Making Beats*: 24). Rose also describes her affinity for the music and associates it with growing up in the Bronx (*Black Noise*: xii) and Roy Christopher recounts his first encounter with *Criminal Minded* by Boogie Down Productions while he was in high school (*Dead Precedents*: 12).
75. Hager, *Hip Hop*: x.
76. Schloss, *Making Beats*: 10.
77. Craig L. Wilkins, "(W)rapped Space: The Architecture of Hip Hop," *Journal of Architectural Education*, 54:1 (2000): 12.
78. Tajai Massey, interview with author, February 11, 2019.
79. Ibid.
80. Ibid.
81. Massey, interview.
82. Ibid.
83. Anthony DeNaro, interview with author, March 2, 2019.
84. DeNaro, "'S' Chair design—Graffiti Futurism," website, https://www.ynotism.com/new-page access June 13, 2019.
85. Carlos Rodriguez, interview with author, February 15, 2019.
86. Ibid.
87. Ibid.

88. Rodriguez as @carlosmare posted, "Part1- 2008 my first of 8 #freestylearchityper installations. This one at Brighton University in England. Influenced by #frankghery" Instagram, February 23, 2017.
89. Boris Tellegen, email to Kokeith Perry II, February 7, 2018.
90. Stéphane Malka, interview with author, March 11, 2019.
91. Ibid.
92. Ibid.
93. According to Malka in his interview, this was his tribute to Radio Raheem, a character from Spike Lee's 1989 film, *Do the Right Thing*.
94. Malka Architecture, "Bow-House," website, https://www.stephanemalka.com/portfolio/bow-house-i-inhabit-the-walls-i-heerlen-2014 accessed June 13, 2019.
95. Ibid.
96. Malka Architecture, "A-Kamp47," website, https://www.stephanemalka.com/portfolio/a-kamp47-i-inhabit-the-wall-i-marseille-2013 accessed June 13, 2019.
97. The book's title has a double meaning in French, with *pari* and *Paris* being homophones: "le petit pari," meaning "the small bet" or "wager," and "le petit Paris" referencing the small parts of the city of Paris.
98. Malka, interview.
99. Ibid.
100. James Garrett, Jr., "Getting Up; at the Scale of the City," at *Towards a Hip-Hop Architecture*, March 20, 2015.
101. Garrett, *Close to the Edge Symposium*, Saint Paul
102. Lauren Halsey, "The Birth—Part 2," *Close to the Edge: The Birth of Hip-Hop Architecture*, public lecture, December 5, 2018, transcribed May 27, 2019.
103. Ibid.
104. Ibid.
105. Jeyifous, *Close to the Edge Symposium*, Saint Paul
106. Ibid.
107. Ibid.
108. Ibid.
109. Ibid.
110. Ibid.
111. Ibid.
112. Ibid.
113. Nathan Williams, "Hip-Hop Ar(t)chitecture Signifyin'," thesis statement sent to author by email, August 3, 2018.
114. Ibid., capitalizations in original text.
115. See Volume II, Section 3: "GODPARENTS."
116. Kendrick Lamar, "King Kunta," 02:12 to 02:16 on *To Pimp A Butterfly* (Interscope Records, 2015)
117. Anonymous comment, "Hip-Hop Architecture: Urbanism + Performance," lecture, July 27, 2017.
118. Wilkins, *The Aesthetics of Equity: Notes on Race, Space, Architecture and Music,* (Minneapolis: University of Minnesota Press, 2007): 174.
119. Forman, *The 'Hood Comes First*: 7.

120. Ibid., 8.
121. Sara Zewde, interview with author, July 11, 2019.
122. Zewde, presentation at *Black in Design* conference, October 10, 2015, *YouTube* video, "Black in Design Day 2 Part 2," posted October 27, 2015, https://youtu.be/mYMvl1P0QWQ transcribed August 15, 2019.
123. Zewde, interview.
124. Zewde, *Black in Design*.
125. Ibid.
126. Ibid.
127. Wilkins, "(W)rapped Space": 7-19.
128. Wilkins, *Close to the Edge: The Birth of Hip-Hop Architecture*, symposium, October 6, 2018, transcribed June 11, 2019.
129. These four criteria are introduced in Volume II, Section 6, "NOSTALGIA."
130. Wilkins, *(W)rapped Space*: 11-13.
131. Ujijji Davis, *Close to the Edge Symposium*, Saint Paul
132. Wilkins, *The Aesthetics of Equity*: 174.
133. Kara Walker, "Ruffneck Constructivism" in *Ruffneck Constructivists*, Institute of Contemporary Art, University of Pennsylvania, Dancing Foxes Press, Brooklyn, 2014: 9
134. Sekou Cooke, "Hip-Hop Urbanist Manifesto," *105th ACSA Annual Meeting Proceedings*, 2017
135. Manifesto written as part of the studio's coursework by Alexander Sheremet.
136. Manifesto written as part of the studio's coursework by Timothy Mulhall.
137. Wilkins, "(W)rapped Space": 11–19.
138. Manifesto written as part of the studio's coursework by Xingyao Wang.
139. Zewde, *Black in Design*.
140. Ujijji Davis, *Close to the Edge Symposium*, Saint Paul.
141. Harry Allen, interview with author, recorded April 6, 2016, transcribed July 23, 2019.
142. Wilkins, "Cuirass Architecture,": 18.
143. Ibid.
144. Forman, *The 'Hood Comes First*: 3
145. Ibid., 25.
146. The Lo-Down Network, "Rooftop Legends Returns," online video, YouTube, posted October 11, 2017, https://youtu.be/zgbQmXXMTDY accessed June 14, 2019.
147. Lineup as published and circulated on event poster via Facebook, http://www.facebook.com/ROOFTOP-LEGENDS-114007275301742/ accessed August 7, 2019.
148. Cooke, *Close to the Edge Symposium*, Saint Paul
149. Wu-Tang Clan, "Supreme Architecture," 00:11 to 00:33 on *Chamber Music* (Universal Music Group, 2009).

VOLUME IV

1. Jon Caramanica, "Behind Kanye's Mask," *New York Times*, New York edition, June 13, 2013: AR1.
2. BBC Radio 1, "Kanye West. Zane Lowe. Part 1," *YouTube* video, September 24, 2013, https://youtu.be/nx3X4r-eCYQ.

3. BBC Radio 1, "Kanye West. Zane Lowe. Part 3," *YouTube* video, September 24, 2013, https://youtu.be/PED4zgjG3Ng.
4. Each of the major architecture and design blogs (ArchDaily, Architizer, Archinect, and Dezeen) published multiple articles on Kanye West's interest in architecture in the days and weeks that immediately followed the Zane Lowe interview.
5. Erica Ramirez, "Kanye West Gives A Lecture at Harvard Graduate School of Design: Watch," *Billboard* website, November 18, 2013, https://www.billboard.com/articles/columns/the-juice/5793245/kanye-west-gives-a-lecture-at-harvard-graduate-school-of-design.
6. Virgil Abloh, Twitter post, November 17, 2013.
7. Kanye West, in "Kanye West speaks with crowd of architecture students at Harvard Graduate School of Design," *YouTube* video by Flavio Sciaraffia, published by Lian Chang, November 18, 2013, https://youtu.be/xDbVz-7WH2o.
8. Common, "Hercules" 01:30 to 01:38 on *Let Love* (Loma Vista Recordings, 2019)
9. A. Williams, *Towards a Hip-Hop Architecture*.
10. Ibid.
11. Cryus Peñarroyo, "The Hype Williams Effect," in *Clog: Guggenheim* (2014): 51.
12. Ibid.
13. Rodriguez, interview.
14. Harry Allen, guest lecture to *3D Turntables* course at Syracuse Architecture, November 29, 2016.
15. Wilkins, *Towards a Hip-Hop Architecture*.
16. Allen, guest lecture
17. Patrick Sisson, "Space is the Place: The Architecture of Afrofuturism," Curbed website, Feb 22, 2018, https://www.curbed.com/2018/2/13/17008696/black-panther-afrofuturism-architecture-design accessed, July 11, 2019.
18. Jehan Latief, "Michelle Mlati's Afrofuturist Approach to Spatial Planning," ArchDaily website, February 15, 2019, https://www.archdaily.com/911518/michelle-mlatis-afrofuturist-approach-to-spatial-planning accessed, July 11, 2019.
19. Amy Frearson, "10 Architects and Designers that are Championing Afrofuturism," Dezeen website, April 6, 2018, https://www.dezeen.com/2018/04/06/african-architects-designers-championing-afrofuturism/ accessed, July 11, 2019.
20. Ekow Eshun, "There is a Desire Among Black People to Make the World Over," Dezeen website, April 9, 2018, https://www.dezeen.com/2018/04/09/ekow-eshun-opinion-afrofuturism-architecture-design/ accessed, July 11, 2019.
21. Edwin Heathcote, "The Afrofuturists with Designs on African Architecture," Financial Times website, June 30, 2019, https://www.ft.com/content/19ce47f4-8b5b-11e9-a24d-b42f641eca37 accessed, July 11, 2019.
22. Mark Dery, "Flame Wars: The Discourse of Cyberculture," in *South Atlantic Quarterly*, Fall 1993 (Duke University Press).

23. Roy Christopher, *Dead Precedents: How Hip-Hop Defines the Future* (London: Repeater Books, 2018): 93.
24. Lisa Yaszek, "Afrofuturism, Science Fiction, and the History of the Future," in *Socialism and Democracy*, Vol. 20, No. 3, November 2006, 41–60.
25. Christopher, interview with Labtekwon in *Dead Precedents*: 94.
26. Eshun, "There is a Desire . . ."
27. Gunseli Yalcinkaya, "Black Panther's "voluptuous" sets are influenced by Zaha Hadid, says production designer," Dezeen website, March 1, 2018, https://www.dezeen.com/2018/03/01/black-panther-film-designer-zaha-hadid/ accessed, July 11, 2019.
28. Manuel Herz, Hans Focketyn, Ingrid Schröder, Julia Jamrozik (eds.), *African Modernism: The Architecture of Independence: Ghana, Senegal, Côte D'Ivoire, Kenya, Zambia* (Park Books, 2015) documents several important civic and institutional buildings constructed during the post-colonial era of the 1950s and 60s in five African nations.
29. Ibid.
30. Exhibition description, "Bodys Isek Kingelez: City Dreams," The Museum of Moderrn Art website, https://www.moma.org/calendar/exhibitions/3889.
31. See Volume III, Section 3, "PROCESS."
32. Christopher, *Dead Precedents*: 26.
33. James Garrett, Jr., artist statement for *Afrofuturism* exhibition.
34. Hancox, *Inner City Pressure*: 21.
35. Ibid.
36. Jeyifous, *Close to the Edge Symposium*, Saint Paul.
37. The exhibition, "Christian Kerez: Contrast and Continuity" showed at the Druker Gallery in Gund Hall at Harvard Graduate School of Design from January 21 to March 20, 2013.
38. Louis Rice, "Informal Architecture/s," in *Transgression: Towards an Expanded Field of Architecture,* Rice, L. and Littlefield, D. eds. (London: Routledge, 2015): 87.
39. Ibid., 95.
40. Ibid.
41. See Volume III, Section 4, "IDENTITY."
42. Jeyifous, *Close to the Edge Symposium*, Saint Paul.
43. Roberto Bedoya, "Spatial Justice: Rasquachification, Race and the City," op-ed on *Creative Time Reports* website, September 15, 2014, http://creativetimereports.org/2014/09/15/spatial-justice-rasquachification-race-and-the-city/ accessed August 17, 2019.
44. Ibid.
45. Rice, "Informal Architecture/s": 100.
46. Charles Jencks, *Le Corbusier and the Continual Revolution in Architecture* (New York: Monacelli Press, 2000): 144.
47. Lawrence Chua, *Towards a Hip-Hop Architecture*.
48. Hager points to the inaccuracies of this notion in describing early b-boy battles: "breakdancing had immediate appeal for the national press, possibly because a quote in the *Voice* credited the dance with replacing

fighting as an outlet for urban aggression. 'In the summer of '78,' said Tee, 'when you got mad at someone, instead of saying, "Hey man, you want to fight?" you'd say "Hey, man, you want to rock?"' The statement was not entirely accurate (break dancers were notorious for getting into fights, especially with each other), but it was just the sort of quote that makes good newspaper copy." Hager, *Hip Hop*: 87.
49. Olalekan Jeyifous, *Towards a Hip-Hop Architecture*.
50. Robin D. G. Kelley, "Kickin' Reality, Kickin' Ballistics: Gansta Rap and Postindustrial Los Angeles," in *Droppin' Science: Critical Essays on Rap Music and Hip-Hop Culture*, (ed.) William Eric Perkins (Philadelphia: Temple University Press, 1996): 16–17.
51. Melle Mel, "Rapper Melle Mel: Delivering 'The Message,'" heard on "Fresh Air," NPR, August 29, 2005, 12:00 AM ET, posted on NPR website, https://www.npr.org/2005/08/29/4821649/rapper-melle-mel-delivering-the-message accessed July 16, 2019.
52. Ibid.
53. *Straight Outta Compton*, Motion Picture, Directed by F. Gary Gray (Los Angeles, California: Universal Pictures, 2015).
54. Christopher, *Dead Precedents*: 31.
55. Schloss, *Making Beats*: 33.
56. DJ Kool Herc, "Introduction," in Chang, *Can't Stop Won't Stop*: xii.
57. Teddy Cruz, "Tijuana Case Study Tactics of Invasion: Manufactured Sites," *Architectural Design*, Vol. 75, No. 5 (2005): 32–7.
58. Louis Rice and David Littlefield, "Introduction," in *Transgression*: 1.
59. Ana María León, "Spaces of Co-Liberation," in *Dimensions of Citizenship*, eds. Niall Atkinson, Ann Lui, Mimi Zeiger (Los Angeles: Inventory Press, 2018): 72.
60. Ibid., 74.
61. G. Britt Eversole, interview with author, February 6, 2019.
62. See Volume II, Section 8: "GRIDS + GRIOTS."
63. Andrés L. Hernandez, *Towards a Hip-Hop Architecture*.
64. Outkast, "Aquemini," 02:38 to 02:41 on *Aquemini* (LaFace Records, 1998)
65. See Volume II, Section 8: "GRIDS + GRIOTS."
66. Charles Jencks, "Contextual Counterpoint in Architecture," *Log* 24 (Anyone Corporation, 2012): 72.
67. Ibid., 74.
68. Ibid., 75.
69. See Volume II, Section 9: "TECHNOLOGY."
70. Jencks, *Adhocism: The Case for Improvisation* (Cambridge: MIT Press, 2013): vii, emphasis in original text.
71. Ibid., viii.
72. Ibid., x, emphasis in original text.
73. Ibid., xii.
74. Ibid., xv.
75. Ibid., xiv.
76. *Log* 26 included an essay by Bryony Roberts titled, "Why There's No Postmodernism 2," in direct response to Jencks' *Log* 24 essay.

77. Kyle J. Miller, "Fundamentals in Architecture: Precedent," Syracuse University, School of Architecture panel discussion, September 19, 2014, YouTube video posted November 24, 2014, transcribed July 18, 2019.
78. Ibid.
79. Ibid.
80. Ibid.
81. Ibid.
82. Ibid.
83. Kyle J. Miller, "The Plan is the Generator," in *Room One Thousand*, Issue 5, 2014
84. Jennifer Bonner, *A Guide to the Dirty South—Atlanta* (London: Artifice books on architecture, 2017): 7.
85. Ibid.
86. Goodie Mob, "Dirty South," 00:57 to 01:02 on *Soul Food* (LaFace Records, 1995).
87. Open Mike Eagle, *Ready or Not, Here I Come: A Conversation on Architecture and Hip-Hop*, panel discussion, June 28, 2018, video posted to *YouTube* by MOCA (Museum of Contemporary Art) July 20, 2018, https://youtu.be/xH3qAFsphQU transcribed August 15, 2019.
88. Kara Walker, "Ruffneck Constructivism," in *Ruffneck Constructivists*, Institute of Contemporary Art, University of Pennsylvania, ed. Kara Walker (Brooklyn: Dancing Foxes Press, 2014): 9.
89. Dr. Ray Dalton may have played the most important role in birthing Hip-Hop Architecture in that he virtually, single-handedly, increased the Black population of student in the architecture program at Cornell during his time there, paving the way for a critical mass of students with similar interests to have meaningful conversations about what it meant to be a minority studying architecture, a predominantly White profession, at a majority institution. I hope to write my next academic title on Dr. Dalton and his legacy as it regards contemporary Blacks in architecture.
90. Anonymous, emails to the author, December 27, 2014 and January 7, 2015.
91. See Volume III, Section 6: "SPACE."
92. "Free Minds, Free People" website, http://fmfp.org/about/ accessed July 21, 2019.
93. Mary-Margaret Zindren, email to author, July 20, 2019.
94. Wilkins, *Close to the Edge: The Birth of Hip-Hop Architecture* symposium, Saint Paul, Minnesota, April 17, 2019, transcribed June 26, 2019.
95. Kyle May, "50 Architects Tell us What They Are Looking Forward to in 2016," ArchDaily website, https://www.archdaily.com/780498/50-architects-tell-us-what-they-are-looking-forward-to-in-2016 accessed July 21, 2019.
96. Lauryn Hill/Fugees, "Zealots" 02:00 to 02:05 on *The Score* (Ruffhouse Records/Columbia Records, 1996).

BIBLIOGRAPHY.

Anzalone, Phillip, Del Signore, Marcella, Wit, Andrew John (eds.), *ACADIA 2018 Recalibration: On Imprecision and Infidelity Proceedings of the 38th Annual Conference of the Association for Computer Aided Design in Architecture,* Mexico City (Mexico, October 2018)

Atkinson, Niall, Lui, Ann, Zeiger, Mimi (eds.), *Dimensions of Citizenship* (Los Angeles: Inventory Press, 2018)

Banks, Adam J., *Digital Griots: African American Rhetoric in a Multimedia Age* (Carbondale and Edwardsville: Southern Illinois University Press, 2011)

Baraka, Imamu Amiri, "Technology & Ethos: Vol. 2 Book of Life," in *Raise, Race, Rays, Raze: Essays Since 1965* (New York: Random House, 1971)

Bayliss, Sarah, "ART/ARCHITECTURE: Museum With (Only) Walls," *The New York Times*, National edition (August 8, 2004)

Betsky, Aaron, and Eeuwens, Adam, *False Flat: Why Dutch Design Is So Good*, (New York, London: Phaidon Press Limited, 2004)

Bonner, Jennifer, *A Guide to the Dirty South—Atlanta* (London: Artifice books on architecture, 2017)

Caramanica, Jon, "Behind Kanye's Mask," *New York Times*, New York edition (June 13, 2013)

Chang, Jeff, *Can't Stop Won't Stop: A History of the Hip-Hop Culture* (New York: Picador, 2005)

Christopher, Roy, *Dead Precedents: How Hip-Hop Defines the Future* (London: Repeater Books, 2018)

Cooke, Sekou, "The Fifth Pillar: A Case for Hip-Hop Architecture" in *Harvard Journal of African American Public Policy*, 2014

Cooke, Sekou, "Hip-Hop Urbanist Manifesto," *105th ACSA Annual Meeting Proceedings*, 2017

Cruz, Teddy, "Tijuana Case Study Tactics of Invasion: Manufactured Sites," *Architectural Design*, Vol. 75, No. 5 (2005)

Dery, Mark, "Flame Wars: The Discourse of Cyberculture," in *South Atlantic Quarterly*, Fall 1993 (Duke University Press)

Dyson, Michael Eric, *Know What I Mean? Reflections on Hip Hop* (New York: Basic Civitas Books, 2007)

Dyson, Michael Eric, *Holler If You Hear Me: Searching for Tupac Shakur* (New York: Basic Civitas Books, 2001)

Du Bois, W.E.B., *The Souls of Black Folk* (New York: Dover Publications, 1903)

Eglash, Ron, Croissant, Jennifer L., Di Chiro, Giovanni, and Fouché, Rayvon (eds.), *Appropriating Technology: Vernacular Science and Social Power* (Minneapolis: University of Minnesota Press, 2004)

Ford, Michael, "What is Hip-Hop Architecture?" in *Platform 2017, Convergent Voices*, eds. Nichole Wiedemann, Charlton Lewis, The University of Texas at Austin

Forman, Murray, *The 'Hood Comes First: Race, Space, and Place in Rap and Hip-Hop* (Middletown: Wesleyan University Press, 2002)

Fouché, Rayvon, "Say It Loud, I'm Black and I'm Proud: African Americans, American Artifactual Culture, and Black Vernacular Technological Creativity," *American Quarterly* 58, no. 3 (2006)

Garland, Jabari, "Flow Tektonics: Re-mixing Architecture to a Hip Hop Beat" in 93rd ACSA Annual Meeting Proceedings, 2005

Godlewski, Joseph, *Introduction to Architecture* (Cognella Academic Publishing, 2019)

Golden, Thelma, *harlemworld: Metropolis as Metaphor* (New York: The Studio Museum in Harlem, 2003)

Gooden, Mario, *Dark Space: Architecture, Representation, Black Identity* (New York: Columbia Books of Architecture and the City, 2016)

Guidice, Emanuela, "L'architettura tra 'Whites' e 'Grays.' Strumenti, metodi e applicazioni compositive," in *FAmagazine* 30, (November-December 2014)

Hager, Steven, *Hip Hop: The Illustrated History of Breakdancing, Rap Music, and Graffiti* (New York: St. Martin's Press, 1984)

Hancox, Dan, *Inner City Pressure: The Story of Grime* (London: William Collins, 2018)

Hernandez, D. and Rehman, B. (eds.), *Colonize This! Young Women of Color on Today's Feminism* (New York: Seal Press, 2002)

Jencks, Charles, "Contextual Counterpoint in Architecture," *Log* 24 (Anyone Corporation, 2012)

Jencks, Charles, *Adhocism: The Case for Improvisation* (Cambridge: MIT Press, 2013)

Lasansky, D. Medina, *Archi.pop: Mediating Architecture and Culture* (New York: Bloomsbury Academic, 2015)

Light, Alan (ed.), *Vibe History of Hip Hop* (New York: Three Rivers, 1999)

Lipsitz, George, "The Racialization of Space and the Spatialization of Race: Theorizing the Hidden Architecture of Landscape," *Landscape Journal*, Vol. 26, No. 1 (University of Wisconsin Press, 2007)

Love, Bettina L., *Hip Hop's Li'l Sistas Speak: Negotiating Hip Hop Identities and Politics in the New South* (New York: Peter Lang Publishing, 2012)

Miller, Kyle J., "The Plan Is the Generator," in *Room One Thousand*, Issue 5, 2014

Miller, Paul D., *Rhythm Science* (Cambridge: Mediawork/The MIT Press, 2004)

Mirzoeff, Nicholas (ed.), *The Visual Culture Reader* (Routledge, 2013)

Oosterhuis, Kas, and Feireiss, Lukas, *The Architecture Co-Laboratory: Game Set and Match II: On Computer Games, Advanced Geometries, and Digital Technologies* (Rotterdam, Episode Publishers: 2006):

Peñarroyo, Cryus, "The Hype Williams Effect," in *Clog: Guggenheim* (2014)

Peoples, Whitney A., "Under Construction: Identifying Foundations of Hip-Hop Feminism and Exploring Bridges between Black Second-Wave and Hip-Hop Feminism," in *Meridians*, volume 8, no. 1 (Duke University Press, 2008)

Perkins, William Eric (ed.), *Droppin' Science: Critical Essays on Rap Music and Hip-Hop Culture*, (Philadelphia: Temple University Press, 1996)

Powell, Kevin, *Step into a World: A Global Anthology of the New Black Literature* (New York: Wiley, 2000)

Rice, L. and Littlefield, D. (eds.), *Transgression: Towards an Expanded Field of Architecture* (London: Routledge, 2015)

Rose, Tricia, *Black Noise: Rap Music and Black Culture in Contemporary America* (Hanover, N.H.: University Press of New England, 1994)

Schloss, Joseph G., *Making Beats: The Art of Sample-Based Hip-Hop* (Middletown, Wesleyan University Press: 2004)

Shabazz, Rashad, *Spatializing Blackness: Architectures of Confinement and Black Masculinity in Chicago* (Urbana, Chicago, and Springfield: University of Illinois Press, 2015)

Steer, Emily, "Theaster Gates: Who Are the Builders?" in *Elephant*, Issue 26, Spring 2016:

Walker, Kara, *Ruffneck Constructivists*, Institute of Contemporary Art, University of Pennsylvania (Brooklyn: Dancing Foxes Press, 2014)

Walsh, Jim, "What's Hip-Hop Architecture? Hip-Hop Culture in Built Form," Minn Post, April 11, 2019

Wilkins, Craig L., "(W)rapped Space: The Architecture of Hip Hop," *Journal of Architectural Education*, 54:1, 2000

Wilkins, Craig L., *The Aesthetics of Equity: Notes on Race, Space, Architecture and Music,* (Minneapolis: University of Minnesota Press, 2007)

Yaszek, Lisa, "Afrofuturism, Science Fiction, and the History of the Future," in *Socialism and Democracy*, Vol. 20, No. 3 (November 2006)

INDEX.

Entries in *italics* refer to titles of literary, academic, or artistic works.

A Friendly Takeover, 143–4
ABC (Another Bad Creation), 60
Abloh, Virgil, 185–6, 188
activist architecture, 207–8
Adams Morgan Recoded, 130–1
Adhocism, 215, 252
African American culture, 27, 70
    Black aesthetic, 35
    Du Bois, 33
    griot, 70
    philosophies of time, 160
    threat to communities, 163
African slaves, 137
Afrika Bambaataa, 20, 32, 59, 129, 200
Afro-Caribbean influences, 31, 51, 70
Afrofuturism, 197–200
    affinities with Hip-Hop Architecture, 198
    Black Panther, 197
A-Kampa47, 145
Allen, Harry, 74, 175, 190, 193
Amalgamated Cypher, 89
Anansi, 70
appropriation
    capitalist consumption, 62, 97
    cultural, 36, 62
    Cyrus, Miley, 36
    linguistic, 114
    marginalized people, 114
    misappropriation, 98
    of hip-hop terminology, 217
    spatial, 23, 156, 161, 180, 202
    tactical, 114
    techniques, 217
Aravena, Alejandro, 204
architectural design, 47, 70, 118, 128, 130
Architecture and the Unspeakable, 106
architecture, definition of, 18
architecture programs, lack of diversity, 120
Astor, Patty, 60
authenticity, 17–20
    architectural practice, 17
    avoiding limiting definitions of, 20
    bridging art and commerce, 59
    Close to the Edge exhibition, 180
    culturally embedded attitudes to, 118

Eminem, 31
    expression of hip-hop truth, 156
    imagery, 97
    Robinson, Sylvia, 31
    Sugar Hill Gang, 17
    visible signs of, 62
    Zvi Belling, 103
Azalea, Iggy, 15, 19, 31, 36, 38, 60

Banks, Adam J., 70–1
Baraka, Amiri, 74–7
b-boying, 175
    Allen, Harry, 177
    appropriation of space, 51
    battle dances, 26, 51, 164, 171
    bodily contortions, 51, 111
    Breaking Space, 121
    graffiti connection, 18, 53, 164, 170, 171, 192
    inspiration for architects, 194
    Latinos, 32
    opposition to the grid, 69
    pillar of hip-hop, 18
    superforce, 177
    violation of boundaries, 140, 164
Beachler, Hannah, 197–8
Beat Street, 51
beats
    Afrodiasporic sound range, 23
    engineered, 111
    hip-hop, 23
    Making Beats, 137, 194
    mixing, 224
    rap, architecturalization of, 49
    Schloss, Joseph, 137, 194
    structure in relation to bars, 128
    West, Kanye, 188
Belcher, Nathaniel, 34, 97
Belling, Zvi, 99, 103, 141
Bey, Yasiin, 20, 49, 68, 69, 71
Black architects, 33, 198, 227
Black Architecture, 5, 33, 45
Black, definition of, 32
Black Panther, 197–8
Black Urbanism, 159
Blow, Kurtis, 137
blues, the, 34, 48, 69
Bonner, Jennifer, 217–19

Bottega, The, 161, 174
Bow-House, 145
Br'er Rabbit, 70
Braithwaite, Fred, 60
breakbeats. *See* breaks
breakdancing, 53, 89, 170
breaker boys. *See* b-boying
breaks, 48, 51, 69–70, 89, 129
Breaks, The, 137
Brooks, Evelyn, 130–1

capitalism, 40, 59, 69, 210
Caribbean immigrants, 137
Carson, A.D., 13
Chang, Jeff
    birthdate of hip-hop, 24, 235
    graffiti, 52
    identity, 137
    Merry-Go-Round, the, 48
    non-black hip-hop, 32
    pioneer of a new canon, 3
    resistance to, 13
Chicago
    Color(ed) Theory (Amanda Williams), 111
    Craig Wilkins' park redesign, 24
    Rebuild Foundation (Theaster Gates), 112
    revolution of pride, 213
    spatial injustice, 212
    Spatializing Blackness (Rashad Shabazz), 237
    (W)rapped Space (Craig Wilkins), 161
    You Say Chi-City (Sekou Cooke), 163, 172
Christopher, Roy
    Dead Precedents: How Hip-Hop Defines the Future, 233
    futures without pasts, 53
    hip-hop as bridge between art and commerce, 59
    identity, 137
    oral traditions, 49
    powerless groups, resistance of, 18
    resistance to, 13
    scholars' relationship with hip-hop, 14
Chua, Lawrence, 26, 68, 71, 205, 210, 223
Cité Frugés, 202
City Thread, 104
Close to the Edge: *The Birth of Hip-Hop Architecture*, 21, 26, 36, 85, 156, 180, 224

Color(ed) Theory, 111
commodification, 7, 60–2
construction
    adaptive and non-traditional techniques, 47, 161, 204
    DELTA, 141, 143
    hip-hop music, 48
    Ivy City typology, 135
    new attitudes for, 62
    NOMA perspectives, 45
    potential of urban voids, 164
    rap, 47
    rap music, 49
    shortage of experts, 175
contradiction, 79–81
    centrality in hip-hop, 13, 69
    cultural basis, 205
    postmodern contradictions, 69
    urban landscape, 159
Cooke John, Nina, 113–14
Corbusier, Le
    Cité Frugés, 202
    five rules, 3
    influence on hip-hop, 24, 27
    Kanye West inspired by, 185
    life and the architect, 204
    low-income living, 202
    social housing, 29
    Villa Savoye copies, 217
    Ville Radieuse, 24
Cornelius, Chris, 118–19, 121, 128
    academic contribution, 26
    making something from nothing, 198
Cornell University, 42, 45, 186, 223
    Dalton, Ray, 223, 250
    Gould, André, 26
    Williams, Amanda, 26
    Williams, Nathan, 23
Corso, Greg, 104
Craddock-Willis, André, 69
crate digging, 70–1
Crenshaw District Hieroglyph Project, 152
Crouch, Stanley, 13
cultural appropriation, 62
Curry, Milton S.F., 34

dance
    criteria of hip-hop consistency, 93
    influence of hip-hop, 5
    philosophies of time, 160
    relationship with architecture, 123
    roots of hip-hop, 51
    translating into form, 119

Dapper Dan, 60
Davis, Ujijji, 161, 175
Deconstructivism, 56, 65, 191–2
deejaying, 18, 23, 48, 75, 208
DELTA. *See* Tellegen, Boris
DeNaro, Anthony (YNOT), 140
Dery, Mark, 197
design process
    DJ analogy, 48, 70
    graffiti applied to, 130
    hip-hop applied to, 85, 111
    hip-hop terminology appropriated, 217
    subjectivity trained, 119
    unpredictability vs. architectural control, 202
Detroit, 29, 31, 161, 174–5, 207
digital fabrication, 76, 119, 121, 141, 186
Dirty South, 218–19
DIY, 204–5
DJ Spooky, 70
DJs
    eccentric musical tastes, 20
    griots, 70
    opposition to the grid, 69
    relationship with b-boys, 51
    roots, 48
    superforce, 177
    technique and technology, 14, 75, 111, 124, 154, 164
Do the Right Thing, 207
down-rock, 111
Dyson, Michael Eric
    hip-hop intellectual, 13
    Holler If You Hear Me, 40
    Know What I Mean?, 13, 59
    pioneer of a new canon, 3
    Tupac Shakur, 40, 41

Eames House, 28, 77, 185
Eglash, Ron, 76
Egyptians, 23, 52, 198, 239
Eisenman, Peter, 65
ELLIS G, 106
Ellis, Bryan (Raydar), 73
Eloheim, Orko, 224
emceeing, 18, 49–50, 75, 152, 224
Eminem, 31, 49
empowerment, 37, 94, 114
empty lots, 27–8, 96, 156, 160, 168, 170, 172
End to End Building, The, 103
Escobar, Van, 140
exhibitions
    A Friendly Takeover, 143
    Afrofuturism, 148, 197
    Close to the Edge: The Birth of Hip-Hop Architecture, 8, 21, 26, 36, 85, 156, 180, 224, 233
    Exothermic, 141
    harlemworld, 33, 97, 223
    Lauren Halsey: we still here, 151
    Postmodernism: Style and Subversion 1970–1990, 69
    Ruffneck Constructivists, 53

Fab Five Freddy. *See* Braithwaite, Fred
fabrication technology, 48, 124
favela, 54, 202
feminism, 13, 40, 42
Fifth Pillar, The, 17, 47, 69, 116, 223
Fisher, Mark, 59
flow
    breakdancing, 90
    challenge to the grid, 69
    consistency in Hip-Hop Architecture, 90
    criteria for formal consistency, 90
    Deconstructivism, 192
    definition of, 50
    discursive bricolage, 51
    Forman, Murray, 51
    Garland, Jabari, 46
    Garret, James, Jr., 46–7
    Harlem landscape, 34
    hip-hop triad, 136
    Jeyifous, Olalekan, 89
    MC's lyrics, 127
    rap music, 50, 90
    Rose, Tricia, 89
Ford, Michael
    academic contribution, 26
    ancestors of hip-hop, 24, 27
form, 85–90
    breakdance, 47, 51
    following function, 192
    inconsistency of, 89
    urban, 210
formalism, of graffiti letters, 53
Forman, Murray
    identity, 137
    spatial imperatives in hip-hop, 159, 177

Fouché, Rayvon
   humanizing technology, 74–6
   technological creativity and resistance, 77
   Technology & Ethos, 74
four elements of hip-hop, 47, 53, 75, 85, 111, 138, 152
Frampton, Kenneth, 65
functionalism, 65

gangs
   breakdancing, roots of, 123
   community pride, 213
   dance forms, 51
   evolution of hip-hop, 81
   loyalty, 54
   marketing of hip-hop, 40
   protection for construction projects, 96
Garland, Jabari
   architectural space of hip-hop, 26
   flow, 50
   Flow-Tektonics, 46
   four principles of hip-hop space, 46
Garrett, James, Jr.
   Afrofuturism, 197–8
   architectural practice and hip-hop, 150, 157
   architectural space of hip-hop, 26
   architecture and social relationships, 29
   Close to the Edge, 224
   four elements of hip-hop, 47
   graffiti, 141
   organization of spaces, 71
   Resonant Spaces/Dynamic Flows: Hip-Hop + Architecture, 238
   Towards a Hip-Hop Architecture, 223
Gates, Theaster, 112–13, 136
Gehry, Frank, 141, 192
gender, 39–43
   contradictions in hip-hop, 40
   Pritzker prize petition, 39
   women architects under-represented, 39
Giudice, Emanuela, 65
Goldberg, David, 14
Gooden, Mario, 35
Gosa, Travis, 15, 42, 223
Goths, 52

graffiti
   architectural outcomes and relationships, 23, 104, 106, 126
   b-boys, 53
   breakdancing, connection to, 53, 123, 170
   Close to the Edge, 226–7
   coding and decoding, 130–1
   design, 53
   flow, 90
   harlemworld: Metropolis as Metaphor, 33–4
   hip-hop pillar and image, 18, 47, 53
   hustle, 60
   incompatibilities, 79
   Jeyifous, Olalekan, 34
   Malka, Stéphane, 24, 147
   motivation of its artists, 52
   political dissent, 207
   Rooftop Legends, 178
   space, 131, 212
   Szot, John, 107
   TAKI 183, 32
   violation of boundaries, 164
   Williams, Amanda, 111
   Zamora, Mauricio, 117
graffiti architecture, 141
graffiti pieces, 99, 147, 153, 164
Grandmaster Flash, 20, 75, 129, 207
Graves, Michael, 65
Grays, The, 65–6
Green, Cee-Lo, 136
grid, the, 65–72
   appropriating the grid, 168–9
   griot attitudes to, 71
   hip-hop response to, 69, 164, 170
   impact on urban culture, 72
   oppressive nature, 68
   ubiquity, 65
   visual dominance, 68
griots, 70–1, 210
   Hip-Hop Architecture, 210
Gwathmey, Charles, 65

Hadid, Zaha, 39, 185–8, 192, 194
Hager, Steven
   anthropology of hip-hop culture, 137
   b-boy dance battles, 51
   graffiti, selling services, 60
   Hip Hop, 17

Hancox, Dan
  academic resistance, 13
  grime as black music, 32, 198
  hip-hop a reflection of reality, 15
  identity, 137
  wigga phenomenon, 31
Harlem, 33–4, 40, 60, 62, 66, 93, 97–8
harlemworld, 33, 97, 223
Hejduk, John, 65, 217
Hernandez, Andrés
  alternatives to modernist principles, 28
  architecture in blackface, 62
  community revolution of pride, 213
  empowerment, 37
  grid, dominion of the, 72
  Hip-Hop Architecture, a way of working, 5
  Hiphopitecture, 10 Points of, 46
  pioneer of a new canon, 3
  Towards a Hip-Hop Architecture, 223
Herzog & de Meuron, 50, 188, 215
Het Wilde Wonen, 98–9
hieroglyph, 95–6, 152, 227
Hip-Hop Architecture, definition, 17–21, 107, 186
  Fifth Pillar, The, 17
  Garrett, James, Jr., 47
  origins of the term, 7
hip-hop, definition, 17
hip-hop fashion, 60, 62, 126
hip-hop process
  architectural applicability, 109, 163
  Close to the Edge, 85
  Cooke John, Nina, 113
  freestyle composition, 136
  Halsey, Lauren, 151
  languages of, 194
  Malka, Stéphane, 145
  Slaughter and Cornelius, 121
  translating into design process, 111
hip-hop space, 8, 177–8, 180
  essential attitudes, 53
  four principles, 46
  guiding philosophy, 54
hip-hop triad, 136
Hip-Hop Urbanism, 8, 159, 162
Hip-Hop Urbanist Manifesto, 163
Hiphopitecture, 10 points of, 45–6
Hive, The, 99, 103, 141
homophobia, 13, 41, 81

hooks, 70
hooks, bell, 3, 40, 212
Hughes, David, 35, 45
Hunker, Molly, 104

Ice Cube, 185, 207
identity, 99, 137–41, 174, 177, 178
  absence of, 65
  authors' identities, 137, 156
  Black identity, 33, 41
  coded identity, 131
  complexity, 40, 137
  creating a new identity, 60, 200
  hip-hop identity, 85, 109, 143, 145, 148, 151, 160
  key feature of hip-hop, 137
  neighborhood identity, 135
  outsiders, 137
  pseudonyms, 60
  struggle for synthesis, 33
  visual identity, 126
image, 97–109
  African past and future, 197
  changing nature of, 97
  Deconstructivism as alternative, 192
  graffiti, 131
  hip-hop as activism, 207
  hip-hop image, 85, 103, 107, 109, 145
  larger-than-life, 60
  masculine image of Black male, 41
  predefined, 109, 178
  reference point, 135–6
  urban form, 210
improvisation
  Close to the Edge exhibition, 180–1
  hip-hop culture, 59
  hip-hop DJs, 48
  hip-hop pioneers, 136
  informal settlements, 204
  Jencks, Charles, 215
  key tenet of hip-hop, 156
  Shanty Megastructures, 154
informal settlements, 201–4
Ingles, Bjarke, 188
Ivy City Redux, 135

J Dilla, 73, 215
Jamaica, 48–9
Jay Dee. *See* J Dilla
Jay-Z, 21, 185
jazz, 13, 34, 38, 69

Jefferies, John, 159
Jefferson, Thomas
    grid, the, 68
Jencks, Charles
    Adhocism, 215
    Postmodernism, 69, 215, 217
Jeyifous, Olalekan
    Afrofuturism, 197–200
    Close to the Edge exhibition, 226
    (Counter)insurgents, 34
    creative energy, 152
    Deconstructivism, 155, 192
    informal settlements, 203
    origin of hip-hop, 207
    pioneer of a new canon, 3
    Political Impermanence of Place (PIMP), 155
    Shanty Megastructures, 89, 154, 200, 203
    Towards a Hip-Hop Architecture, 223
Juxtaposition Arts Center, 224

Kanye West. *See* West, Kanye
Kerez, Christian, 201, 204
Know What I Mean? (Dyson), 13, 59
Koohaas, Rem, 188
Kool Herc
    eccentric musical tastes, 20
    hip-hop pioneer, 32, 74–5
    origin of hip-hop, 24, 48
    power of hip-hop, 208
Krabath, Scott, 87, 128
Kris Kross, 60
KRS-One, 52

Lamar, Kendrick, 15, 156, 207
layering
    breakdancing, 90
    Deconstructivism, 192
    flow, relationship to, 90
    graffiti, 53, 104, 106, 126
    hip-hop triad, 136
    Malka, Stéphane, 145
    Rose, Tricia, 90
    ruptures in line, relationship to, 90
    Szot, John, 106
    temporal, 126
    Williams, Nathan, 156
Le Petit Pari(s), 147
Lee, Spike, 207
Lefebvre, Henri, 172, 173

locking. *See* popping and locking
Love, Bettina, 13, 40–1
low-income housing, 130, 202

making do, 71, 161
Malka, Stéphane
    A-Kampa47, 145
    architect, 143
    graffiti artist, 24
    Le Petit Pari(s), 147
    rejected by art school, 24
    sampling and layering, 145
manifesto
    Hip-Hop Architecture, 5
    Hip-Hop Urbanist Manifesto, 163
    Roughneck Constructivism, 55–7
    students', 166
mapping, 92, 118, 155, 164
MARE 139. *See* Rodriguez, Carlos
marginalized
    communities, 46, 56, 154
    people, 5, 32, 53, 114
Marsalis, Wynton, 13
masculine image, 41, 98
mashup, 217
Massey, Tajai, 81, 138, 140, 143
Maurer, Marc, 98
Maurer, Nicole, 98
Maurer United Architects, 89, 98
Meier, Richard, 65
Melle Mel, 50, 207
Miller, Kyle, 217
Miller, Paul, 70
misogyny, 13–14, 40–1, 81, 98, 211
mixed-use development, 79, 130
mixing, 34, 71, 90, 98, 215
mixtape, 71, 116
modernism
    African Modernism, 198
    destroyed, 29
    Enlightenment, the, 193
    rejection of, 69
    space, 28
    utopianism, 56, 69
Mos Def, 20, 71–2. *See also* Bey, Yasiin
Moses, Robert, 24, 27–8

Nas, 59
National Organization of Minority Architects (NOMA), 45
Neo-Postmodernism, 215–21
neutrality, 68–71

New Chocolate City, 128, 162, 172
New York Five, The, 65
NWA (Niggas With Attitudes), 207

oral tradition, 49, 70, 173

Parliament Funkadelic, 92, 198
PHAT, 34, 97
physical space, 94
Political Impermanence of Place, 155
popping and locking, 69, 90
Postmodernism, 69, 71, 215, 217
Potter, Russell, 59
Pough, Gwendolyn, 41, 71
primary objective of Hip-Hop
    Architecture, 5
Pritzker Architecture Prize, 39
process, 111–21
    Cooke John, Nina, 114
    graffiti artists' tactics borrowed, 111
    improvisational spirit, 136
    leveraging of, 109
    predefined, 178
    reassessment, 131
programmatic flexibility, 138
pseudonyms, 60
Public Enemy, 207
public housing, 3, 68, 156
public programming, 128
public space
    absence of, 212
    appropriating, 51
    breakdancing, 51
    designing, 114
    empowerment, 114
    graffiti, 126
    leftover space, 114
    reinterpreting, 123
    transforming, 163
    underused space, 104

Quinta Monroy, 204

R&B, 69
race, 31–5
    architecture and, 35–6
    Azalea, Iggy, 31
    imbalance in Pritzker laureates, 39
    marketing, 40
    space and place, 177, 210–11
    urban as metaphor for, 210
    Whites and Grays, 65

Ramela, Renata, 89, 128
Rammellzee, 52, 197
rap music
    black cultural expression, 31
    Black Noise, 69
    cultural values, 40
    exemplar of hip-hop, 18
    flow, 50–1, 90
    marketing, 40
    media attention, 14
    philosophies of time, 160
    postmodern contradictions, 69
    sampling and coded references, 151
    sexism, 40
    Sugar Hill Gang, 17
    technology as catalyst, 75
    urbanism, 159
    white supremacy, 14
rapping, 31, 47, 68, 81, 90, 140, 188
Rasquache, 204
Raydar. *See* Ellis, Bryan
remix
    appropriation, 217
    Close to the Edge, 180
    critical interpretation, 71
    Hip-Hop Architecture, 168
    Jeyifous, 153
    reinvention, 217
    renovation, 48
    technique and attitude, 71, 219
renovation, 47, 48
Represent Represent, 126
restoration, 48, 203
reverse colonization, 52
rhyme schemes, 111, 168
rhythm and blues. *See* R&B
Rich, Adrienne, 71
Rickenbacker, Shawn, 27, 71, 223
riffs, 70
Robinson, Sylvia, 17, 31, 34, 60
Rodriguez, Carlos (MARE 139), 26, 141
Rooftop Legends, 178
Rose, Tricia
    Black Noise, 40
    contradictions in hip-hop, 69, 81
    hip-hop style, 87
    identity, 40, 137
    pioneer of a new canon, 3
    pseudonyms as identity framing, 60
    rap music, 31
    resistance to, 13
    sexism, 40–1

Sugar Hill Gang, 17
technology and black culture, 75
urbanism, 159
Rothelowman Architects, 87
Rowe, Colin, 65
rudeboy, 53
ruffneck, 53, 114
Ruffneck Constructivists, 26, 53–4, 114
ruptures in line, 89–90, 136
Russian Constructivists, 53
RZA, 181

sacred geometry, 140
sampling
    criterion of hip-hop, 90
    Halsey, Lauren, 95, 151
    inconsistency of form, 90
    Malka, Stéphane, 145
    Maurer United Architects, 98
    reclamation of undervalued spaces, 164
    Schloss, Joseph, 194
Schloss, Joseph
    African aesthetics in hip-hop, 32
    deejaying, 208
    hip-hop, lack of categorization, 20
    Making Beats, 194
    origin of hip-hop, 24
    researchers' social world, 137
SCHMO: stratum, surface, time, 141
scratch, 23, 48, 69, 75, 111, 180, 192
Scully, Vincent, 65
sellout, 17, 59
sexism, 13, 40–1, 69, 211
Shabazz, Rashad, 41
Shakur, Tupac, 41
Shanty Megastructures, 89
Shine, 70
shoutout, 70–1
signifyin, 49
Signifyin Monkey, the, 70
Simmons, Kyle, 133
Slaughter, Stephen
    academic contribution, 26
    digital fabrication, 121
    Harlem: The Ghetto Fabulous, 34, 97–8
    harlemworld: Metropolis as Metaphor, 97–8
    studio course, 119
Smalls, Biggie, 13

social housing, 29, 143
Soja, Edward, 210
South Bronx, 20, 27–9, 51, 53, 66, 68
space, 172–5
spatial injustice, 210–11
spatial practices, 29, 79, 161, 177
Spittin' Bars, 127
SPORTS Collaborative, 104
squatting, 202
Stagger Lee, 70
Stanescu, Oana, 188
stealing space, 114
steeping period, 106–7
Stern, Robert, 65
street art, 79, 106–7, 161
Sugar Hill Gang, 17, 31, 60
Sun Ra, 197, 212
Surface Armatures, 153
surfaces
    dissociation from structure, 192
    graffiti, 111, 147, 151
    gridded, 69
    SCHMO: stratum, surface, time, 141, 148
    transformation of, 53, 111
    two-dimensional, 126
Syracuse University, 31, 45, 121, 123, 128, 224
Szot, John, 104, 106–7

tag
    graffiti, 178, 192
    graffiti structure, 24, 69, 133
    layering, 104
    space, 143, 150, 162, 174
TAKI 183, 32, 52
Tate, Greg, 34, 52
technology, 73–6
    adaptation of, 76, 124
    attitude to, 48, 77
    fusion with mastery and style, 60
    humanizing technology, 75
Tellegen, Boris (DELTA), 141
tenement row houses, 68, 71
Third Space, 89, 128
3D Turntables, 124, 192
throw up, 133
toprock. *See* uprock
Towards a Hip-Hop Architecture, 26, 31, 65, 223
Tower of David, The, 202

Transgression: Towards an Expanded Field of Architecture, 208
Travis, Jack, 27, 35, 45, 77, 223
Tupac Shakur. *See* Shakur, Tupac

universality, 5, 13, 69
uprock, 51
urban design, 8, 33, 128, 148, 159, 164
urban development, 154–5, 203
urban landscape, 14, 33, 159, 161, 215
urban planning, 118, 128
Urban Porch, The, 114
urban renewal, 65, 68, 97
urban space, 72
urbanism, 159–62
    Afrofuturism, 197
    black urbanism, 159
    hip-hop urbanism, 8, 128, 159
    landscapes, 161
    towers-in-the-park, 24
    transformation of neighborhoods, 129
    Zewde, Sara, 159
utopianism, 68, 154, 178, 190, 210, 223

Vanilla Ice, 31, 60
Venturi, Robert, 39, 65
violation of boundaries, 171
violence, 13–14, 40–1, 81
visualization, 153

Walker, Kara
    baby mama of Hip-Hop Architecture, 191
    pioneer of a new canon, 3
    Ruffneck Constructivists, 26, 53, 163
West, Kanye, 186, 188, 190, 211, 223
    defense of, 41
white spatial imaginary, 5, 204
Whites, The, 66
Wilkins, Craig L., 29, 36, 57, 78, 228
    anthropomorphism, 170
    attitudes of hip-hop space, 53
    books, 26
    breakdancing, 170

Cuirass Architecture, 53
Deconstructivism's lineage, 192
DIY ethos, 205
four principles of hip-hop space, 46
graffiti, 170
Hip-Hop Park, 161
Hip-Hop Urbanism, 159
identity, 137
model for architectural practice, 228
pioneer of a new canon, 3
redesign of Chicago park, 24, 161
Ruffneck Constructivists, 26, 53
space, 177
Towards a Hip-Hop Architecture, 223
understanding our world, 72
urbanists, 159
(W)rapped Space, 46
Williams, Amanda, 43, 63
    Color(ed) Theory, 111
    early inspiration, 26
    forefathers of hip-hop, 191
    Pink Oil Moisturizer, 226
    progressive vision of Black architecture, 45
    Silver Shoe Mantra, 34
    thought leader, 65
    Towards a Hip-Hop Architecture, 197
Williams, Hype
    forefathers of hip-hop, 191
Williams, Nathan
    conflicts, 27
    Hip-Hop Ar(t)chitecture Signifyin, 155
    pioneer of Hip-Hop Architecture, 24
    undergraduate thesis, 23–4
Williams, Pharrell, 186
Wilson, Mabel O., 3, 35, 68
(W)rapped Space, 26
    four principles of hip-hop space, 53

YNOT. *See* DeNaro, Anthony
You Say Chi-City, 163, 172

ZEDZ, 99
Zedzbeton, 98–9
Zewde, Sara, 160, 173
Zindren, Mary-Margaret, 224